THE INKA EMPIRE

AND ITS ANDEAN

ORIGINS

AMERICAN MUSEUM OF NATURAL HISTORY

THE INKA EMPIRE

AND ITS ANDEAN

ORIGINS

CRAIG MORRIS

ADRIANA VON HAGEN

OBJECT PHOTOGRAPHS BY
JOHN BIGELOW TAYLOR

ABBEVILLE PRESS   PUBLISHERS

NEW YORK   LONDON   PARIS

FOR CONNY AND FRED LANDMANN

Jacket front: Long-haired llama formed of crimped silver sheet metal. Inka period, Lake Titicaca, Bolivia (see page 182).

Jacket back: Male and female ceramic figurines. Chancay period, central coast, Peru (see page 144).

Frontispiece: Ceramic whistling bottle in the form of a Muscovy duck. Late Sicán style, north coast, Peru (see page 130).

Editor: Jacqueline Decter
Line Editor: Diane D'Andrea
Designer: Rebecca Daw
Art Director: Monika Keano
Production Editors: Paul Macirowski, Owen Dugan
Production Manager: Matthew Pimm
Maps: Joe Le Monnier (map of the Inka Road System redrawn after John Hyslop, 1984)

First edition

Library of Congress Cataloging-in-Publication Data

Morris, Craig.
    The Inka Empire and its Andean origins / by Craig Morris and Adriana von Hagen ; object photographs by John Bigelow Taylor.
        p.   cm.
    "Sponsored by the American Museum of Natural History."
    Includes bibliographical references and index.
        ISBN 1-55859-556-2
        1. Incas—History. 2. Incas—Politics and government. 3. Incas—Antiquities. 4. Andes Region—Antiquities. I. Von Hagen, Adriana. II. American Museum of Natural History. III. Title.
F3429.M843   1993
980'.012—dc20   93-26610

ACKNOWLEDGMENTS

Financial support for this book, and for the Hall of South American Peoples at the American Museum of Natural History, was provided by the National Endowment for the Humanities.

It is not possible to acknowledge here the contributions of all the many colleagues and friends who have assisted directly and indirectly with this book. Although we have tried to rely on the published literature, casual conversations in the field and elsewhere are important in forming perspectives that inevitably find their way into a general book like this. Morris in particular is indebted to the people who have worked with him over the years in field research in Huánuco and Chincha and to the National Science Foundation, the Tinker Foundation, the Richard Lounsbery Foundation, and the National Geographic Society for their sponsorship of that research.

Of the people who most specifically helped us, our first thanks must go to John Hyslop. He helped assemble the bibliography, organized photographs and captions, and tirelessly read drafts. We are also indebted to John Bigelow Taylor, whose photographs of the objects bring alive the cultures that produced them. We extend thanks as well to Anahid Akasheh, Richard Burger, Joan Buttner, Barbara Conklin, William Conklin, Anita Cook, Margaret Cooper, Jeanne D'Andrea, Rebecca Daw, Jacqueline Decter, Dianne Dubler, Paul Goldstein, Monika Keano, Heather Lechtman, Scarlett Lovell, Thomas Lynch, Carol Mackey, Donna McClelland, Patricia Moore, Matthew Pimm, Vuka Roussakis, Diana Salles, Idilio Santillana, and Helaine Silverman.

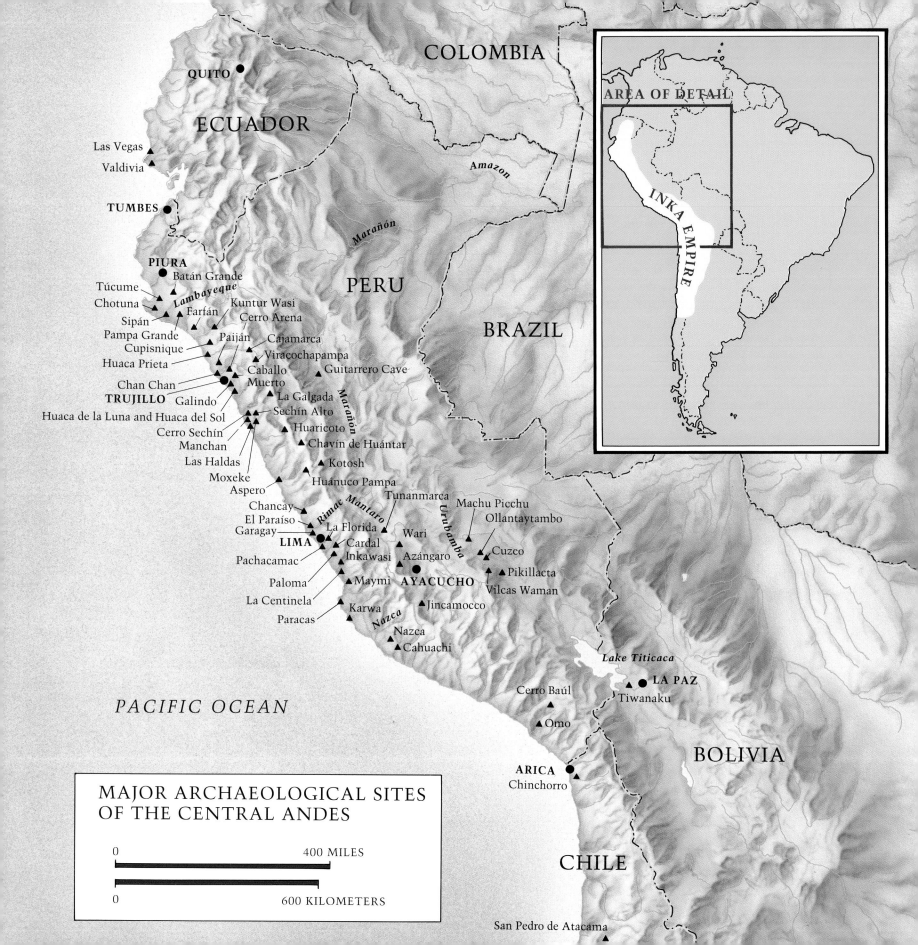

COLOMBIA

QUITO

ECUADOR

Las Vegas
Valdivia

PERU

TUMBES

Amazon

Marañón

PIURA
Batán Grande
Túcume
Chotuna   *Lambayeque*
                Kuntur Wasi
Sipán   Farfán   Cerro Arena
Pampa Grande   Paiján
Cupisnique   Cajamarca
Huaca Prieta   Viracochapampa
                Caballo   Guitarrero Cave
                Muerto
Chan Chan
TRUJILLO   Galindo   La Galgada
Huaca de la Luna and Huaca del Sol   Sechín Alto   *Marañón*
Cerro Sechín   Huaricoto
Manchan   Chavín de Huántar
Las Haldas
Moxeke   Kotosh
Aspero
                Huánuco Pampa
Chancay   Tunanmarca   Machu Picchu
El Paraíso   *Rímac* *Mantaro*   Ollantaytambo
Garagay   La Florida   Wari
LIMA   Cardal   *Urubamba*   Cuzco
Pachacamac   Inkawasi   Azángaro
Paloma   Pikillacta
La Centinela Maymi   AYACUCHO   Vilcas Waman
Karwa   Jincamocco
Paracas   *Nazca*
                Nazca
                Cahuachi

BRAZIL

Lake Titicaca

Cerro Baúl   LA PAZ
                Tiwanaku
Omo

BOLIVIA

PACIFIC OCEAN

ARICA
Chinchorro

CHILE

San Pedro de Atacama

MAJOR ARCHAEOLOGICAL SITES
OF THE CENTRAL ANDES

0   400 MILES

0   600 KILOMETERS

CONTENTS

AUTHORS' NOTE

The idea for this book grew out of the planning and installation of the archaeological sections of the Hall of South American Peoples at the American Museum of Natural History in New York City. These portions of the permanent exhibition undertake to tell the story of Andean civilization, using the material collected at the museum over a century. More than ten thousand objects were examined to see how they might throw light on Andean prehistory, allowing the extraordinary objects created by these ancient peoples to tell part of their own story. The same approach was chosen for a book, to be extensively illustrated with the objects shown in the hall, and with the advantage of a fuller text and more photographs of sites and landscapes than a museum accommodates. This book is intended to complement the exhibition for some of the millions of people who visit the museum and to stand alone as an up-to-date source on early Andean cultures for a general audience.

Our challenge was to organize a discussion of twelve thousand years of cultural development over an area extending more than 4,200 kilometers (2,600 miles) along the coast of South America. The difficulties of achieving this goal are compounded by the remarkable range of Andean cultures. During certain epochs stylistic similarities among the arts of different areas probably indicate linkages among religious and political organizations. Archaeologists have long used a system for organizing Andean prehistory based on these stylistic linkages, or "horizons." During most of prehistory, however, diversity was as evident as homogeneity. Certain regions, such as the north coast of Peru, the highlands of Bolivia and southern Peru, and the south coast of Peru, enjoyed relatively uninterrupted courses of development. Even within these smaller regions, however, there seems to have been much diversity and uneven growth. To approach the story from a strictly chronological perspective risks obscuring geographical and environmental diversity. Using a regional, geographic perspective does not do justice to those periods when art, religion, and perhaps political control were shared over a large area. Neither perspective alone allows us to emphasize several special areas of achievement by the Andean peoples: notably textiles, metallurgy, and music. Therefore, an approach based on cultures organized somewhat loosely in space and time has been chosen for this volume, with separate consideration given to these special achievements in the last three chapters.

Covering such a large area with so rich a cultural development is not possible without omitting much worthwhile information. Further, far more information is available for some periods and geographic areas than others. This imbalance necessarily leads to a somewhat uneven treatment of cultures, regions, and topics. A volume of larger scope would also treat the areas around the core of the central Andes. The prehistories of Argentina, Chile, Colombia, and Ecuador, mentioned here only in passing as we deal with metallurgical technology or the expansion of the Inka empire, are fascinating and deserve books of their own. Most books of this nature cannot accommodate every point of view where there is controversy, and controversy is especially common when evidence is meager. We have tried to provide a list of important readings related to each chapter and hope that the reader will find the story of Andean civilization sufficiently interesting to pursue it further.

Many readers will be struck by our spelling of *Inka* with a "k" instead of a "c." Scholarly works have almost universally shifted away from *Inca,* based on the way the word is spelled in modern Spanish. While the Inka had no written language, modern spelling in Quechua, or Runasimi, the language the Inka spoke, uses *Inka* for the name of both the ethnic group and the "king" who ruled the Inka Empire. We have tried to use the same principles of spelling for other words in the Quechua language: thus *Wari* instead of *Huari* and *Tiwanaku* instead of *Tiahuanaco.* Readers may be relieved by these new spellings, as they are much closer to the way an English speaker would pronounce these names than those derived from Spanish. We have made an exception for place names that are commonly found on maps, retaining Cuzco, instead of Cusco, and Nazca, instead of Nasca.

While we both accept responsibility for the text as a whole and each made suggestions for revision of the other's work, we decided that the best plan was a division of major responsibility on the basis of chapters. Adriana von Hagen wrote chapters 3, 4, 5, 6, and 12; Craig Morris wrote chapters 1, 2, 7, 8, 9, 10, and the epilogue. We are grateful for Peter Kvietok's contribution of chapter 11. He devoted great effort to the exhibition that inspired this book and much to advance the idea of a book that will be a companion to the Hall of South American Peoples.

THE ANDEAN PEOPLES

THE EVIDENCE OF THEIR HISTORY AND ACHIEVEMENTS

More than twelve thousand years ago people moved out of Asia, across the land bridge that crossed what later became the Bering Strait, through North America, and down to the tip of South America. The people who settled throughout the New World produced a remarkable series of cultures and civilizations. Their achievements in art, technology, and social organization rank with those of other continents.

Unfortunately, our vision of Native American accomplishments has been hampered by a serious lack of information and clouded by the European perspective of the conquering culture that came to dominate and, in many cases, destroy the indigenous cultures.

One of the most remarkable series of cultures in the Americas developed in the Central Andes. In this region, some of the most spectacular and diverse landscapes in the world were brought into productive use: steep mountain slopes, high grassy plateaus, warm intermontane valleys, and a dry strip of coastal desert. By the time Francisco Pizarro invaded the Andes in 1532, destroying the Inka rulers of the last independent Andean state, the region had an impressive list of achievements. Andean farmers had domesticated dozens of plant species, including the potato, one of the world's major food plants. Weavers were producing cloth of unsurpassed beauty and technical virtuosity. Metallurgists had developed a series of sophisticated technologies for smelting, casting, joining, and gilding metals. Architects had built enormous monuments and planned great cities in stone and adobe. Planners had overseen the construction of massive irrigation projects and road systems that,

under the Inka, exceeded 25,000 kilometers (15,500 miles).

A series of important states had arisen. Best known was that of the Inka. Extending more than 4,200 kilometers (2,600 miles) down the coast of South America, it became the largest empire in the New World. Vast economic wealth was accumulated. In addition to the cloth and precious metals so admired by Europeans, there was a rich supply of food, some of it stored in an impressive system of warehouses. By any standards the Andean achievements were notable.

European and European-American ethnocentrism has led us to assume that Native American societies were primitive and often poor. Five hundred years after Europeans discovered the Americas we are beginning to understand that in many ways, perhaps most, Native American cultures were at least equal to those that "conquered" them.

One skill not developed in the Andes was writing. But, while Andean societies had no code for recording speech, they had several admirable substitutes. Arrangements of knotted strings, sometimes numbering in the hundreds, contained records of censuses, contents of warehouses, and the numbers of taxpayers in various provinces. Calendars also may have been recorded on these knotted-string records, which are known as *khipu*. Khipu may also have aided those charged with remembering official accounts of battles, dynasties, and other aspects of what we call history. If so, all knowledge of how to interpret such accounts has been lost.

Only three sources remain as a basis for understanding what was clearly a complex civiliza-

1 The majestic snow-capped peaks of the Cordillera Blanca were but the summit of the greatly varied landscapes that fostered thousands of years of native Andean civilization. North-central highlands, Peru.

tion. The first source is in the records set down by the invaders. Although Francisco Pizarro was illiterate, the scribes who accompanied him recorded the conquerors' amazement at the culture they were destroying. Later, there were more complete accounts, admirable in their attempts to grasp the nature of a foreign world. There were also bureaucratic records, compiled by the colonial administration or by inspectors sent by the Spanish Crown. Although it was not their primary purpose, the inspections often provide remarkable firsthand information on native people and their customs. Later still, Church officials collected and recorded information on native beliefs and religious practices as part of the campaign to stamp them out. All these European written sources have limitations in both their completeness and their point of view.

The second source of information comes from present-day descendants of pre-Columbian inhabitants of the Andes, most of whom continue to live there. Five hundred years of domination has obliterated all vestiges of the upper, or state, level of native Andean societies. It has not erased the ability of these people to produce intricate and beautiful textiles, or their complex ideas about the cosmos and the world, or their ability to manage a diverse and fragile environment. These people can explain many of the principles and customs that had evolved for thousands of years before the European invasion.

The third source of information is archaeology. The Andean region is dotted with thousands of sites of pre-Columbian occupation. The study of these sites and their contents provides our most

direct link with ancient Andean cultures. By examining the nature of the objects recovered from archaeological sites, their relationship to other objects, bones, botanical remains, and other material left behind long ago, we can partially reconstruct ancient ways of life. When many archaeological sites over large areas are compared, patterns of distribution of objects and sites begin to shed further light on the practices and events of the past. Archaeology in the Andes is relatively young, compared to that in other parts of the world. Moreover, there has been far more looting than scientific excavation of Andean archaeological sites. The information obtained from looted objects is only a sad hint of the wealth of understanding that can come from carefully recorded patterns of artifacts and other objects found together in an archaeological site. But even objects deprived of their context provide evidence of Andean manufacturing technologies and artistic accomplishments. Unfortunately, it is precisely the modern admiration of those artistic and technological achievements that fuels the commercial market for ancient objects, resulting in the destruction of invaluable archaeological information.

Most of this book is based on archaeological information and methods. Only at the end of the story—the brief period of the Inka themselves—were there European witnesses who wrote down their observations. Native informants could reliably go back no further than their own memories. Similarly, the further back we move in time, the less certain we can be of any continuity with living Andean peoples. For the great sweep of Andean history, we must rely on fragmentary material remains, interpreted through carefully tested ideas based on what we know from the Inka and their modern descendants.

Fortunately, many of the objects that early Andean peoples left behind speak eloquently of their makers and users. This volume relies heavily on photographs of this visual heritage, so that readers may see the richness of Andean cultures for themselves. These pieces tell us primarily about art and technology, since so many have been torn from their archaeological context by looters eager to profit from their beauty. Other photographs are of landscapes, architecture, and in situ stone sculpture. These illustrations show the setting of the peoples and the objects they made. They also demonstrate an unusual sensitivity to and use of the natural landscape. The Nazca lines and Machu Picchu are the two most famous examples of large-scale human modification of the landscape that seem to transcend any ordinary utilitarian purposes.

We still do not know as much about the ancient cultures of the Andes as we do about many other cultures contemporary with them and of like importance. Much more research has been done on the civilizations of the ancient Orient, the Near East, and Mesoamerica. Only in the past two decades has archaeology in the Andes begun to reach a par with studies of other ancient cultures. As the story becomes more complete, the true dimensions of the Andean achievement emerge: weaving, as fine and virtually as early as any in the world; monumental buildings, contemporary with the pyramids in Egypt; an early empire, rivaling in size the extensive Old World empires.

CAMÍNA EL AVTOR

TIME AND GEOGRAPHY

VERTICAL LAND AND BOUNTIFUL SEA

In this book the word *Andes* is used primarily as a cultural term that refers to the general area where Andean civilization spread. The setting was both vast and varied. While the Andean region certainly included warm valleys with moderate temperatures and adequate rainfall, it is more notable for its extremes: deserts that may be without rain for more than twenty years; cloud forests with almost impenetrable vegetation; and high, windy plains, where daybreak brings summer and nightfall brings winter. The image of jagged peaks evoked by the word *Andes* also describes the region accurately.

Andean history, or more properly prehistory, is as complex as the geography of this large region. Like the geography, the history of the Andes consists of many pieces and extremes. The trajectory moves from hunting, fishing, and gathering societies to those that irrigated whole valleys, built temples with adjoining gardens of golden plants, and formed empires. But this path fluctuates between expansion and contraction, between war and peace, between bursts of creativity and times of stagnation. Major cities were often built on virgin terrain, expanded rapidly and then abandoned. To a degree such unevenness and oscillation characterize the history of societies everywhere, but the pattern was especially marked in the Andes.

A map (page 6) shows the core area of Andean civilization and identifies the major archaeological sites discussed in this book. The inset outlines the extent of the Inka Empire. That empire encompassed the largest area ever brought together under a single rule. For certain purposes, we also discuss the northern Andean area, in what

is now Colombia, home in pre-Columbian times to some of the principal gold-working peoples. Most of our discussions omit many of the Andean areas in Ecuador, northwestern Argentina, and northern Chile. Although these areas were conquered by the Inka in the last century before the arrival of Europeans, their inhabitants seemed to have been in only sporadic contact with the core area of Andean civilization during the long epoch preceding the Inka Empire.

A chronological chart (page 18) places Andean cultures, defined by their artifact styles, into a temporal and geographic framework. In reading later chapters, reference to the chart and the map will help to locate particular cultures in time and space and see their interrelationships. We emphasize that the chart is based on dates from many sources. The age of archaeological sites and the levels within them are usually determined by radiocarbon dating, but the ways of measuring the dates have changed somewhat as radiocarbon techniques have become more precise over the forty or so years they have been in use. As we will see in subsequent chapters, the coverage of reliable dates is much better for some areas and time periods than for others. As more and better dates become available, this chart is likely to be modified.

Even in this simplified version of Andean diversity, the sheer number of different names and the ways in which regions and periods so often are divided into small units immediately signal the complexity of the Andean world. That world was a kaleidoscope of cultures, societies, and languages. Throughout Andean prehistory and history, societies seem to have come together to form

3 On the high Andean mountain slopes farmers cultivated potatoes and other native tubers. Chinchero area, south highlands, Peru.

collaborating groups, only to break apart again or realign with other groups. The chart shows that at three points in Andean prehistory related styles spread over a large geographic area, a phenomenon archaeologists noted long ago. The meanings of these stylistic expansions were probably somewhat different in each instance (chapters 5, 7, and 9 discuss this question). In no case did the spread of object styles indicate a destruction of cultural diversity. Local peoples always retained many of their own customs and their arts. Diversity was a continuing hallmark of the Andes, as were almost continual change and a tendency to form shifting cultural alignments.

From very early times, patterns emerge of what seem to be periods of relatively close communication between various regions, followed by periods of conflict and division. Whatever the situation at any given moment, it was almost certain to change within a few generations. While states and empires existed, there was as yet no sense of a regional identity that encompassed the Andes as a whole. Indeed, specific groups and regions carefully maintained their individual identities during the time of the Inka Empire (see chapter 9). The Andean peoples apparently saw benefits in diversity as well as in unity. We cannot know, of course, whether a greater sense of unity would have developed had the Andes continued its autonomous development without the heavy yoke of European domination.

The naturally fragmented Andean landscape may have encouraged this constant search for more productive combinations of goods and resources, and more workable relationships with neighboring peoples. Although the Andes was an area of incredible wealth, many of its most important riches were unevenly distributed or difficult for a single people to dominate. Strategies had to be invented that went beyond narrow zones, bringing together diverse products, peoples, and technologies to forge economies rich in subsistence goods and objects of artistic complexity. Reaching this goal required political structures capable of coordinating the efforts of many people and achieving peace over large areas.

Symptomatic of Andean diversity is the large number of languages people spoke. Before the success of Spanish efforts to reduce the number of native languages, or even to eliminate them altogether, there were certainly dozens of Andean languages. Unfortunately, we have no accurate list, or even count, of the number. Millions of people continue to speak Quechua, the language of the Inka, largely in Peru. Aymara, the other surviving Andean language, is spoken mainly in Bolivia. Linguists believe that while the Inka introduced Quechua as a language of prestige and administration in the areas they conquered, they made no attempt to displace the local languages. On the contrary, they may even have encouraged the preservation of these languages as part of a strategy to maintain diversity. The Inka followed a principle of introducing new political groups (such as members of the Inka ruling class) into a region. The new arrivals occupied a position independent of and perhaps superior to the local people. The extent to which these interlinked peoples spoke one another's languages and the nature of their interaction are not clear.

The kaleidoscope of diverse cultures arranged over an equally diverse landscape created a patchwork of political, ethnic, and linguistic groups that did not occupy a single, contiguous territory. Particularly in parts of the highlands, groups spread out like islands, often separating members of the same group. At times members of certain groups had to travel more than two days to reach some of their far-flung territories. Anthropologist John V. Murra has studied and outlined this strategy of occupying "islands" as a way of taking maximum advantage of various levels in the vertical Andean ecology, which differs sharply with altitude.

The Andean area displays some of the most spectacular landscapes on earth. The three most distinct regions are the narrow strip of western coastal desert; the rugged mountains with high peaks, broken by warm valleys; and the heavily forested eastern foothills. Within a relatively short west-to-east span, they provide environments of striking contrasts. The contrasts include rainfall, temperature, length of the growing season, nature and range of vegetation and other available natural resources, and, ultimately, human use of the land.

Since so much of the character of cultures relates to their interaction with the landscape, an outline of the major environmental zones is useful. The basis for this classification was developed by the Peruvian cultural geographer Javier Pulgar Vidal. It stresses landscape features as they relate to human use, rather than strictly physical or biological features.

In the Pacific Ocean off the coasts of Peru and Chile, currents of cold water flow north from the Antarctic and well up from a deep tectonic trench. These currents, known collectively as the Humboldt, or Peru, Current, are unusually rich in nutrients and many species of marine plants and animals. For millennia, Andean peoples living near the coast have exploited one of the richest stretches of ocean in the world. In addition to the wealth of marine life that helped sustain large coastal populations from very early times, the ocean waters also carried a rich trade up and down the coast, and shells from the sea were worked into prized ornaments. A source of constant danger as well as wealth, the ocean played a major role in myth and religion.

People fished both from the shore and from seaworthy boats, using line and hook, nets, traps, and harpoons. By the time of the Inka, fishing in some areas had become a specialized full-time activity for people, who even spoke their own "fishers'" language. Dried and salted fish was a common item of trade. In the sixteenth century Father José de Acosta wrote: "There were many fishermen, each one sitting in his raft courageously cutting through the waves of the sea that is very choppy and turbulent where they fish. . . . They looked like tritons or neptunes" (Acosta, 1954 [1590]: 74).

The sea's abundance also yielded shellfish, sea lions, seabirds and their eggs, and marine algae. *Guano,* or bird droppings, collected from the offshore islands and rocky parts of the coast, fertilized agricultural fields. Long-distance trade by sea was common among coastal groups. Shells, gold, and other goods of both land and sea often were carried by full-time traders on large, keeled rafts with capacities of more than twenty sailors.

4 The Peruvian coast is primarily a desert strip with abundant offshore marine resources. Chincha Valley, south coast, Peru.

THE DESERT COAST

The Humboldt, or Peru, Current strongly influences climatic conditions along the coast. It cools the air over the ocean, keeping evaporation to a minimum. Cool air moving inland toward the steep Andes becomes steadily warmer, increasing its capacity to hold moisture and thereby inhibiting rainfall. The Peru Current thus accounts for both the rich coastal waters mentioned above and a coastal region that forms a narrow desert strip. The ancient settlers of this region eventually made the dry, but rich, coastal soils productive through irrigation. Among the plants they cultivated were maize, beans, squash, and cotton. The crops of the irrigated valleys, combined with the abundant resources from the sea, gave the coastal peoples a relatively independent food supply (fig. 4).

THE WESTERN FOOTHILLS

Rainfall is scant on the western face of the Andes, and here river valleys become increasingly narrow as the land rises, offering little space for cultivation. Effective farming requires irrigation and often terracing. But the warm temperatures provide ideal conditions for native fruits, such as *lucuma* and chirimoya (fig. 5).

THE DEEP INTERMONTANE VALLEYS

The deep, warm river valleys that cut through the mountains are prized as zones for growing varieties of Andean maize. Farmers sometimes increased the relatively small usable area by terracing and irrigating the valley slopes. These valleys became major suppliers of maize to highland centers of

MAJOR ARCHAEOLOGICAL CULTURES OF THE ANDES

TIME SCALE	NORTH COAST	CENTRAL COAST	SOUTH COAST	NORTH HIGHLANDS	CENTRAL AND SOUTH-CENTRAL HIGHLANDS	SOUTH HIGHLANDS	
1532							Spanish Invasion
1450							Inka Empire
1350						Inka Killke / Aymara Kingdoms	
1250	Chimú	Chancay	Chincha	Cajamarca	Wanka		Late Kingdoms
1150						Chanka	
1000	Sicán	Pachacamac					
800					Wari		First Empires
600							
400	Moche / Vicús	Lima	Nazca	Recuay	Huarpa	Tiwanaku	
200	Gallinazo / Salinar					Pukará	Early Kingdoms
0			Paracas				
200							Chavín cult
400						Chiripa	
600					Kotosh Religious Tradition		
800	Cupisnique						Early Ceramic
1000			Chinchorro				Cotton Preceramic
2000							
4000					Puna hunters		
6000	Paiján Tradition						Early Peoples
8000							
10,000							

political power, at several times in Andean prehistory. For example, the Inka built elaborate terraces in the valley of the Urubamba River, a principal source of maize for Cuzco (fig. 5).

THE HIGH MOUNTAIN CULTIVATION ZONE

Formed mostly of steep and broken terrain, and marked by warm days and cold nights, the high Andean mountain slopes were used for cultivating many food crops. In addition to potatoes, farmers grew native tubers such as *mashua, ullucu,* and *oca.* Quinoa provided a highly nutritious grain, and the domesticated guinea pig was a source of protein and the basis of ceremonial meals. Though the Andean peaks themselves rise above the limits of human habitation, seen from a distance they remain the subjects of veneration (fig. 3).

THE HIGH GRASSLANDS

The major resources of the high grasslands, called *puna,* were herds of domesticated llamas and alpacas and wild vicuñas and guanacos. Unlike cotton, alpaca fiber takes dye easily, providing textiles of brilliant colors. The llama carried cargo over long distances and its meat was dried into *charqui* (similar to the "jerky" used by the natives of North America), which resisted spoilage. Great wealth was accumulated in herds of llamas and alpacas often numbering thousands of animals (fig. 8).

THE EASTERN FOOTHILLS

The eastern face of the Andes is frequently shrouded in clouds. Almost impenetrable vegetation usually covers its humid, undulating terrain. During Inka times, this region formed the eastern frontier of Andean civilization. Its principal product was the coca leaf, valued for its ability to increase physical endurance (fig. 7).

THE TROPICAL RAIN FOREST

Great rivers leading to the Amazon cross the relatively flat tropical rain forest. Its wealth of plants and animals supported cultures whose characteristics differed in many respects from those of the Andes to the west. Though Andean peoples never directly controlled the rain forest, they nevertheless obtained several important products from it, such as the feathers of exotic birds to adorn their clothing (fig. 9).

DIVERSITY THROUGH TIME

The diversity of the Andean climate and landscape is almost as marked in time as it is in space. Changes from year to year are nearly as great as the changes from one season to another. The tropical latitude of the Andes tempers seasonal variation. In most of the region there are seasonal variations in cloud cover and rainfall, but seasonal variations in temperature are far less extreme than in temperate latitudes. For example, the median February (southern hemisphere summer) temperature in Lima in 1990 was 22.4°C (72.3°F), and in Huancayo, in the central highlands of Peru, it was 13.3°C (55.9°F). In July (winter) it dropped to 15.9°C (60.2°F) in Lima and 10.8°C (51.4°F) in Huancayo. Summer (February) rainfall in Huancayo was 134 mm. (5¼ in.) while winter (July) rainfall was 10 mm. (⅜ in.). On the coast, rainfall is near zero year round, but during the winter (June-August) an almost constant cloud cover with frequent fog and mist makes the air humid and is a major factor in lower winter temperatures.

Severe fluctuations in air and ocean currents sometimes produce dramatic environmental changes that seriously threaten life and society and must have affected the developmental history of Andean culture. The most extreme of these fluctuations is known as El Niño, named after the Christ child because its onset is usually noted near Christmas. El Niño produces devastating rainfall along the northern coastal deserts and serious drought with consequent famine in the highlands. Some of these periodic fluctuations last for more than a year, and in modern times cause population movements and other compensatory reactions, as people adapt to adverse conditions.

Sediment layers in ice cores taken from the Quelccaya ice cap have begun to provide a more precise record of the climatic irregularities, and the archaeological record has yielded evidence of destruction from climatic events, particularly on the north coast. Moreover, tectonic activity connected with movement of the Nazca plate has also

7 Almost impenetrable vegetation usually covers the eastern foothills of the Andes, which are often shrouded in clouds. Manu National Park, southeastern Peru.

9 The tropical rain forest is crossed by great rivers leading to the Amazon. Cocha Salvador, Manu National Park, Peru.

produced a long history of earthquakes and volcanic eruptions. Both the climatic irregularities and the tectonic activity have caused destruction and disaster in modern times and must have influenced ancient societies. Several anthropologists and archaeologists have suggested that the ebb and flow of political and economic prehistory are somehow related to the periodic natural disasters and generally high level of geologic stress in the Andean environment. Some have speculated that major floods and drought brought an end to important kingdoms such as Moche. Others have claimed that the superior ability of large states to coordinate production in several distinct ecological zones favored the growth of empires like those of the Wari and the Inka.

Certainly, a climate and environment so bold and, in a sense, so severe exerted a strong influence on the growth of cultures. Much more information is needed on the details of both the cultures and the environmental sequences to understand this obviously intricate relationship. Some things are clear, however. For example, there were obvious architectural adaptations to such dangers as earthquakes. Environmental challenges were met by increasingly sophisticated technologies—such as irrigation, terracing, and other artificial field systems—that increased the amount of cultivatable land and overall food production. By Inka times the management of resources through a massive storage system offered potential protection from years of bad crops. The lands were molded by technology, but the environment was respected just as it was modified and managed. The famous Inka site of Machu Picchu is one of the world's outstanding examples of marrying the architecture of a human settlement to a spectacular, and probably sacred, landscape.

Andean civilization rose out of these incredibly diverse and somewhat unstable landscapes. The wealth to build it was there, not to be simply taken from a single zone but to be developed by coordinating several environments. What Andean civilization forged in these landscapes was, on the one hand, a set of technologies that transformed the available natural resources into a reliable food supply along with an abundance of manufactures and, on the other hand, a series of principles of social organization that motivated production and merged the resources of various zones. A system was developed for putting order into time, space, human affairs, and the goods that constitute and create wealth.

The evidence of material wealth amazed the invading Europeans, who came almost to equate the Andes with wealth, as the phrase *vale un Perú* (worth a Peru) implies. The emergence of the technologies and organizational principles that underlie the Andean achievement was a gradual and somewhat uneven process. In spite of the progress of the past decades, many aspects of this growth trajectory remain obscure. The main events, however, can now be sketched to provide a profile that is as varied and spectacular as the Andes themselves.

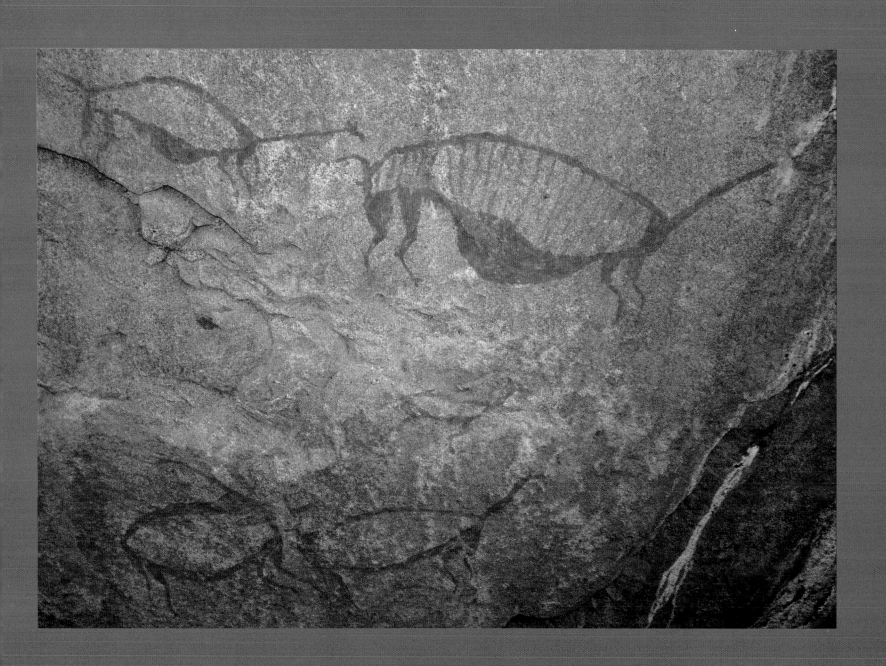

THE EARLY PEOPLES

ACROSS THE LAND BRIDGE AND DOWN TO CAPE HORN

About twenty thousand years ago, small groups of people began to cross the Bering land bridge that once connected Asia to the northwestern tip of the American continent. These migrations by America's first peoples ended some twelve thousand years ago, when global climatic and environmental changes caused glaciers to melt and sea levels to rise, submerging the land bridge and creating what we now call the Bering Strait. Large Pleistocene animals, such as the American mastodon, horses, and giant sloths became extinct as people expanded their range southward through North America, Central America, over the Isthmus of Panama, and to the southernmost tip of South America, which they reached about 9000 B.C.

A handful of claims exists for settlements earlier than those established in South America about 10,000 B.C. There is little compelling evidence to substantiate such claims, however, and the debate continues over when people began to settle in the Americas. While few scholars agree on when the Bering Strait migrations took place, many think that three distinct migrations occurred and that only one of those reached southern South America. These early peoples, hunters of wild game and collectors of seeds and plants, roamed windswept Patagonia. Others established themselves in the lush, tropical Amazon basin rain forests, the bleak highland plains, or Andean puna, and the arid coastal deserts.

The search for early peoples in the Americas has been fraught with controversy ever since the 1926 discovery in Clovis, New Mexico, of projectile points in association with extinct Pleistocene bison. These ten-thousand-year-old finds, whose hallmark is the distinctive, fluted Folsom projectile point, spurred others to search for evidence of early human occupation in the Americas.

Soon, archaeologists established the Clovis horizon, beginning five hundred years earlier and often associated with extinct elephants. In 1934, Junius Bird led an expedition sponsored by the American Museum of Natural History to the Straits of Magellan and Tierra del Fuego. There, in rock shelters and caves on the windswept plains of Chilean Patagonia, Bird discovered the earliest-then-recorded human cultural remains in South America. At Fell's Cave (fig. 11) and Palli Aike, he found simple stone tools and fluted fishtail points (fig. 12) along with bones of the extinct native horse and ground sloth as well as those of the guanaco, a relative of the llama, which still roams the desolate, treeless Patagonian plains. Radiocarbon dates of organic remains from the cave sites range from 9000 B.C. to historic times, which places the discoveries well within the range of dates obtained for similar Palaeo-Indian finds in North America. Bird traced an uninterrupted sequence of occupation in the area from the prehistoric era down to the descendants of the historical Ona.

Most scholars accept the Fell's Cave and Palli Aike dates as the earliest evidence for Palaeo-Indians in southernmost South America. But more recent discoveries in south-central Chile and northeastern Brazil have led others to claim even earlier dates. At the site of Monte Verde in the rain-drenched, temperate pine forests of Chile, archaeologist Tom Dillehay discovered wooden

10 An ancient rock painting from Cuchimachay in the highlands east of Lima. The scene depicts Andean camelids, possibly a family of vicuñas. The large figure with internal patterning probably portrays a pregnant female. Preceramic period. W. 1 m. (39.4 in.)

11 Fell's Cave in Chilean Patagonia. First excavated in the 1930s by Junius Bird, this cave provided the first scientific evidence for the early arrival of humans in South America. The cave's earliest occupation is dated 10,000–9,000 B.C.

and stone tools as well as remains of log and plank structures dating to about 13,000 B.C. Other finds from the site have been dated twenty thousand years earlier. Dillehay believes that the people of Monte Verde hunted camelids and other game, and collected wild potatoes, seeds, nuts, berries, leafy vegetables, rhizomes, and tubers.

In Peru, environmental changes brought on by the Pleistocene-Holocene transition, the end of the Ice Age, led to the demise of large animals that once thrived on Peru's north coast. Fossil remains found there include giant armadillos, horses, camelids, and mastodons. Before 14,000 B.C. coastal water sources nourished coastal meadows in what is today one of the world's driest deserts. Mangrove swamps extended as far south as Piura. But by 6000 B.C., rising sea levels and diminishing rainfall caused the mangroves to shrink to their present range—northernmost Peru and Ecuador. The end of the Pleistocene also brought major climatic and environmental changes to the Andes, where the last major ice advance in the central Andes has been dated to about 10,000 B.C.

Between 11,000 and 8000 B.C. in the Piura-Chira valleys of far-northern Peru, people estab-

lished camps along the shore where they collected shellfish from the mangrove swamps. To the south a group of people living ten thousand to seven thousand years ago, in the arid desert near the modern city of Trujillo, created a highly specialized stone industry known as the Paiján tradition. The distinctive, long, slender Paiján points, argues French archaeologist Claude Chauchat, are far too delicate to have penetrated the hides of long-extinct Pleistocene fauna. Chauchat believes that the people of Paiján used the points to spear fish. Similar points, however, are found far inland as well, in the mountains of Ecuador and northern Peru.

The Paiján people consumed abundant fish, crabs, and land snails, and they hunted lizards, birds, fox, and viscacha. Judging from the few excavated burials, they covered their dead with a thin layer of ash. Burial offerings are rare. One grave, that of a man in his twenties, dated to 8250 B.C., contained a stone tool and a bead. Today the shoreline sites of the Paiján lie underwater, but archaeologists also have found some one hundred inland camps, stone tool workshops, and quarries.

12 Stone "fishtail" points like these, probably used to tip hunting spears, are among the earliest recorded human cultural remains from South America. These examples were found with the bones of extinct native horse and ground sloth. 10,000–9,000 B.C. **Fell's Cave, Chile.** H. 6.7; 5.4; 4.2; 3.6 cm. (2.6; 2.1; 1.7; 1.4 in.) 41.1/1979

Farther north, on Ecuador's Santa Elena Peninsula, archaeologist Karen Stothert's excavations at the site of Las Vegas uncovered camps and settlements dating from about 8000 to 4000 B.C. The people there constructed circular houses with floors of plastered mud, and they made simple stone tools. Deer accounted for more than half of the animal portion of their diet, but the people of Las Vegas also fished and collected mollusks from mangrove swamps three kilometers (two miles) away. They supplemented their diet with wild plants and may have cultivated the bottle gourd. Grave goods were rare in the 192 burials excavated by Stothert, but the occasional funerary offerings included shell spoons, perforated conch shells, flat pebbles, and stone tools.

In the Andes to the east, early Peruvians established a base camp at the site of Guitarrero Cave perhaps as early as twelve thousand years ago. Located at 2,850 meters (9,350 feet) above sea level, the site overlooks the Santa River in the Callejón de Huaylas. The major occupation at Guitarrero Cave dates back ten thousand years, with most dates closer to 9000 B.C. Lithics, or stone tools, found there are similar to those from the contemporary sites of Lauricocha, in Huánuco, and Pachamachay, in Junín. While living at Guitarrero, people consumed viscacha, tinamou, dove, and deer. Deer remains outnumbered camelid bones seven to one. By 8600 B.C. the people of Guitarrero had begun to produce twined mats and mesh containers made of fiber as well as cordage for textiles and weaving. Vegetal remains found at the cave include rhizomes, tubers—ancestor of the modern potato—squash, lucuma, and *pacae*. Guitarrero

may also provide some of the earliest evidence in the Andes for domesticated beans and peppers. These finds have been dated to 8500 B.C.

Guitarrero Cave, however, was not a permanent settlement. According to Thomas Lynch, Guitarrero's excavator, during the December–March rainy season the cave's occupants moved up to the puna, at about 4,000 meters, (13,120 feet) to hunt camelids, especially vicuña. The Peruvian puna environment is not as bleak as it looks. Game was readily available, and people also collected wild plants, as evidenced by carbonized seeds found in puna excavations. According to archaeologist John Rick, who excavated several puna sites in Junín, the earliest phase of the puna hunting groups may date from 10,000 to 7000 B.C., a period characterized by roaming hunting groups.

The earliest puna occupants camped within natural caves and rock shelters, but later peoples built structures at cave entrances. They also decorated cave and shelter walls with painted hunting scenes that portrayed humans and camelids, as well as with geometric designs in black and red mineral pigments. These hunting scenes are some of the earliest examples of art in the Americas.

About 8000 B.C. the inhabitants of the lakeside puna site of Lauricocha used leaf-shaped projectile points to hunt deer, supplementing their diet of deer with roots and tubers. Lauricocha lies at an elevation of 3,900 meters (12,800 feet) at the neck of a glacial valley not far from rich camelid pastures. By about 7500 B.C. it may have been one of the earliest permanent settlements in the Andes. By 6000 B.C. camelid bones far outnumber

13 Detail of an ancient rock carving at Ichucollo, Lake Titicaca region, Peru. The carving may date back to several thousand years B.C. Except for a young llama (top center), all of the llamas depicted face in the same direction, and they may be led by the humans at right. South highlands, Peru.

14 A miniature wooden raft and paddle that may represent an actual raft used by fisherfolk who lived in the coastal desert of northern Chile in the third millennium B.C. H. 32.3 cm. (12.7 in.) 41.2/5289, 5290

15 Barbed pointed harpoons like this one were used by fisherfolk in ancient Chile to hunt for sea lions. Northern Chile. L. 32.4 cm. (12.8 in.) 41.1/7033

deer remains in the finds. Three child burials excavated at Lauricocha by Peruvian archaeologist Augusto Cardich contained offerings of food, stone tools, and beads.

At Uchumachay, in Junín, a puna site occupied between 8000 and 7000 B.C., people hunted deer until about 5500 B.C. At this time camelid remains begin to replace those of deer, indicating that at Uchumachay as at other puna sites—Telarmachay, for instance—the domestication of camelids was under way. By the third millennium B.C. camelid remains far outnumber those of deer. Telarmachay, also in Junín, was occupied from 7000 to 4000 B.C. A team of archaeologists led by Danièle Lavallée uncovered burials and also found bone needles and stone perforators used for working camelid skins.

In the next phase, from 7000 B.C. onward, permanent populations occupied the area. By 6000 B.C. groups of specialized hunters and collectors had emerged and established themselves in the varied ecosystems of the Andes. During the fifth millennium B.C. a switch from generalized to specialized hunting took place. This heralded the domestication and, eventually, the herding of camelids. Evidence from Telarmachay indicates that by 3500 B.C. camelids were already domesticated. Guinea pigs also seem to have been domesticated in the highlands about this time; remains dating to 7000 B.C., however, are probably from wild guinea pigs. By this time, the specialized puna hunters exploited a wide range of plant resources as well, gathering plants from lake shores and stream beds and collecting grains, cactus fruits, and medicinal plants.

During the age of specialized hunting on the coast, people exploited the *lomas*—pockets of vegetation nourished by the winter fogs that once extended all along the Peruvian and northern Chilean coastline. In northern Chile, fisherfolk consumed fish and shellfish and hunted inland for deer, using leaf-shaped projectile points, some made of obsidian. About 5000 B.C., Chile's Chinchorro people hunted for deer and collected plants inland, while on the coast they hunted seabirds and harpooned sea lions with barbed harpoons. Archaeologists also have found remains of fishing nets and fishhooks made of cactus thorns, shell, and later, bone.

The Chinchorro people carried out sophisticated practices to preserve their dead, providing some of the earliest evidence in the Americas for an ancestor cult. Indeed, their sophisticated, elaborate mummification techniques are the earliest in the New World. The Chinchorro flourished 7,800 to 3,800 years ago, refining their mummification techniques over the millennia. The most elaborate Chinchorro mummies are roughly contemporary with, but independent of, ancient Egypt's similarly treated burials.

Studies by palaeopathologist Marvin Allison of sixty-nine Chinchorro mummies found at the site of El Morro near Arica indicate that the mummies were not buried but propped up in groups. Judging by frequent repairs, the mummies were maintained for years above ground before they were buried.

Chinchorro specialists used stone and shell tools and sharpened pelican bones to remove the internal organs and major muscles and cut away

the skin of the dead person. In some cases, they took out the brain through a cut in the skull or hooked it out through the foramen magnum. Sometimes they filled the body cavity with ash and coal and allowed it to dry. Elbow and knee joints were bound, the chest tied, the spinal column made rigid by implanting cane supports, sticks inserted into the ankles, and the body cavity filled with feathers, grass, shells, and earth. At times the entire body of the deceased was covered with clay, which was molded to the body's shape. A face of clay with a modeled nose was sculpted and a wig of human hair was placed on the head. The clay-covered body was painted with red or black pigment.

Contemporary with the flowering of the Chinchorro, the site of Paloma, just south of Lima, was occupied from 5700 until about 2800 B.C. Paloma is located near lomas meadows on the edge of the Chilca River valley, a few kilometers from the river floodplain and three to four kilometers (about two miles) inland. Midden (refuse) at the site covers fifteen hectares (thirty-seven acres). The people of Paloma lived in semisubterranean flat-roofed huts, oval or quadrilateral in shape, made of bunches of cane poles set into the earth. Cross poles probably supported the structure and bunches of grass or reeds were wedged between the poles. The Palomans carpeted their floors with reed mats and may also have used these mats to insulate the walls of their huts.

Archaeologist Jeffrey Quilter studied more than a hundred burials excavated at the site by Robert Benfer and Frédéric Engel. Most burials were flexed and wrapped in reed mats, the hands placed over the pelvis or face. The bodies were buried in shallow pits in the floors of the huts or just outside. Most of the burials were of infants. Indeed, studies indicate that 42 percent of the Palomans did not live past childhood. Life expectancy at Paloma was twenty to thirty-five years; but there were some exceptions, notably one woman who lived to the age of fifty. Diet and health may have improved over time as evidenced by the decrease in infant mortality.

Burial offerings at Paloma are rare, although some burials contained shells, gourd fragments, shell disks, pieces of red pigment, and grinding stones. In one burial a cache of mussel shells filled with hair was found. Hearth stones often were placed over the tombs. Reed mats, often the only offerings in tombs, were made from *junco*. Palomans crafted twined textiles from the fibers of the succulent *Furcraea occidentalis andina*, known as *cabuya*, or maguey.

The people of Paloma used the bones of sea mammals, deer, or camelids to make beads, pins, and fishhooks. On the floor of one house, archaeologists found a fishing kit that included three bone fishhooks, cordage, and a fragment of netting. Ground-stone tools, such as *manos* and *metates*, and chipped-stone tools were fashioned from locally available basalt. Archaeologists also uncovered obsidian flakes and one complete obsidian projectile point. The nearest known source for obsidian is 400 kilometers (250 miles) away. Obsidian was not the only exotic item found at Paloma. Quilter also discovered the worked femur of a spider monkey, whose habitat lies in the tropical rain forest far to the east.

Although marine resources provided the bulk of the Paloman diet, people also exploited the nearby lomas for their wild game, trees and bushes, sedges and fruits, and the tuber of a begonia species. They also may have gathered guava fruit and grown squash and beans on the nearby river floodplain. But the lomas meadows are especially vulnerable to overexploitation, and Quilter believes that this fragile habitat, particularly its trees, which help contain moisture and reduce evaporation, was already overexploited in antiquity.

By 2500 B.C., people had begun to shift from wide-ranging hunting and gathering and to focus instead on tending and harvesting locally available resources. Although few sites from this period have been excavated and archaeological evidence is slim, the increasing number of permanent settlements reflects the change in subsistence strategies. As the next chapter shows, this shift culminated in such specialized Cotton Preceramic sites as Huaca Prieta and Aspero.

16 Nourished by winter fogs, lomas meadows once flourished all along the Peruvian coast. These lomas near Lima are some of the few that remain after centuries of overgrazing and deforestation. Lomas de Lachay, central coast of Peru.

THE FOUNDATIONS OF CIVILIZATION

EMERGING COMPLEX SOCIETIES, THEIR ART AND TECHNOLOGY

The foundations of Andean civilization can be traced back five thousand years to developments on the Peruvian coast and in the highlands that began in the mid-third millennium B.C. New evidence suggests that monumental architecture in the Andes may be the earliest in the New World, predating by one thousand years that of the Olmec in Mexico, whose public constructions were long thought to be the most ancient in the Americas. The first such examples in the Andes are contemporary with the earliest pyramids of Egypt, about 2500 B.C. In the past decade, data from excavations at coastal and highland Preceramic sites pinpoint the Andes as one of the centers where civilization first arose in the world.

Most of what we know about the late Preceramic is based on data from excavations at a handful of well-preserved sites on the arid central and north coast. Fewer contemporary sites have been studied in the highlands, where rainfall is often high and preservation consequently poor. The data thus reflect both a preservation bias as well as a research emphasis on coastal sites with monumental architecture.

The subsistence base of Preceramic peoples is the subject of a long-standing debate. Debated is whether late Preceramic complexes depended primarily on a marine subsistence base or on domesticated plants and animals. In the highlands, people hunted for deer and wild camelids, supplementing their diet with local plants. Late Preceramic coastal peoples subsisted on a combination of marine resources—mainly fish and mollusks—and wild and domesticated plants.

First proposed in the 1960s and 1970s by archaeologists Michael Moseley and Edward Lanning, the argument for dependence on marine resources is based, in part, on the fact that cotton and bottle gourds are some of the earliest cultigens (cultivated plant with an unknown wild ancestor), found at coastal Preceramic sites. Both cotton and bottle gourds were industrial crops widely used in the manufacture of fishing nets, lines, and floats. This marine hypothesis for the origins of Preceramic civilization does not explain the emergence of complex societies in the highlands, however.

Archaeological evidence, in fact, indicates that coastal peoples depended primarily on farming and fishing for their protein, while highland dwellers still relied heavily on hunting. Chipped-stone tools, such as projectile points, are rare on the coast in late Preceramic times but common in the highlands, where they were used to hunt deer and wild camelids.

Peru's rich shoreline abounds in fish and shellfish: people gathered rock-perching and sand-dwelling mollusks and crustaceans, such as crabs, and they fished for shark, catfish, herring, anchovy, and sea bass. The Preceramic inhabitants hunted seabirds such as penguins, and sea mammals, including sea lions and fur seals. They also exploited the occasional beached whale, incorporating whale ribs into the roofs and walls of their houses.

At the same time, coastal people cultivated cotton and gourds on seasonally inundated river floodplains. They also grew squash, chili peppers, and beans and gathered fruits, such as lucuma (from an evergreen tree; the fruit has a dry, mealy

17 A 4,000-year-old gourd from Huaca Prieta, northern Peru, engraved with human faces that recall designs on ceramics of the same period from Valdivia in coastal Ecuador.
H. 4.2 cm. (1.7 in.) 41.2/2555

pulp), pacae (from *Inga feuillei,* a shade tree;
the long green seed pods are surrounded by a
sweet white pulp), and guava (*Psidium guava,* a
globular yellow fruit). There is increasing evidence to suggest that maize was present at some
places in late Preceramic times. Most scholars
agree that a primitive form of maize was introduced about 3000 B.C. from Mesoamerica to the
Andes, where it adapted to numerous Andean
ecosystems.

There are strong indications for contact at
this time among peoples of the coast, highlands,
and tropical forest. Coastal dwellers exchanged
products such as dried and salted fish, shellfish,
salt, seaweed, and chili peppers for highland goods,
such as potatoes. Long-distance trade was undertaken to acquire exotic prestige goods, such as
obsidian, the coral-rimmed Spondylus shell, and
colorful feathers of tropical birds.

By 2500 B.C. people had shifted away from
hunting and gathering, and were focusing instead
on locally available resources. This shift is
reflected in an increasing number of permanent
settlements. The latter part of the Preceramic
period, from 2500 to 1800 B.C., is often called the
Cotton Preceramic, an epoch before the appearance
of pottery, when ancient Peruvians first began
crafting cotton textiles and building large, permanent settlements.

The Cotton Preceramic is known for its
large architectural complexes. Often these complexes contained ceremonial structures, burials
accompanied by grave offerings, cotton textiles,
domesticated plants and animals, and specialized
artifacts.

THE COTTON PRECERAMIC

One of the best documented Cotton Preceramic
sites is Huaca Prieta, a small fishing settlement
located on Peru's north coast near the mouth of the
Chicama River (fig. 18). Directed by Junius Bird,
the excavations at Huaca Prieta in 1946–47 were
part of the Virú Valley Project, an ambitious
archaeological and anthropological investigation of
the nearby Virú Valley sponsored by the Institute of
Andean Research in New York. The American
Museum of Natural History covered Bird's field
expenses. Today the dark-colored mound of Huaca
Prieta rises twelve meters (approximately forty feet)
above a sandy plain bordering the Pacific. The
mound, or *huaca,* consists of a late Preceramic
midden, or refuse heap, topped on the northern side
by later occupations. The Preceramic occupation of
Huaca Prieta dates from about 3000 to 1200 B.C.

In addition to gathering wild plants, the
people of Huaca Prieta cultivated squash and
gourds, by far the most common vegetal remains
encountered by archaeologists; and they harvested
lucuma, *achira* (a plant of the Canna family, cultivated for its starchy tubers), *ciruela del fraile* (*Bun-
chiosa armeniaca,* an orange, plumlike fruit),
cotton, chili peppers, and beans. They also gathered mollusks and crabs, fished, and hunted for
birds on the nearby beach.

Judging by the high incidence of "surfer's
ear," or exostosis of the external auditory canal,

many inhabitants spent a lot of time in the cold ocean water. Exostosis results in hearing impairment and loss, is characterized by swelling, and indicates prolonged exposure to water temperatures below 17.5 degrees Celsius (63.5 degrees Fahrenheit). A high incidence of surfer's ear at Huaca Prieta reveals that more time was probably spent diving for shellfish in deeper waters than net fishing nearer the shore.

Huaca Prieta's inhabitants fashioned twined mats and looped baskets of *junco,* a kind of sedge that grew along the nearby Chicama River. Mats were used for sleeping, for floor coverings, and for roofs. Some of the baskets have cotton wefts. Bottle-shaped gourds served as fishing-net floats. Bird found the remains of a large fishing net still attached to eight bottle-gourd floats. Gourds were also used to hold food. Simple stone tools and worked pebbles were used as fishing line sinkers, and fishhooks were made from mussel shells or thorns.

Huaca Prieta's weavers used twining techniques to produce the earliest decorated textiles in the Americas. Unlike true weaving, in which weft and warp yarns interlace, in twining the weft yarns turn around the warp (see chapter 10). Twining was the most common technique used in the Andes before heddle weaving began, about 1800 B.C. Textile colors at Huaca Prieta were varied. They included the naturally pigmented Peruvian cotton, *Gossypium barbadense,* in shades of white, brown, and tan. Some cloth was dyed blue or rubbed with red pigment. No examples of sewn clothing were found, which suggests that people probably wrapped themselves in cloth. Footwear included sandals made of coarse fiber cord.

When Bird first found textiles at Huaca Prieta, the cloth appeared ordinary and undecorated. But in his New York laboratory, where he painstakingly traced the paths of the warps with a microscope, Bird and his assistant were able to reconstruct a wide array of natural and geometric designs. Huaca Prieta's weavers created the designs by crossing warps of different colors from one face of the fabric to the other. These designs—a condor with a snake in its stomach, double-headed snakes, cats, crabs, and a rare human figure—are considered some of the earliest art in the Americas (see chapter 10). Some of the Huaca Prieta motifs, like the double-headed snake and interlocking images, continued to be

used by Andean weavers for the next four thousand years.

The people of Huaca Prieta buried some of their dead in the floors of their simple, stone-lined subterranean houses, while others were interred in the midden. Bird unearthed a total of thirty-three burials. The bodies were flexed and buried with sleeping mats and fragments of textiles. Some graves contained offerings, such as a gourd pyroengraved (engraving with a heated tool) with geometric designs (figs. 17, 19). Some archaeologists have linked the designs found on two Huaca Prieta gourds to designs made by potters at the Ecuadorian site of Valdivia. The Valdivia 4 style dates to 2100 B.C., and the similarity in design may provide further evidence of far-ranging contacts among ancient Andean peoples (fig. 20).

Some 360 kilometers (220 miles) separate Huaca Prieta from Aspero, one of the largest coastal Preceramic centers. Aspero sprawls over twelve hectares (thirty acres) on a bluff overlooking the Pacific, near the northern edge of the Supe Valley. Constructions at Aspero include ceremonial mounds, plazas, and terraces. The deep midden deposits indicate a large resident population at the site, beginning about 2800 B.C.

The Aspero site includes seven large mounds and six lesser ones, rising only a few meters above the desert floor. Aspero's builders modified low-lying hills to build their mounds. Two of the larger

18 Huaca Prieta, a seaside Preceramic mound in the Chicama Valley. Textile fragments found there are among the oldest in the Americas. Except for rock painting, the designs on these textiles represent the earliest art in South America. North coast, Peru.

19 Designs on two pyroen-
graved gourds, found with a
burial at Huaca Prieta, may
be related stylistically to
objects from Ecuador. The
design on the right is that for
the gourd in fig. 17. Decorating gourds is a 5,000-year-
old Andean tradition.
Drawing by Miguel
Covarrubias.

mounds, Huaca de los Idolos and Huaca de los Sacrificios, measure about 30 by 50 meters (98 by 164
feet). Excavations have revealed walls made of
large blocks of basaltic rock quarried nearby and
set in mud mortar. On the summits of both
mounds, archaeologists found rooms of varying
sizes with remains of plaster on the walls and
traces of red and yellow pigment. The largest room
on Huaca de los Idolos served as the mound's main
entrance and looked like an open courtyard.

Aspero's builders also constructed with bags
made of looped sedge fibers and filled with loose
rubble, river cobbles, or quarried stone. This technique, known as *shicra,* was used to fill in rooms
for other constructions as well as to rebuild and
form the cores of mounds. The use of bagged fill is
one of the hallmarks of late Preceramic and Early
Ceramic period architecture. Shicra bags are also
found at El Paraíso in the Chillón Valley and at Las
Haldas near Casma.

Significantly, no shicra bags have been found
with domestic architecture. The use of shicra and
other architectural features—such as restricted
access to the summits of Aspero's larger mounds,
and niches, friezes, and wall paint on mound
walls—point to the ceremonial function of these
constructions.

The ceremonial importance of Aspero's
main mounds is also evident from the dedicatory
caches and burials found on Huaca de los Sacrificios and Huaca de los Idolos. Offerings include
small textile scraps held in scallop shells, featherwork, and string and cane *ojos de Díos.* Archaeologist Robert Feldman also uncovered burnt and
unburnt cotton seeds and carved wooden sticks.
On Idolos, a dedicatory cache included more than a
dozen female and male figurines fashioned of
unbaked white clay. These are some of the earliest
examples of figurative art from Peru. The largest
figurine, a male, wears a kind of wraparound skirt,
a bead necklace, and a tasseled hat (fig. 21). An
infant burial excavated on Sacrificios contained
over five hundred beads of shell and stone, a
bundle of textiles, and a four-legged grindstone.
Another cache found on Sacrificios included the
remains of a wooden bowl, its inside carved with
frogs that look over the rim.

As at other sites, the main industrial crops
cultivated by Aspero's Preceramic residents were
cotton and gourds. The population subsisted on
gathering, fishing, and limited planting on the
nearby Supe River floodplain. Using digging
sticks, they cultivated cotton and bottle gourds.
Archaeologists also uncovered remains of squash,

20 Ceramic and stone figurines of standing women that may be fertility symbols. 2100–1700 B.C. Valdivia 4–6 style, Ecuador.
H. 3.7; 4.2; 6.3; 6.7 cm. (1.5; 1.7; 2.5; 2.6 in.) 41.2/8389, 8390, 8387, 8388

chili peppers, legumes, and achira from the midden. Analysis of the Preceramic midden at Las Haldas, an important Preceramic center twenty kilometers (twelve miles) south of the Casma Valley, indicates that the site's dwellers consumed abundant amounts of shellfish. Some gourd rinds, cotton seeds, and fiber, and a few examples of guava and beans were also found.

The Preceramic occupation of El Paraíso (fig. 22) dates to about 1800 B.C. Sometimes called Chuquitanta, the site is Peru's largest Preceramic monument. Its builders used more than 100,000 tons of quarried stone to construct its platform mounds and stone buildings. El Paraíso lies 2 kilometers (1.2 miles) inland on the southern side of the lower Chillón Valley, and it covers more than 50 hectares (125 acres). Its buildings are scattered across a gently sloping plain.

Some archaeologists argue that the late Preceramic site of El Paraíso marks the earliest use of the U-shaped architectural plan that became widespread at Early Ceramic sites on the central coast a few centuries later. According to architect Carlos Williams, an idealized U-shaped complex is composed of a central pyramid at the base of the U, flanked by two lateral wings that enclose a large courtyard.

El Paraíso is important, too, because it signals the shift inland of late Preceramic populations. While earlier sites like Huaca Prieta and Aspero were located only hundreds of meters from the shore, El Paraíso is one of the earliest examples of an inland Preceramic site. When irrigation agriculture became widespread in the Early Ceramic period, people had to move even farther inland,

sometimes near the valley neck, where they could better control the source of irrigation waters. While there is no evidence for irrigation systems at El Paraíso, the site is located a few kilometers from the coast, so that its people could exploit marine resources as well as practice floodplain agriculture.

One of El Paraíso's excavators, Jeffrey Quilter, estimates that the site was occupied for only about two hundred years and that most of its constructions are Preceramic in date. He argues that the site's large midden deposits identify El Paraíso as a major late Preceramic population center in the Rimac-Chillón valleys. Residents ate mostly fish; but they cultivated squash, beans, chili peppers, *jicama*, lucuma, and pacae; and they collected sedges and cattails from the river's edge. Along the river floodplain they cultivated cotton, their major crop, which they used to make fishnets and fishing lines and to fashion simple clothing.

The site's two largest mounds together may form a U; each measures more than 50 meters (165 feet) wide, and they run parallel for almost 300 meters (980 feet). At the base of the U-shaped mounds lies a small, stone structure measuring about 50 meters (165 feet) square and 8 meters (approximately 26 feet) high. Two separate stairways gave access to the summit. The sunken floor area contains four circular pits, each about 1 meter (3 feet) in diameter, where archaeologists found the remains of charcoal. The presence of these curious circular pits may point to a highland connection, where firepits in ceremonial structures often contain charred remains of offerings.

21 Unbaked clay figurine from Aspero, a Preceramic site in the Supe Valley, Peru. Among the earliest figurative art from the Andes, it depicts a male wearing a skirt, a bead necklace, and a tasseled hat. Central coast, Peru.

22 An extensively reconstructed set of rooms at El Paraíso, Chillón Valley. These rooms and nearby constructions may have formed the largest Preceramic architectural complex in the Americas. Central coast, Peru.

Another feature that dominated ceremonial architecture in the Early Ceramic period, but also had its origins in the late Preceramic, is the sunken circular plaza. These plazas are distributed over some 600 kilometers (370 miles), from the Mala Valley south of Lima to the Moche Valley. They also occur at some highland sites. The earliest examples are found on the north coast at Alto Salaverry, Salinas de Chao, and at several sites in the Supe Valley. The plaza at Alto Salaverry, lined with stone and clay mortar, is associated with a nearby pyramid. The twined-cotton textiles and lack of ceramics indicate a late Preceramic occupation, dating to about 1480 ± 110 B.C. The greatest concentration of these pits is in the Supe Valley, where they exist at some thirty sites. According to Williams, this plaza type probably developed somewhere near the Santa Valley, predominated in the Supe Valley, and spread south. The sunken circular plaza and the U-shaped plan culminate in the Old Temple of Chavín de Huántar several centuries later (see chapter 5) and their earlier appearance on the coast suggests that both of these architectural features had a coastal origin.

THE HIGHLAND PRECERAMIC

Preceramic ceremonial centers at the highland sites of Kotosh, La Galgada, and Huaricoto share many features with contemporary sites on the coast. But while the ceremonial focus of coastal sites emphasized large, flat-topped mounds with multichambered structures on their summits and accompanying plazas and courtyards that could hold many people, highland ritual focused on small chambers with central firepits that could accommodate only a few worshippers. In the firepits are charred remains of burnt offerings, such as peppers, marine shells, meat, and precious—often exotic—items, such as feathers, deer antlers, and rock crystal.

The burning of offerings is an ancient Andean ritual and formed part of a Preceramic ceremonial rite, which archaeologist Richard Burger has called the Kotosh Religious Tradition. Burger's term refers to the site of Kotosh, in the Huallaga drainage, where the ritual firepits were first recognized, although the rite did not necessarily originate there. The sphere of influence of the Kotosh Religious Tradition has been traced some 250 kilometers (155 miles) to the north and south of Kotosh, and evidence for the rite has been found at highland sites on both the eastern and western slopes of the Andes. The tradition included the ritual entombment of ceremonial structures, which were carefully and deliberately sealed and then covered over by new ones. At the site of La Galgada, in the Santa drainage, the sealed structures were later used to hold burials, while at Huaricoto in the Callejón de Huaylas and at Kotosh the chambers were sealed and never used again.

Kotosh lies five kilometers (three miles) west of Huánuco in the north-central highlands at 2,000 meters (6,560 feet) above sea level. The complex includes stone constructions and terraced mounds. The site's most famous monument, dating to the Preceramic Kotosh Mito phase, is the Temple of the Crossed Hands, a nine-meter-square (thirty-foot-square) structure with rounded corners, built about 2000–1500 B.C.

The Temple of the Crossed Hands is named for the sculpted clay panels—each with a plastered mud frieze of human arms crossed at the wrists—below two central niches in one of the temple's walls. The frieze is a rare example of public Preceramic highland art. Nothing like it has been found at either La Galgada or Huaricoto. Constructions similar to the Temple of the Crossed Hands are ceremonially buried beneath it. Before the people of Kotosh buried the temple itself, however, the builders protected its reliefs with a thick layer of fine black sand and then sealed the entire enclosure with boulders and small stones. The Temple of the Niches was built over this base.

The ubiquitous central firepit is found in the Temple of the Crossed Hands, the Temple of the Niches, and the White Temple. In the midden of the Temple of the Crossed Hands, archaeologists found baked clay figurines. Formed of flattened lumps of clay, each figurine has punctuated eyes and an appliquéd nose. Two stone disks with incised geometric designs were found on the temple floor, and stone figurines were discovered at an associated mound. In the White Temple, excavators found other baked clay objects, including a clay disk, figurines, a small bowl, and a clay object shaped like a bottle gourd. The site also contained bone and shell artifacts, including bone beads, bone needles with decorated heads, and polished shell ornaments.

Kotosh is strategically located midway between the eastern slopes of the Andes and the tropical forest, which begins only thirty-five kilometers (twenty-two miles) away. Evidence of strong links with the tropical lowland forest can be seen in the mandible of a piranha found at the site and in early ceramic decoration from Kotosh.

La Galgada, another site within the Kotosh Religious Tradition's sphere of influence, perches 1,000 meters (3,280 feet) above sea level, in a narrow, dusty canyon overlooking the Tablachaca River, a tributary of the Santa. Occupied for about five centuries, between 2400 and 1900 B.C., La Galgada has well-preserved constructions that include two mounds flanked by a circular courtyard and topped by ritual chambers, ceremonial hearths, and tombs. The last occupants transformed one mound's summit into a U-shaped structure that included three platforms set around a central court.

The earliest structures, built of river cobbles set in mud mortar, had plastered walls. Later walls, dating to about 2300 B.C., were built of broken fieldstones and plastered white. La Galgada's temple walls are unusual for their ornamental construction on both sides. Exterior decoration includes dados, corbels, and a series of horizontal niches.

The earliest ritual chambers date to the site's first occupation, and they contain firepits, ventilator shafts, and interior walls with niches and low benches. Within the firepits, archaeologists found the burnt remains of chili peppers; white, orange, and green feather down; and the lower half of a deer antler. The chambers were ceremonially buried and later reused as tombs, and groups of ritual chambers were stacked over each other.

Excavators uncovered twenty-seven adult burials and several juvenile and infant burials at La Galgada. Unlike Preceramic coastal burials, these bodies were extended and placed in the stone-lined chambers previously used for ceremony. Early Ceramic burials were flexed, however. The burial chambers held from three to five bodies, and grave goods sometimes included bone pins inlaid with a greenish, turquoiselike stone, stone cups, and red stone beads.

Because little rain falls at La Galgada, textiles, baskets, and other organic remains are well preserved. Most were recovered from the tombs. Almost all the cloth was made of cotton, although weavers also used some other plant fibers. Sleeping mats were made of twined cotton, while bags were produced by looping. Netting, knotted looping, and interlooping techniques were used as well. La Galgada's weavers decorated the looped bags with designs of birds and snakes as well as with curvilinear patterns and with what archaeologists Terence Grieder and Alberto Bueno, who excavated La Galgada, describe as an anthropomorphic deity. Designs were executed in shades of red, yellow, blue, and black as well as in naturally pigmented cotton tones of brown and white.

Unlike people at Preceramic sites on the coast who depended heavily on marine life for subsistence, inland populations at sites like La Galgada turned to agriculture and hunting, supplementing their diet with dried fish and shellfish. Located midway between the Pacific and the Marañon River, La Galgada is well placed for exchange between coast and highlands. People hunted deer and planted some crops on the narrow strip of land that bordered the river. Remains of irrigation canals point to La Galgada as one of the earliest sites in the Andes that shows evidence of irrigation agriculture.

Huaricoto, at 2,750 meters (9,020 feet) above sea level in the Callejón de Huaylas, served as a ceremonial center from about 2000 to 200 B.C. The site contains small, one-room structures with single entrances, plastered floors, and central firepits. By 1800 B.C., when ceramics were first introduced there, Huaricoto's residents had transformed their ritual chambers into rectangular, square, or round structures, with a perishable superstructure and split-level, plastered floors. A bench surrounded the firepit, and a stone-lined ventilator shaft passed under the bench to the outside.

Two radiocarbon dates indicate Huaricoto's earliest occupation: 3290 ± 120 B.C. and 2820 ± 200 B.C. During the site's second occupation Huaricoto became a small temple. One of two ceremonial hearths, dating to 2020 ± 110 B.C., contains a stone-lined circular pit, dug into clay and filled with ash and carbon. Archaeologists found pieces of burnt bone and quartz among these charred remains.

Unlike the firepits enclosed within stone chambers at La Galgada and Kotosh, those at Huaricoto lay out in the open, topped by perishable wattle-and-daub (bundles of cane plastered with mud) superstructures. Nor were the ceremonial hearths fed by ventilators or surrounded by benches or niches. The Kotosh Religious Tradition continued to flourish at Huaricoto long after the introduction of pottery. Two ritual hearths there date to the late Early Ceramic period and others date to the Chavín Period, when the Kotosh Religious Tradition was practiced alongside ceremonies tied to the Chavín cult.

By 1800 B.C., the onset of the Early Ceramic period, ceramics became widespread throughout the Andes. Pottery had appeared earlier in the Amazon basin and in northern South America, and archaeologists believe that ceramic technology may have spread from these regions to the Andes. The growth of irrigation systems throughout the middle sections of the valleys also dates to the Early Ceramic period. Sites moved inland, away from shoreline settings. Although people still relied on marine resources, they began to depend more and more on agriculture for subsistence. New cultigens appeared, too: avocado, potatoes, sweet potatoes, and peanuts. The production of cloth increased, with the invention of the more efficient heddle loom. Ceremonial architecture on the coast and in the highlands became truly monumental. Large, U-shaped pyramids and sunken, circular forecourts became common on the central and north coast, and temple façades were adorned with impressive, colorful abode friezes. Llamas, early highland domesticates, are found on the coast for the first time, although in small quantities, indicating increasing ties to the highlands. Developments in the Preceramic period provided the foundations for the startling innovations of the Early Ceramic period.

CHAVIN AND ITS ANTECEDENTS

THE SPREAD OF ART STYLES AND IDEAS

Chavín de Huántar was—and is—one of the most renowned ceremonial centers in the Andes. Few sites in Peru have received as much scholarly attention. Recent studies have shown, however, that Chavín de Huántar was not the inspiration for the startling architectural and technological innovations that occurred on the coast and in the highlands. On the contrary, it was the culmination of those earlier developments. But Chavín de Huántar's architects skillfully blended coastal traits—the U-shaped, truncated pyramid and sunken circular and square forecourts—with local traditions, such as the masterful carving of stone. The result was an imposing ceremonial center that provided the basis for a widespread cult that would unite previously isolated regions with a shared religion and technology (fig. 24).

By 1800 B.C., a thousand years before building began at Chavín de Huántar, the beginnings of irrigation agriculture spurred many peoples to move from their shoreline settlements to prime agricultural lands in lower and mid-valley habitats. There, people clustered their villages around monumental ceremonial centers and began to build irrigation systems. These systems originated near the valley neck, where the Andean foothills rise imposingly and the valley narrows. This is an optimal location for canal intakes. More land can be irrigated efficiently in the mid-valley than in the lower valley areas, where rivers flow more slowly as they reach the sea and canal construction requires greater labor.

The spread of irrigation agriculture in the Early Ceramic period allowed people to plant more than one crop per year. The plentiful food supply contributed to the widespread adoption of ceramics throughout the Andes. Ceramic containers served not only to store foods but also for cooking and for brewing fermented beverages such as *chicha*, or maize beer.

The gradual switch from a primarily marine to a farming economy is reflected in the contents of middens from these newly established lower- and mid-valley centers, where more agricultural products than marine remains are found. Shoreline settlements still existed, but the diet clearly emphasized domesticated plants.

Bountiful crops led to population increases, which in turn provided labor for building monumental complexes. Indeed, sites built during the period leading up to the Chavín florescence are some of the largest ever constructed in ancient Peru, surpassing the number built during the Preceramic period. Specialized craft production also emerged during the Early Ceramic period. For the first time in Andean prehistory, people began to produce pottery and cloth on a large scale. The switch from floodplain agriculture to irrigation farming allowed abundant cotton harvests, and the plentiful supply of cotton, as well as the widespread introduction of the heddle loom, led to increased production of cotton cloth.

Massive monumental architecture was also a characteristic of highland centers, although it was less imposing than that along the coast. Highland communities depended on rainfall agriculture, herding, and hunting. Llamas, domesticated some two to three thousand years earlier in the bleak altiplano, appeared on the coast for the first time. Not only were these camelids used as pack

23 Nose ornaments, like this one of thin hammered gold representing a four-legged creature, were probably worn by priests or political leaders. Chavín style, north coast, Peru. L. 5.9 cm. (2.3 in.) 41.2/7758

45

animals to transport trade goods but their meat became an important protein source and their fiber was used in weavings.

The architecture of this period, however, remains its most impressive monument. Architectural canons established in the Preceramic period became widespread at central, north coast, and highland centers. The U-shaped plan, developed in the Preceramic, is found at coastal sites from the Mala Valley in the south to the Supe Valley in the north. Rectangular mounds with their adjacent sunken courtyards proliferated at north-coast ceremonial centers.

Unlike Preceramic ceremonial centers, where temple adornment was rare, the façades of Early Ceramic temples and ceremonial structures were often colorfully decorated. Polychrome friezes and freestanding adobe sculptures of fearsome fanged creatures are a distinctive hallmark of Early Ceramic period ceremonial architecture. These Early Ceramic sites share another feature: many are similarly aligned, and the open ends of almost all U-shaped complexes face upvalley toward the Andes and the rivers' sources of water. In addition, most of the sites are located on what is today prime agricultural land. This settlement pattern began to change two thousand years ago, when population pressures forced people to move to the edges of the fertile valleys, away from agricultural land.

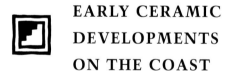

EARLY CERAMIC DEVELOPMENTS ON THE COAST

By 1750 B.C., construction had already begun at the Rimac Valley site of La Florida, where monumental building started in the Early Ceramic period and continued until the site was abandoned several centuries later.

This U-shaped platform mound is located 11 kilometers (7 miles) inland with the open end of the U oriented toward the Rimac River. The central platform today stands 17 meters (56 feet) high. Two wings that extend 500 meters (1,640 feet) and rise 3 to 4 meters (10 to 13 feet) above the valley floor, frame a 120,000-square-meter (1,291,680-square-foot) area. In the middle of the central plat-

24 The renowned ceremonial center of Chavín de Huántar flourished from 850 to 200 B.C. at the confluence of two rivers in the Callejón de Conchucos, north-central highlands, Peru. The Old Temple is honeycombed with rooms and interior passages.

form, archaeologists uncovered the remains of an atrium connected by a staircase to a low-walled, square courtyard in front of the central mound.

La Florida's inhabitants made distinctive ceramics, in shapes that included simple, neckless pots and shallow bowls, embellished by appliqué and modeled decorations. Archaeologists also found fragments of an unfired clay figurine, a grinding stone with traces of red pigment, and an incised-stone spindle whorl. Studies of La Florida's midden revealed that people subsisted on fruits and vegetables, fish, shellfish, and the occasional guinea pig.

Some three hundred years later construction began at the site of Garagay, occupied from about 1500 to 600 B.C. The open end of the U-shaped structure there faces another water source, the Chillón River. Garagay lies 6 kilometers (3.7 miles) inland. At its base, the central pyramid measures 385 by 155 meters (1,260 by 510 feet). The pyramid rises 23 meters (75 feet) above the valley floor. Two wings enclose a large plaza of 90,000 square meters (968,760 square feet). The central pyramid has a U-shaped atrium with a rectangular, sunken forecourt. Archaeologists William Isbell and Rogger Ravines found remains of a striking frieze painted in blue, red, black, and white on the atrium's northeast corner. According to archaeologists Richard Burger and Lucy Salazar-Burger, the frieze portrays an anthropomorphized spider deity. Spiders, the Burgers say, are commonly associated with rituals and offerings to ensure fertility and the availability of water.

Meanwhile, at Cardal, a site in the Lurín Valley south of Lima, construction began about 1100 B.C. on a monumental U-shaped central platform. Cardal occupies some 20 hectares (50 acres) on the south side of the valley, on a natural terrace. The central, flat-topped platform measures 145 by 60 by 17 meters (475 by 197 by 56 feet). Two wings enclose a 3-hectare (7.5-acre) terrace forecourt. Again, the open side of the U is oriented northeast toward the Lurín River.

Burger unearthed sixteen burials in the atrium, built into the center of the main platform. The most distinctive funerary offerings were found with the burial of a man, among them a necklace made of sea-lion teeth and earspools crafted of dolphin vertebrae. Remains of a polychrome clay frieze on the atrium walls show a strip of meter-long, giant interlocking teeth with traces of cream,

yellow, and rose-colored paint. This snarling frieze would have been visible to worshippers standing in the forecourt below. Later, Cardal's architects used fiber fill bags to cover the frieze and atrium.

One of Burger's goals when he began excavations at Cardal was to determine whether architect Carlos Williams was correct in hypothesizing that sites like Cardal served as agro-religious complexes. In the sacred fields and orchards of such complexes, Williams believes, people may have carried out the ritual cultivation of crops. Burger's excavations, however, uncovered only a prepared earthen floor and revealed no furrows or other evidence of cultivation. Neither did he find any traces of canals that would have watered the hypothetical sacred fields. His excavations did show that Cardal's residents swept the courtyard clean. This paucity of artifacts in Cardal's central courtyard ties in with age-old Andean conventions, still observed today, of sweeping sacred space clean.

Ten large circular courts ring the site. In the center of one court Burger unearthed an offering, a ceramic bottle decorated with an incised design of interlocking, two-headed serpents. This circular court is 13 meters (43 feet) in diameter and its stone walls have traces of plaster. In the center of another court Burger found the cranium of a child. Yet another has walls with traces of red, white, and black plaster and a stone-lined hearth with remains of ash at its center. Archaeologists encountered few artifacts and little debris in the circular plazas, whose floors, like that of Cardal's large central plaza, seem to have been kept purposely clean. Although these circular courts probably had a ceremonial function, they were not part of Cardal's original plan; a rectangular room with high walls was found beneath one court and traces of a road lay beneath another.

Excavations revealed an extensive domestic occupation south of the central mound, indicating that Cardal was not solely an uninhabited ceremonial center. This area yielded remains of structures as well as undecorated cooking pots and bowls, fragments of female figurines, agricultural tools, cotton seed, and pottery spindle whorls. Cardal's potters made single-necked bottles with flaring rims and round-bottomed bowls decorated with stamped circles, zoned punctuation, and incised geometric designs. Remains of clams, mussels, fish bones, sea mammals, deer, and birds reflect the diet at Cardal. People also consumed guava, pacae,

25 The Tembladera style of the Jequetepeque Valley is known for its incised and resin-painted decorations. This ceramic bottle is modeled with a human figure wearing a jaguar skin. North coast, Peru.

H. 19.6 cm. (7.7 in.) 41.2/7717

tuna (a succulent fruit of the cactus family), chili peppers, bottle gourds, peanuts, and squash.

Cardal's monumental structures were built over a span of three hundred to four hundred years that ended about 850 B.C. The site seems to have been one of four or five monumental centers that flourished in the Lurín Valley during Early Ceramic times, along with Manchay Bajo, a kilometer northwest of Cardal, Mina Perdida, and Parka, less than five kilometers (three miles) distant.

To the north of Cardal, construction continued at the shoreline site of Las Haldas, just south of the Casma Valley. During the third Early Ceramic occupation phase at Las Haldas, the inhabitants began building the site's ceremonial complex. This included the central mound and a long series of plazas and smaller mound-and-plaza complexes, including two sunken circular forecourts. As at Cardal, the circular courts appear to be later additions to the main ceremonial building phase. Pre-temple domestic constructions had double-faced cobblestone walls. Potters decorated their simple neckless pots, jars, and bottles with combing, incising, and punctuation. The inhabitants of Las Haldas still depended largely on marine resources, but studies of their midden showed that since Preceramic times their diet had expanded to include lucuma, peanuts, beans, potatoes, lima beans, chili peppers, pacae, ciruela del fraile, wild plants, and land snails collected from the nearby lomas.

Just north in the Casma Valley, a boom in monumental construction took place. Here archaeologists have documented some of Peru's most spectacular Early Ceramic sites. Thomas and Shelia Pozorski postulate that the Casma Valley may have been a center of regional authority during the Early Ceramic period. But others argue that there is little evidence for social stratification, such as lavish funerary offerings and personal wealth, that would indicate the existence of such an authority. Religion, they say, may have been the unifying force that inspired the construction of these monumental ceremonial centers. At the same time, age-old Andean conventions of *mit'a,* or communal labor, might have provided the manpower to build these monumental centers.

At the Casma Valley site of Pampa de las Llamas-Moxeke, first excavated in 1937 by Peruvian archaeologist Julio C. Tello, recent research has shown that construction of the site's two major complexes began about 1400 B.C. Located eighteen kilometers (eleven miles) inland, the site covers some 220 hectares (540 acres) near the confluence of the Sechín and Casma rivers. Two large mounds—Moxeke and Huaca A—face each other across a kilometer-long series of plazas, the largest 350 meters (1,150 feet) long. Low mounds and domestic constructions flank the plazas.

Moxeke's architects designed the Moxeke pyramid with a bilaterally symmetrical plan. Constructions on the summit form a U. Almost square—170 by 160 meters (560 by 530 feet)—the mound stands 30 meters (100 feet) high. The building's corners are rounded, an Early Ceramic trait, and conical adobes form the core of the mound. Tello uncovered elaborately carved free-standing figures and colossal heads, 2.4 meters (8 feet) wide, that once stood 3 meters (10 feet) high. These were painted red, blue, white, green, and black and could have been seen by worshippers gathered in the plaza below. Only the bottom halves of the freestanding figures survive. These figures represent individuals wearing kiltlike skirts and holding the knotted ends of tunics in their hands. One wears a ropelike belt, and the heads of four serpents coil around the figure's body.

The Pozorskis, Moxeke-Pampa de la Llamas' most recent excavators, have interpreted the Moxeke mound as the complex's sacred structure, while they assign Huaca A a secular function. Moxeke's southern façade faces Huaca A, which measures 140 by 140 meters (462 by 462 feet) and rises only 9 meters (about 30 feet) above the valley floor. On the summit, which was accessible from either side, archaeologists uncovered numerous rooms with rounded corners. The central rooms are largest, and the rooms become progressively smaller as they near the southeastern and north-western sides of the Huaca. All the rooms have niches set high up in the thick, white-plastered walls that once rose 4 to 7 meters (13 to 23 feet) high. Many rooms appear to have been carpeted with reed mats. The Pozorskis believe that Huaca A was used to store agricultural products, trade goods, and textiles. In some of the rooms they found turquoise beads, a jet mirror, a wooden fig-urine, and scraps of finely woven textiles. Access to Huaca A's storage facilities may have been tightly controlled, because at many doorways exca-vators found remains of wooden beams that once served as gates.

On the walls of Huaca A's northeast atrium, the Pozorskis hypothesize that two snarling feline images may have once guarded an entrance set into the walls of a recessed courtyard leading into one of the summit's larger rooms. Only the felines' feet, tails, and certain decorative elements survive to record the frieze. A reconstruction, based on contemporary feline depictions in other media along with the atrium's estimated wall height, indicate that the hypothetical felines were origi-nally 10 meters (33 feet) long and 5.5 to 6 meters (18 to 20 feet) tall. White and traces of red and pos-sibly blue pigment cover much of the remaining frieze. Each feline's tail ends in a fanged serpent head.

The plazas off Huaca A's southwest and northeast sides both measure 125 by 110 meters (410 by 360 feet) and 2 meters (about 7 feet) deep. A raised platform, 40 by 60 meters (130 by 200 feet) and 3 meters (10 feet) high, lies off the northeast plaza. In the center of this platform the Pozorskis discovered a badly preserved sunken circular court, ranging from 32 to 39 meters (105 to 130 feet) in diameter.

According to Williams, sunken circular courtyards first appear about 2500 B.C., from the Moche Valley in the north to Mala in the south, with some examples in the highlands. The courtyards are either isolated structures or associated with truncated pyramids. They average 18 meters (60 feet) in diameter by about 3 meters (10 feet) in depth and are accessible by stairways or ramps built into the courtyard walls. The Supe, Casma, Huarmey, and Pativilca valleys have the heaviest concentration of circular courtyards, but Williams believes that they may have originated farther north in the Santa Valley. These courtyards became especially popular in the Supe Valley, while in the south they became secondary elements of U-shaped ceremonial structures. At some sites they seem to be later additions, because they are not aligned with the U-shaped central pyramid. At Sechín Alto, in Casma, and the Old Temple at Chavín de Huántar, however, circular courtyards form an integral part of the ceremonial design.

Excavations by the Pozorskis of the domestic area flanking the large plaza of Moxeke-Pampa de las Llamas uncovered small, stone-walled structures. Ceramics found here and in other areas include neckless pots, bowls, jars, bot-tles, solid figurines, and spindle whorls. Many of these objects are decorated by punctuation, incising, incised appliqué, and modeling. Several pieces of stone vessels were also recovered. Some were decorated with incised lines, while others served as mortars for red pigments. People here subsisted on a largely marine-based diet of shellfish and fish, as well as deer, along with peanuts, squash, lucuma, potatoes, sweet potatoes, achira, manioc, avocado, hot peppers, guava, and beans.

At the site of Sechín Alto, which is roughly contemporary with Moxeke-Pampa de la Llamas, there is a massive, solid, truncated pyramid that archaeologists consider the largest stone construction of its time in the Americas. According to archaeologist Michael Moseley, Sechín Alto is fifteen times larger than Chavín de Huántar, which flourished centuries later. The mound measures 300 by 250 meters (980 by 820 feet) and stands 44 meters (145 feet) high. The site, fifteen kilometers (nine miles) inland, is oriented northeast, and the main entrance faces the water source upvalley. Sechín Alto's builders used quarried stone set in silty, clay mortar. A 20-meter-deep (65-foot-deep) looter's pit in the center of the mound reveals an inner core of conical adobes, indicating an earlier adobe construction of about 1500 B.C. or even before. Remains of a frieze were found near this adobe core. At least four plazas extend out over a kilometer northeast of the central mound. Three of them contain sunken circular courtyards aligned with the central mound's axis. Smaller constructions flank the plaza area, but remains of domestic occupation have been largely obliterated by modern cultivation. Confusion surrounds the

26 Andean ceramics often portray individuals with coca leaves in their mouths. This man pours from a gourd into a container. Early Ceramic, north coast, Peru.
H. 26.4 cm. (10.4 in.) 41.2/7768

27 This Tembladera-style ceramic bottle decorated with resin-based pigments portrays a supernatural being with stylized feline features. North coast, Peru.
H. 29.9 c:n. (11.8 in.) 41.2/7518

dating of the later stone-construction phase, but ceramics found at the site resemble those from Moxeke and Las Haldas.

The nearby site of Cerro Sechín, perhaps Casma's most renowned monument, lies thirteen kilometers (eight miles) inland, nestled against a low hill. The main structure measures 50 meters square (180 feet square), and the corners of the complex are rounded. The site was first explored scientifically by Tello in 1937. More recent excavations indicate two building phases: a three-stage period of construction with conical adobes and a later stone construction. Again, much confusion surrounds the dating of Cerro Sechín because firm ceramic associations are lacking. But a recent radiocarbon date based on remains of a wooden post indicates a late Early Ceramic date of about 1290 B.C. for the stone-construction phase. Two felines brandishing enormous claws and painted black, reddish orange, and white, guard an entrance to the central chamber of the lower platform, which is associated with the first adobe building phase. An adobe frieze of an incised and painted fish, on a wall of the lowermost terrace west of the central stairway, is contemporary with the third adobe building phase. The site's most unusual feature is its façade of over four hundred stone slabs carved in low relief. They portray a macabre procession of what look like victorious warriors and a jumbled array of disarticulated human heads, arms, legs, and entrails.

North of Casma in the Moche Valley, construction began about 1300 B.C. at Huaca de los Reyes, one of eight platform mounds that form the Caballo Muerto complex. Huaca de los Reyes is the best preserved structure within this complex, lying twenty kilometers (twelve miles) inland on the north side of the valley. The plan is U-shaped, with a central platform and lateral wings framing a spacious central courtyard. The open side of the U faces east, or upvalley. Colonnades of rectangular pillars, semisunken rectangular courtyards, and rectangular rooms with multiple entryways were made of river cobbles set in mud mortar. The walls were then plastered.

In the northern section of Los Reyes, near the main façade of the central platform, archaeologists discovered four colossal adobe heads modeled in relief. The heads are set into 60-centimeter-deep (24-inch-deep) niches and measure 2.2 meters (7.2 feet) in width and 1.3 meters (4.3 feet) in height. Shown in frontal view, the heads portray snarling, fanged creatures with feline features and interlocked canine teeth. Traces of red and white pigment remain on the canines, lips, and cheeks (fig. 28). A series of friezes that adorned the entry colonnade portray standing, two-legged figures flanked by fanged heads shown in profile.

No domestic architecture was found near Huaca de los Reyes, although people probably lived on the hills flanking the site to the west. Marine resources formed an important part of the diet as did llamas and deer, but no plant remains were preserved.

In the La Leche Valley 200 kilometers (120 miles) north, excavations by Izumi Shimada revealed that occupation at Batán Grande's Huaca Lucía dated to about 1300 B.C. This well-preserved temple had been carefully "entombed" in white sand. Ritual burial of ceremonial sites is another practice that originated in the Preceramic and continued into the Early Ceramic and later periods. Ceramic fragments and remains of a polychrome mural, painted in black, gray, and red, identify Huaca Lucía as part of the Cupisnique tradition. This north coast style is marked by monumental architecture, colonnades, and elaborately modeled and incised ceramics. At Huaca Lucía, columns painted red formed three parallel rows above a three-level platform that once spanned a U-shaped enclosure, and polychrome murals decorated the enclosure walls. Dubbed Temple of the Columns

28 A large felinelike figure on one of several adobe reliefs at Huaca de los Reyes, Moche Valley. The site is Early Ceramic, but the frieze shows features of what later became the Chavin style. North coast, Peru.

by Shimada, the enclosure sat on top of a two-level rectangular platform that measured 52 meters (170 feet) east to west.

Like the temple itself, a well-preserved adobe stairway of twenty-two steps was buried in clean sand. Shimada believes that Huaca Lucía represents the northernmost extension of the U-shaped platform/sunken plaza tradition.

For many years Cupisnique was mistakenly thought to be a coastal culture contemporary with the florescence of Chavín de Huántar. This culture was first noted by Peruvian archaeologist Rafael Larco in the arid Cupisnique drainage south of Pacasmayo. Ceramics range in color from brown to carbon black, and their shapes include the stirrup-spout bottle and simple bowls. Potters made patterns of geometric incisions that represented human as well as fantastic and naturalistic animals. Sculptural ceramics depicting humans, birds, vegetables, fruit, and architectural forms were adopted later by Moche potters (fig. 29; see chapter 6). But unchecked looting in the Cupisnique heartland and flooding of many Cupisnique sites in the Jequetepeque Valley, following the completion of the Gallito Ciego Dam, have destroyed scores of monumental complexes and cemeteries of this poorly understood culture.

Archaeologists were led to a Cupisnique site, near the modern fishing village of Poemape just south of San Pedro de Lloc, after intensive looting at Poemape's ancient cemetery in 1988–89 saturated the antiquities market with Cupisnique ceramics. In 1990 excavators uncovered the remains of a low-lying, stone-fronted temple platform approached by a stairway on its north side.

THE EARLY CERAMIC PERIOD IN THE HIGHLANDS

To the east, in the highlands of Cajamarca, excavations by Japanese archaeologists at the sites of Huacaloma and Layzón have uncovered architecture reminiscent of Kotosh and Huaricoto (see chapter 4). Early Huacaloma period (1500–1000 B.C.) walls at Huacaloma were made of fieldstones set in clay mortar. Walls and floors were plastered. Archaeologists found a hearth, apparently

29 Ceramic vessel in the form of a manioc tuber, with an incised design of human heads and a feline figure. North-coast Cupisnique art inspired the later Chavín cult, which dominated much of the Andean area from 400 to 200 B.C. North coast, Peru. H. 26 cm. (10.2 in.) 41.2/7516

plastered, that contained traces of a fine, white ash powder. During the Late Huacaloma period (1000–500 B.C.) at Layzón, inhabitants carved six platform mounds into the bedrock. A stairway connected four of the platforms, and there were carved geometric figures on the lower stairway. Excavators also found remains of polychrome plaster. At Layzón, two temple structures contained the remains of concentric circles and a stone-lined hearth.

At the site of Kuntur Wasi, first excavated by Rebecca Carrión Cachot and Tello, further excavations in 1989 by Yoshio Onuki uncovered four lavish tombs. Occupation of this site near the town of San Pablo, west of Cajamarca, dates from the Early and Late Huacaloma periods through the Layzón period. Onuki also found Cupisnique-style ceramics contemporary with the Late Huacaloma period.

About 1000–700 B.C., Kuntur Wasi's earliest occupants constructed a central platform, painting the walls and floors of the structure white. In a small room on a low platform, west of the central mound, excavators uncovered fragments of paint and a mudbrick statue whose face and fangs are painted red, green, yellow, and black. During the site's second construction phase, from 700 to 500 B.C., builders erected a U-shaped structure whose summit was approached by a central stairway. A 24-meter-square (79-feet-square) sunken courtyard, reached by two stairways, lies in front of the central mound. Ceramics from recently excavated Kuntur Wasi tombs show strong affinities to Cupisnique, while the goldwork has decorative elements that relate it to gold objects from Chon-

goyape, a site in the upper Lambayeque Valley (see chapter 12) contemporary with the early florescence of the Chavín cult.

Onuki discovered the four tombs, each about 2 meters (7 feet) deep, on the platform summit. One tomb, that of a man, contained an 18-centimeter-high (about 7-inch-high) crown, hammered from a single sheet of gold. Fourteen gold human heads dangle from the crown. In the same tomb, archaeologists excavated a stirrup-spout ceramic vessel that portrays a birdlike figure, a pair of earspools carved from a greenish-blue stone, and three Strombus shells, one of them incised with a figurative design. In an adjacent tomb they found another gold crown, an H-shaped gold pectoral 17.5 centimeters (7 inches) high depicting a snarling, fanged being, and several smaller gold pectorals.

Meanwhile, studies of the Early Ceramic occupation at the sites of Kotosh, Huaricoto, and La Galgada, in the highlands of Huánuco and Ancash, respectively, show that these sites remained important centers after the Preceramic florescence (see chapter 4). Pottery of the Kotosh Waira-jirca phase, the site's earliest ceramic phase, dated about 1850 B.C., includes triangular bowls decorated by incising, burnishing, and rocker stamping. Some ceramics were decorated after firing with red, yellow, and white paint. Spindle whorls were found as well. The next phase, known as Kotosh-Kotosh, is dated 1120 B.C. and 890 B.C. About this time maize was introduced to the site. Ceramic shapes include bowls with convex sides, bowls with lateral flanges, and figurines also decorated by postfire painting.

30 An incised bone spatula
    decorated with stylized
    feline, bird, and human
    designs, shows traces of red
    pigment, probably hematite
    or cinnabar. Ancient Andean
    peoples valued these mineral
    ores for their bright red
    color. Chavín style, north
    coast, Peru.
    L. 30.7 cm. (12.1 in.) 41.2/7734

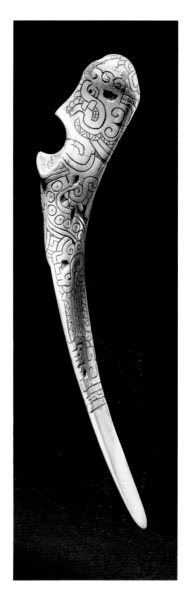

At La Galgada, people rebuilt the summit of the site's main platform in a U-shaped configuration. Burials were placed in gallery crypts that flanked a forecourt. Grave goods found here are some of the richest pre-Chavín examples, and the tombs may be the earliest elite burials in the Andes. Offerings included elaborate textiles and jewelry, such as shell disks carved with birds as well as a Spondylus shell disk with traces of red pigment. Archaeologists also uncovered a stone disk inlaid with a stone mosaic. At Huaricoto, the Toril phase, dated about 1800 B.C., coincides with the introduction of pottery. Simple shapes made by Huaricoto potters include neckless pots and bowls. Decoration is rare. People subsisted on a mixed diet that included deer and wild camelids. More variety in ceramic shapes is found in the subsequent Huaricoto phase as potters began to use red slip, hatching, and red postfire paint. Burger, Huaricoto's excavator, sees similarities to Kotosh phase Kotosh and Urabarriu phase Chavín de Huántar. The Kotosh Religious Tradition continued at Huaricoto throughout the Early Ceramic period and the Chavín expansion period, even at the apogee of the Chavín cult.

At Chiripa, on the Bolivian side of Lake Titicaca, construction of the site's ceremonial platform mound began during the Middle Chiripa phase, 900–600 B.C. The ceremonial structures there consist of a sunken courtyard surrounded by sixteen one-room rectangular structures that may have been used to store food. The walls of houses were painted and rooms had interior wall niches. Double-jambed doorways framed the entrances to the houses. Architect William Conklin believes that the Chiripa architectural style foreshadows the Titicaca architectural tradition, which culminated at the later sites of Pukara, Wari, and Tiwanaku (see chapters 6 and 7). By 500 B.C. many lakeside sites, with links as far north as Chumbivilcas, had stelae carved in the style of a local Titicaca religious tradition that featured supernatural images, serpents, and frogs.

After Chiripa, the most notable culture on the altiplano was Pukará, which flourished at the end of the first millennium B.C. and was still functioning about A.D. 200, the time of the rise of Tiwanaku south of the lake. Located north of the lake at an altitude of 3,950 meters (13,000 feet), and covering an area of about 6 square kilometers (2.3 square miles), Pukará was the largest settlement of its time on the altiplano. The midden, remains of houses, and extensive surface remains indicate that the site was residential as well as ceremonial. The best-known part of Pukará is a set of U-shaped patios of fine masonry rooms that rest high on steep terraces. There are many smaller sites related to the culture of Pukará throughout the northern end of the Lake Titicaca Basin.

THE RISE OF CHAVIN DE HUANTAR

The transition from the Early Ceramic period to the Chavín florescence took place about 800 B.C. It is marked by the decline of the main coastal centers like Huaca de Los Reyes and Las Haldas in the north and Cardal in the south. These sites may have been abandoned in the wake of a Niño, the cyclical and often devastating weather complex that forces warm Ecuadorian ocean currents south, brings torrential rains and floods to the north coast, and causes drought in the southern highlands. Indeed, there is increasing evidence for a major Niño about 500 B.C. that would have decimated cold-water marine life, destroyed irrigation canals, and wiped out field systems, causing famine and bringing disease to the once flourishing Early Ceramic centers. People suddenly abandoned most of the major Casma Valley sites. Camelids and guinea pigs appeared, changes in architecture occurred, and new ceramic shapes and decorative techniques were introduced.

Construction began about 800 B.C. at the highland site of Chavín de Huántar in the Callejón de Conchucos during the Urabarriu phase. The initial date for the onset of Chavín expansion was thought to be much earlier, but research over the past twenty years has shown that much of what was thought to be Chavín-influenced art and architecture developed on the coast and highlands several centuries before Chavín became the important center of a widespread cult.

Ethnographic evidence shows that mountains were worshipped in antiquity and are still revered today, to ensure the fertility of crops and herds. One hypothesis proposes that the functions and locations of Andean ceremonial centers, such as Chavín de Huántar, relate to the practice of mountain worship. Johan Reinhard, author of this hypothesis, argues that Chavín's location between two rivers symbolically linked the site to Huantsan, one of the highest peaks in the Cordillera Blanca to the west. The waters of the Wacheqsa river, one of two rivers that flow by Chavín de Huántar, originate in Huantsan's glaciers. Ethnographical sources indicate that Huantsan was worshipped in antiquity as well as today.

Chavín de Huántar's location between two rivers also allowed the construction of underground canals that ran below Chavín's temple and other structures. Pilgrims may have associated the sound of rushing water with the roar of Chavín de Huántar's oracle. Underground canals have also been discovered at Tiwanaku, the ceremonial center that flourished south of Lake Titicaca in the first millennium after Christ (see chapter 8).

At the same time, Chavín de Huántar is ideally situated on an important trade route midway between the coast and the lowland tropical forest and lies at the end of an easy pass through the Cordillera Blanca. Indeed, just as Chavín de Huántar's architecture drew on the older coastal centers, its religious symbols featured the animals of the tropical north coast and forest: the jaguar, harpy eagle, and monkey along with the serpent and the caiman.

Chavín de Huántar was never exclusively a ceremonial center but was a bustling highland community, well located for rainfall agriculture and trade with coastal and tropical-forest peoples. At its apogee the ceremonial center and its associated village covered 42 hectares (105 acres). The temple area occupies 5 hectares (12 acres) of terraced and leveled land at the confluence of the Mosna and

31 A famous image from Chavín de Huántar is the staff god. Engraved on a slab of granite almost 2 meters (6.5 feet) long, it is known as the Raimondi Stela.

Wacheqsa rivers. Burger estimates that some two thousand to three thousand people lived at Chavín de Huántar during the Janabarriu phase (390–200 B.C.). In his view, the building of the Old Temple began during the Urabarriu phase (850–460 B.C.).

The Old Temple, lying north of the New Temple, is a seemingly solid stone construction. But its interior is honeycombed with rooms and passageways, known as galleries. The galleries are connected by stairways, vents, and drains. Smaller truncated pyramids serve as the wings of the U and flank a sunken circular courtyard embellished by slabs of stone carved in low relief that portray Chavín de Huántar's pantheon. The main object of worship, perhaps Chavín de Huántar's earliest oracle, was a knife-shaped monolith 4.5 meters (15 feet) tall set in an interior gallery. Unlike most of Chavín's stone sculpture, it still occupies its original position. This monolith, variously called the Lanzón, the Great Image, or the Snarling or Smiling God, portrays a human form, its right hand raised and its feet and hands ending in claws. The deity's almost human earlobes hang heavy with pendants, but the face has feline attributes: a snarling, thick-lipped mouth drawn back to display fearsome upper canine teeth. The eyebrows and hair end in snake's heads. The deity wears a tunic-like garment and a belt of human faces. The top of the monolith reaches through the ceiling into an unexplored gallery above, from which Chavín de Huántar's priests, acting as the voice of the oracle, may have spoken to supplicants.

During the next phase, Chakinani (460–390 B.C.), the lower, or northern, residential sector was abandoned. In the Janabarriu phase that followed, the ceremonial complex of Chavín de Huántar became one of the largest religious centers in the Americas. Chavín's architects enlarged the original temple, shifting the ritual focus of the complex to the south. They created an immense stone construction that stands ten meters (thirty-three feet) high. Known as the central pyramid, or New Temple, it faces two rectangular courtyards that sweep eastward down to the river's edge and are flanked by buildings on the northern and southern sides. The entire temple façade was decorated with projecting human and zoomorphic heads, and the underside of the cornice was carved in low relief. Steps led to the summit of the New Temple through a black-and-white stone portal. The columns and stones on the portal's south side were of carved white granite, while those on the north side were carved of black limestone. The low-relief carvings on the columns portray humanoid figures with bird attributes.

By this time, some archaeologists believe, the Lanzón, or snarling image, worshipped at the Old Temple may no longer have been Chavín de Huántar's primary cult image. The deity that replaced it has not been found, however. The Old Temple image may have been replaced by a less awesome one, known as the staff god. This deity is portrayed on an almost two-meter-long slab of granite discovered at Chavín in the 1840s and known as the Raimondi Stela (fig. 31). Another monolith, carved earlier than the Raimondi Stela, is the so-called Tello Obelisk. It portrays a flayed caiman with intricate carvings that include depictions of Strombus and Spondylus shells, and manioc, gourd, and chili pepper.

Janabarriu ceramics from Chavín de Huántar are characterized by flat-bottomed, stirrup-spout bottles, bowls with beveled rims, and neckless pots. Potters decorated ceramics with stamps and seals and made incisions, circles, and concentric circles. On the south coast, Janabarriu traits are found in phases 3 and 4 of the Paracas ceramic sequence, resulting in motifs painted in varied hues. Potters often applied resin colored with pigment to pots after firing.

 ## THE CHAVIN CULT

At its apogee, the Chavín cult and its art spread as far south as the Nazca drainage and north to Puerto Eten. In the northern highlands, Chavín-inspired art has been found at Pacopampa north of Cajamarca; south of the Callejón de Conchucos it spread to the Mantaro Valley and to Huancavelica and Ayacucho. The symbols of the Chavín cult, images derived from stone sculptures at Chavín de Huántar's New Temple, were reproduced on ceramics, textiles, goldwork, and stone (fig. 32). As a result, ancient Peru became united for the first time by a shared religion and technology. And, like the Wari and Inka, the two other great unifying Andean cultures that followed centuries later, the Chavín cult united previously unrelated cultures in the highlands and on the coast. Symbols of this cult were incorporated into the local pottery styles, such as the resin-painted pottery of Paracas on the south coast, polychrome slip-painted pottery of the north, and monochrome polished

32 The modeling of this north-coast ceramic bottle portrays the head of a supernatural being with awesome fangs and serpents emerging from the eyes. Chavín style.
H. 20.7 cm. (8.2 in.) 41.2/8555

33 A spotted feline and cacti are modeled on this Chavín-style ceramic bottle. The San Pedro cactus represented here is still used by folk healers for its hallucinogenic properties. North coast, Peru.
H. 26.8 cm. (10.6 in.) 41.2/7517

34 As the Chavín cult spread, goldsmiths created objects displaying Chavín iconography. This vessel of hammered sheet gold is decorated with a geometric design. North coast, Peru.
H. 25.8 cm. (10.2 in.) 41.0/3698

35 At its peak, the Chavín cult had widespread influence on coastal and highland art styles. The half image of a seated man modeled on this ceramic vessel points to Chavín influence, as do the slip paint, the vertical eye band, and the fanged mouth. North coast, Peru.
H. 21.5 cm. (8.5 in.) 41.2/7970

36 Ceramic *ocarina*, or whistle, decorated with a painted face. The mouth of the face forms the blowhole and its eyes are the finger holes. Ocarinas were common musical instruments in ancient Peru. Paracas, south coast, Peru.
L. 11 cm. (4.3 in.) 41.2/7560

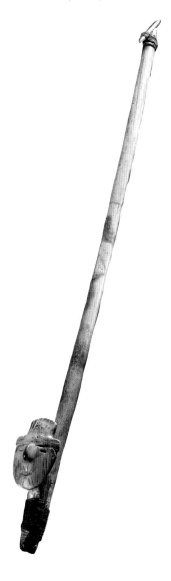

37 Atlatl, or spear-thrower, from Cerro Uhle, Ica, with a carved whalebone shaft, stone contact point, and thumb rest of sperm-whale tooth carved in the form of a human head wearing a forehead ornament. Paracas, south coast, Peru.
H. 51 cm. (20.1 in.) 41.2/6017

ceramics of the central coast. Although Chavín's influence lasted only about two centuries, its effects on the well-established patterns of the Early Ceramic period changed the face of Andean culture forever.

Burger believes that the Chavín cult may have spread in much the same way as the later cult of Pachacamac, an important ceremonial center that flourished for many centuries in the Lurín Valley, on the central coast. Ethnographic sources and archaeological evidence have pinpointed Pachacamac as the center of a highly revered oracle and vast ceremonial network that had spread throughout much of sixteenth-century Peru on the eve of the Spanish invasion. Sixteenth-century Spanish documents reveal that far-flung communities petitioned Pachacamac's priests for permission to set up branch oracles. Once granted, the communities set aside agricultural lands and herds to support the regional cult center, with part of the produce paid to Pachacamac as tribute. A much-feared deity, Pachacamac was thought to punish offenders by sending earthquakes. Tribute to him included cotton, maize, dried fish, llamas, and guinea pigs, as well as precious goods, such as finely woven textiles, and raw materials, such as gold. Branch shrines of Pachacamac were viewed as the wives and daughters of Pachacamac.

Applying the Pachacamac model to the Chavín cult, Burger suggests that the south-coast site of Karwa may have been a regional Chavín cult center. Karwa lies eight kilometers (five miles) south of Paracas, where Chavín-style motifs appear on early Paracas ceramics, pyroengraved gourds, and textiles. Looters discovered Karwa in the 1970s, digging up a cache of painted textiles and ceramics. The iconography of these objects is unquestionably Chavín. On cotton cloth from Karwa there are symbols from Chavín de Huántar, painted in shades of red orange, tan, brown, olive green, and blue. Karwa ceramics have been likened to the fourth-century B.C. early Ocucaje pottery style from the Ica valley. Some pottery fragments even show similarities to Janabarriu-style ceramics from Chavín de Huántar.

Resist techniques, innovations linked to the spread of the Chavín cult, also were used to decorate Karwa textiles. The most common image found is that of a staff-bearing deity. But unlike the staff god portrayed on the Raimondi Stela, Karwa's staff deity is invariably female. Karwa textiles seem too large to be worn as clothing and may have been used as wall hangings or banners at shrines dedicated to the Chavín cult. One cloth, for instance, is estimated to have measured more than 4 meters (13 feet) wide and almost 3 meters (10 feet) long.

The spread of the Chavín cult also is tied to innovations in metallurgy and weaving technology. Conklin believes that innovations in weaving techniques and textile decoration were first used to display Chavín designs. Indeed, these innovations may be directly connected to the spread of portable Chavín-style objects crafted in metal and cloth. One innovation is the introduction of painted textiles, such as those from Karwa, as well as the spread of resist techniques, such as batik and tie-dye. Camelid fibers, which absorb dyes more readily than cotton, begin to appear in cotton-warped textiles. New weaving techniques,

38 Late Paracas potters modeled naturalistic images of fruits and vegetables. This vessel may depict the sweet, melon-like fruit *Solanum muricatum*. South coast, Peru.
H. 11.7 cm. (4.6 in.) 41.2/5966

39 Polychrome ceramic vessel in the form of a monkey holding his penis. The vessel was painted with resinlike pigments after firing, a distinctive trait of the Paracas Cavernas tradition that extended from the windswept Paracas Peninsula south to the Ica Valley. South coast, Peru.
H. 17.8 cm. (7 in.) 41.2/8637

40 LEFT

Gourd rattle with pyroengraved design that features a human figure in ceremonial attire. The cane handle is wrapped in cotton cord. Paracas ritual specialists and supernatural beings are often shown holding such rattles. South coast, Peru.

L. 16.2 cm. (6.4 in.) 41.2/7674

41 RIGHT

Ceramic figurine with painted face and wig of human hair. Perforations in the earlobes may have held pendants. Freestanding human figures are rare in Paracas art. South coast, Peru.

H. 33.6 cm. (13.2 in.) 41.2/7664

42 Camelid-fiber mantle with decorated border of double-headed, stylized birds and feline figures. Embroidery of stem stitches with crossed looping on the edges. Paracas style, south coast, Peru.
L. 238 cm. (93.7 in.) W. 136 cm. (53.5 in.) 41.2/632

43 Detail of Paracas mantle border (fig. 42), embroidered with double-headed stylized, birds and feline figures.

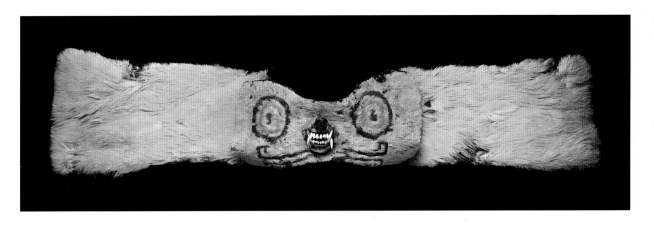

44 Feather-covered ornament. Its central face includes the muzzle of an animal, possibly a fox. Part of an elaborate headdress—a long camelid-fiber turban—that was placed on top of a cloth-wrapped mummy. Feathers from the blue-and-yellow macaw and other tropical birds. Paracas style(?), Cerro Uhle, Ica Valley, south coast, Peru.

L. 46 cm. (18.1 in.) 41.2/6010 a, b, c

such as tapestry, appear for the first time on the coast (see chapter 10). In metallurgy, the Chavín cult was accompanied by innovative techniques that included soldering, sweat welding, repoussé decoration, and the alloying of gold and silver (see chapter 12).

Trade in exotic goods, such as obsidian, increased significantly. Burger, who has studied the Andean sources of this volcanic glass, says that almost all the obsidian used in the Andes at this time came from a single source in Huancavelica. During the Janabarriu phase at Chavín de Huántar all the obsidian came from Huancavelica, 470 kilometers (290 miles) distant, and it occurred as far north as Pacopampa. Cinnabar, too, a compound containing mercury that was valued in antiquity for its bright red color, exists only in Huancavelica, although it has been found as far north as Kuntur Wasi.

Only two hundred years after its rise, the Chavín cult began to languish. But the vacuum left by the fall of this unifying cult was filled by regional cultures that arose throughout the Andes and culminated in the regional florescence of well-known cultures, such as Recuay, Vicús, Moche, Paracas, and Nazca.

45 Ceramic bottle with polished black areas and painted color panels. Paracas style, Cerro Uhle, Ica Valley, south coast, Peru.

H. 17.6 cm. (6.9 in.) 41.2/6000

LORDS, WARRIORS, AND ARTISTS

THE WEALTHY EARLY KINGDOMS

The centuries that followed the decline of Chavín influence in the Andes are marked by regional developments culminating about the turn of the millennium in the rise of two of Peru's most famed pre-Inka cultures: Moche, in the fertile northern coastal valleys, and Nazca, in the drier valleys of the south coast. Both cultures are renowned for their lively, decorated ceramics, intricately woven, colorful textiles, and sophisticated metallurgy. Because of the appeal of their art and its widespread distribution, Moche and Nazca are two of the best-documented and most extensively studied pre-Inka cultures. But the popularity of these styles among dealers and collectors has also led to the unrelenting destruction by *huaqueros*—looters—of thousands of archaeological sites, and archaeologists are often left to sift through the ransacked remains.

 ## THE MOCHE

The origins of Moche civilization are still poorly understood, but there is little doubt that it owes much to the Salinar and Gallinazo cultures. Salinar and Gallinazo flourished in the Moche Valley and in valleys immediately north and south during the centuries before the Moche realm reached its apogee. Salinar (c. 200–50 B.C.) is best known for its distinctive ceramics, first identified by Peruvian archaeologist Rafael Larco at a cemetery at the Chicama Valley, and later found in the Virú Valley by archaeologists of the Virú Valley Project (fig. 47). In Virú the Salinar lived in small villages and fortified hilltop settlements. The largest known Salinar site is Cerro Arena on the south side of the Moche Valley. Perched on a steep ridge, the site covers two square kilometers. Excavations there by Curtis Brennan recorded two thousand separate structures built of quarried granite that ranged from crude one-room residences to elaborate twenty-room structures. People subsisted on a variety of crops, shellfish, llama, and guinea pig. Salinar sites located upvalley, near the intakes of canals that irrigated Cerro Arena's fields, hint at some kind of alliance with Cerro Arena.

The Gallinazo phase that followed (c. 50 B.C.–A.D. 300) was first identified in the Virú Valley just south of Moche. Best known for its distinctive negative-painted ceramics, Gallinazo in many ways continued Salinar, and it flourished in the Moche heartland until the Moche realm began to expand. Gallinazo settlements in the lower Virú Valley include villages associated with large irrigation canals and mounds as well as monumental terraced platform constructions. Terraced platforms on hillsides, such as Huaca Licapa in the Chicama Valley, were often embellished by geometric adobe friezes, a tradition continued by the Moche. The finest Gallinazo pottery is modeled and resist-painted, resulting in black geometric designs of lines, circles, and triangles on an orange surface (fig. 48). Potters incised, punctuated, and appliquéd their ceramics. Moche art also borrowed many of the characteristics of the earlier Cupisnique culture, and it has many similarities to the highland Recuay culture, centered in the Callejón de Huaylas and Santa Valley drainage.

46 This Late Nazca ceramic figurine is a rare example of a naturalistic human form in Nazca art. Around its neck is a pendant of Spondylus shell—an exotic trade item from the warm waters of the Gulf of Guayaquil in Ecuador. The slanted forehead illustrates the popular Nazca practice of skull deformation. South coast, Peru. H. 38 cm. (15 in.) 41.2/7955

48 Ceramic bottle modeled in the form of a standing feline, decorated with resist-painted designs. Gallinazo style, northern Peru.

H. 22 cm. (8.7 in.) 41.2/8672

47 Part of this ceramic bottle represents a house enclosure with painted walls. It was modeled by Salinar potters, who lived in the former Cupisnique heartland about the second century B.C. Moche potters borrowed many design elements from Salinar, such as the bottle's bridgelike handle. Salinar style, northern Peru.

H. 15 cm. (5.9 in.) 41.2/8671

Moche flourished on the coast parallel to the highland Recuay culture of the Callejón de Huaylas. Recuay ceramic artists portrayed an array of supernatural figures holding human trophy heads and resembling serpents, felines, and condors. This pottery was usually made of kaolin paste and embellished with negative painting, modeling, and painted decoration in black, white, and red (figs. 49, 50, 51, 52, 53). Some vessel shapes recall Moche shapes and point to extensive contact between the two cultures. Indeed, Recuay ceramics have been found in Moche tombs in the Santa Valley. In the highlands the Recuay people excelled at stone sculpture, such as tenoned heads that recall their Chavín ancestry and freestanding sculptures that generally portray humans.

Some of the most interesting and enigmatic of Moche art objects were unearthed by treasure hunters in the Vicús cemeteries at the edge of the Sechura Desert, in the upper Piura Valley. The Vicús tombs became famous both for their fine metal objects (see chapter 12) and for their ceramics—usually hand modeled and rich in whimsical human and animal representations (figs. 54, 55, 56, 57, 58, 59, 60). Tombs were dug to the extraordinary depth of more than nine meters (twenty-nine feet). The graves consisted of narrow round shafts that widened into a chamber for the body and grave goods. While some of the ceramics found in the Vicús tombs are early Moche in style, many of the ceramics and metal objects seem also to have been influenced by regions to the north, in what is now Ecuador and Colombia.

At its apogee about A.D. 400, the Moche realm stretched from Huarmey in the south to Piura in the north, a 600-kilometer-long (370-mile-long) swath of desert coastline sliced by fertile river valleys. The culture is named after the Moche, or Trujillo, Valley where this archaeological culture was first identified. Several hundred thousand people may have lived in these lush, coastal valleys, in both fishing villages and inland settlements as far as fifty kilometers (thirty miles) from the shore. The Moche tapped the rivers to build sophisticated irrigation systems. Indeed, their canals and aqueducts watered considerably more land than is cultivated today. Farmers grew maize, squash, beans, cotton, and other crops as well as avocados and chili peppers. They fertilized the fields with *guano*—bird droppings—collected from coastal islands by far-ranging Moche seafarers. The Moche fished from totora-reed boats and hunted for deer in the once-flourishing inland meadows. Their realm was connected by roads that nine hundred years later became part of the Inka road system. An extensive sea and overland trade network provided the Moche with alpaca fiber, metal ores, and produce from the highlands, lapis lazuli from Chile, turquoise from northwestern Argentina, and exotic seashells from waters off the coast of what is now Ecuador.

Construction of the Pyramids of Moche, the political and ceremonial center of the Trujillo Valley in Moche times, began about A.D. 100. Excavations in 1899 by the German archaeologist Max Uhle, the "grandfather of Peruvian archaeology," revealed a long occupation at the site, extending from pre-Moche to historical times. The pyramids are the largest Moche settlement in the valley, occupying an entire square kilometer (.4 square

49 Cotton textile, possibly a panel from a tunic of interlocked and dovetailed tapestry with a design of stylized five-legged animals. Textiles from the Recuay region are exceptionally rare and sometimes closely resemble other contemporary styles. Recuay style, north highlands(?), Peru.
L. 166.7 cm. (65.6 in.) W. 27.5 cm. (10.8 in.) 41.2/7898

Highland Recuay ceramics are commonly found in the lower Santa Valley. Their distinctive style and iconography influenced Recuay's coastal counterparts, the Moche. This modeled and painted ceramic vessel represents two elaborately attired people apparently dancing or wrestling. North coast, Peru. H. 11 cm. (4.3 in.) 41.2/8024

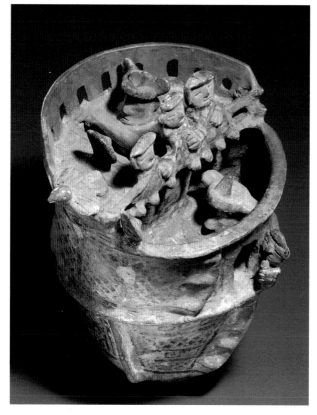

50 Distinctive Recuay ceramics were made from a white kaolin clay and decorated with resist, or negative, painting or with black and red slip painting over a kaolin paste. This vessel represents a llama led by a man holding a shield or staff and wearing an elaborate headdress, earspools, and decorated tunic. Northern Peru. H. 23.5 cm. (9.3 in.) B/8816

52 Highly detailed Recuay portrayals of houses and ceremonial structures provide clues to pre-Hispanic architectural forms. This ceramic vessel represents a multistoried structure with resist-painted surface designs. One stairway leads to a door opening into a two-roomed patio; a second reaches the roof, which is occupied by six people and two birds. Northern Peru. H. 23.2 cm. (9.1 in.) B/8264

54 The Vicús style of northern-most Peru flourished from about A.D. 100–400, apparently influenced by early cultures in Ecuador and Colombia to the north as well as by Moche, a southern neighbor. This ceramic vessel portrays a man whose posture suggests swimming. Northern Peru.
H. 17.5 cm. (6.9 in.) 41.2/7077

53 This Recuay-style ceramic vessel is modeled and painted in the form of a crouching man holding a cup to his mouth. He wears a patterned tunic, large earspools, and a headdress with a spout through which liquid can be poured. Northern Peru.
H. 13.1 cm. (5.2 in.) 41.2/8577

55 This Vicús whistling vessel represents a man wearing a bird headdress. A whistle hidden inside the man's hollow head sounds when water is agitated inside the vessel. Ceramic whistling vessels like this one were common in the ancient Andes. Northern Peru. H. 26 cm. (10.2 in.) 41.2/6645

57 FACING PAGE
In this unusual Vicús ceramic piece, the figure of a man partly merges with the body of the vessel. His nose ornament represents the typical Vicús bimetallic nose ornament. Northern Peru. H. 22 cm. (8.7 in.) 41.2/6643

56 Vicús burial offerings included an array of ceramic vessels and elaborately crafted metal objects. This gold nose ornament has a repoussé animal design. Northern Peru. L. 11.5 cm. (4.5 in.) 41.2/8900

mile). Construction began on the smaller of the two pyramids, the Pyramid of the Moon (Huaca de la Luna) in Gallinazo times. The Pyramid of the Moon is a terraced adobe structure, 95 meters (312 feet) long by 85 meters (279 feet) wide by 20 meters (66 feet) high in its first construction stage. It is composed of three mounds connected by courts. More than fifty million adobe bricks went into its construction, and murals and friezes decorated many of the walls. The pyramid stands beneath imposing Cerro Blanco, where archaeologists uncovered remains of stone-walled residential architecture at its base and ceremonial structures on its summit.

A 500-meter-wide (1,640-foot-wide) plain, pockmarked by looters' pits and the remains of residential architecture, separates the Pyramid of the Moon from the larger Pyramid of the Sun. The largest adobe brick structure ever built in the Americas, the Pyramid of the Sun measures some 342 meters (1,122 feet) long by 159 meters (522 feet) wide and it once stood over 40 meters (131 feet) high. A ramp, 6 meters (20 feet) wide by 90 meters (295 feet) long, led to a rectangular platform, 18 meters (59 feet) high. A series of terraces and ramps connected this platform to the summit. Little remains of the Pyramid of the Sun's cross-shaped plan, however. In 1610 enterprising Spanish treasure hunters diverted the waters of the Moche River, washing away roughly two-thirds of the pyramid (fig. 61).

Moche architects built the Pyramid of the Sun in several stages over a period of many centuries. A total of eight construction phases are visible in a cut, or cross section, on the pyramid's largely destroyed northern side. The earliest construction phase dates to Moche I, about A.D. 100. The entire pyramid was built of more than 143 million mold-made adobe bricks, arranged in tall, columnlike segments. Certain adobes have so-called maker's marks impressed into their tops. These markings range from hand- and footprints to circles and squiggles. According to archaeologists Michael Moseley and Charles Hastings, who recorded more than a hundred of these marks, the adobes probably served to distinguish bricks made by different groups and may have been the local, or subject, population's tribute or labor obligation to the Moche ruler. This would imply the existence of a highly organized, well-established central authority.

60 Whistling jar modeled and painted in the form of an owl. The whistle is located in the owl's neck. Vicús culture, northern Peru.

H. 21 cm. (8.3 in.) 41.2/6639

58 Vicús potters hand-modeled a lively assortment of animals, such as this vessel in the form of a sharp-toothed, unidentified beast, embellished with resist and white slip painting against an orange clay background. North coast, Peru.

H. 18.5 cm. (7.3 in.) 41.2/7434

59 Resist-painted ceramic jar modeled in the form of a frog. Vicús culture, northern Peru.

H. 14.5 cm. (5.7 in.) 41.2/6635

61 Construction of the Pyramid of the Sun, on the southern side of the Moche Valley, in northern Peru, began about A.D. 100. The largest adobe construction ever built in the Americas, it once stood about 40 meters (131 feet) high and contained more than 140 million adobe bricks. Diversion of the Moche River by seventeenth-century Spanish treasure hunters washed away about two-thirds of the pyramid.

Recent discoveries in the Lambayeque and Jequetepeque valleys have modified the traditional idea of a Moche realm controlled from the Pyramids of the Sun and Moon in Trujillo. Indeed, according to Moche scholar Christopher Donnan, there may have been two separate Moche kingdoms: a northern and a southern realm, separated by the inhospitable, forty-kilometer-wide (twenty-five-mile-wide) Pampa de Paiján just north of the Chicama Valley. In this scenario each valley housed a separate principality or court that followed Moche religious, social, architectural, and artistic conventions. Like European royalty, the local Moche lords may have been related, but they ruled independently. Unlike the royal families of Europe, the descendants of the Moche elite did not inherit the lavish gold ornaments. Instead, these treasures accompanied the Moche lords to the afterlife (fig. 62).

Each Moche-controlled valley produced highly distinctive ceramics that provide some of the liveliest and most informative records of Moche life. Combined with data from burials, decorated ceramics offer insight into Moche social organization, indicating status by dress and head ornaments in portrayals of lords, warriors, priests, prisoners, and craftspeople. These scenes also tell us something about the complex Moche pantheon of awesome, half-human gods. Many of these gods have serpent and feline attributes, and they often are shown brandishing knives and holding severed human heads.

Moche scholar Rafael Larco divided the Moche period into five sequential phases, keyed to changes in the forms and decoration of ceramic vessels. He derived his relative chronology from ceramics found in the Moche and Chicama valleys,

the traditional Moche heartland. But in the past twenty years, archaeologists working in other Moche areas have found that the five-phase sequence inadequately reflects the regional variations in Moche art. Finely crafted ceramics from the site of La Mina in Jequetepeque, for example, show stronger affinities to those of the Loma Negra site near Piura than to ceramics from the Moche or Chicama valleys. According to Donnan, the iconography of metalwork from the early Moche site of Sipán in Lambayeque also exhibits closer ties to local gold-working traditions—as well as connections with Loma Negra—than to the traditional Moche heartland. Larco's sequence has not yet been further refined, however, and the scheme continues to be widely used.

Moche I, in the Larco sequence, is seen as a continuation of the earlier Gallinazo style. Vessels are modeled, showing Cupisnique influence, and painting, although rare, is geometric, reflecting its Salinar origins. The short, wide spout has a pronounced beveled lip. By Moche II, the lip has become smaller, mold-made vessels first appear, and low relief often replaces painting. In Moche III, the spout has a pronounced flare, the lip has almost disappeared, and we see the onset of fineline drawing. Moche III style is more widespread in the valleys north and south of Trujillo. The famous Moche portrait heads date to this phase (fig. 64), when the realm reached its greatest extent. By Moche V, painted decoration becomes more intricate and often overcrowded. By the onset of this phase, the Moche abandoned their largest administrative, urban, and ceremonial center at the Pyramids of the Sun and Moon and moved upvalley, to the right bank of the Moche River, where they established Galindo.

This shift inland about A.D. 600 may signal the onset of a severe drought in the Andes that forced the Moche to settle closer to irrigation canal intakes. Galindo, which occupies five square kilometers (three square miles), became the major urban center in the Moche valley in Moche V times. Galindo has no massive adobe constructions like the imposing Pyramids of the Sun and the Moon. Instead, its layout heralds a pattern of rectangular compounds culminating, hundreds of years later, at Chan Chan, the Chimú capital. North of Trujillo in the Lambayeque Valley, the focus of Moche power centered on Pampa Grande, a sprawling urban center that occupied 4.5 square

62 Mosaic designs on earspools with copper-alloy rims represent a warrior holding a club and shield. These mosaics are composed of iron pyrites, malachite, gilded copper alloy, and Spondylus shell. Moche style, north coast, Peru.

D. 5.5 cm. (2.2 in.) 41.2/9019 A, B

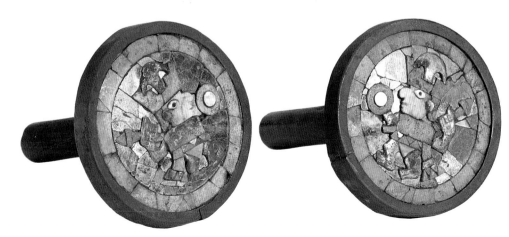

63 Mold-made ceramic bottle that represents an elaborately dressed man seated on a stepped throne or bench. Moche potters often used molds to mass-produce ceramics. North coast, Peru. H. 24.6 cm. (9.7 in.) B/8916

64 Moche potters excelled at fashioning realistic images of the human form. The details of facial features, headdress, and other items of ornament lead archaeologists to believe that models of the human head, such as this one, may have been portraits of actual people. North coast, Peru. H. 29.4 cm. (11.6 in.) B/4914

65 Bound prisoners often appear in Moche ceramic art and were central to the so-called Sacrifice Ceremony, a ritual involving the sacrifice of captives and offering of blood. This vessel is modeled and painted in the form of a man with a rope around his neck that terminates in a snake head. North coast, Peru. H. 28.2 cm. (11.1 in.) 41.2/623

kilometers (1.7 square miles). The site, which also controls the valley neck and thus the canal intakes, may once have housed ten thousand people. Pampa Grande's 55-meter-high (180-foot-high) adobe pyramid is almost as large as Moche's Pyramid of the Sun.

Thus each valley had a major Moche ceremonial and/or administrative center: Pañamarca in Nepeña; El Brujo and Mocollope in Chicama; Pacatnamu and San José de Moro in Jequetepeque; and Sipán, and later Pampa Grande, in Lambayeque. The principal huaca, or temple mound, was often embellished with polychrome friezes or murals. A newly discovered adobe frieze at El Brujo, the late Moche ceremonial center in the Chicama Valley, covers two sides of a house set into one of the temple terraces. The house, similar to those shown crowning the summits of pyramids portrayed in Moche ceramics, has a gabled roof (fig.70). A frieze on the house walls—painted in red and yellow ochre, blue, black, and white, includes almost the entire Moche bestiary as well as crowned figures and fishermen holding nets. Above the fishermen is a rainbowlike arc surmounted by foxes. Another terrace frieze includes a procession of life-size, nude prisoners, while a third frieze portrays a group of men wearing fringed costumes and holding hands. On the uppermost terrace archaeologists uncovered the remains of a spiderlike figure, holding a ceremonial knife, that recalls the fanged spider-decapitator god from Sipán.

The site of Sipán may have been the seat of a regional Moche court. After the discovery by *huaqueros,* in February 1987, of two tombs filled with

66 Moche art is known for its naturalistic images of animals. Crayfish, depicted on this ceramic bottle, live in Peru's coastal rivers. North coast, Peru.

H. 16.9 cm. (6.7 in.) 41.2/7780

67 Ceramic bottle modeled in the form of a land snail. The Moche ate land snails, gathering them during winter months from inland meadows watered by dense fogs. North coast, Peru.

H. 18 cm. (7.1 in.) 41.2/8903

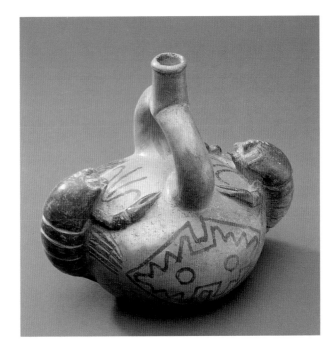

68 A ceremonial scene painted in fine line on this ceramic bottle includes two reed boats with standing costumed human figures. One figure holds a sea creature on a long line and the other receives a bowl from a birdlike creature. A sea lion, ray, and three kinds of fish are in the water. Human legs are shown under the boats. Moche culture, north coast, Peru.

H. 25.5 cm. (10 in.) 41.2/8386

69 This ceramic bottle in the form of a ceremonial structure recalls the Sacrifice Ceremony in which figures seated inside temples receive goblets containing the blood of sacrificed captives. Moche culture, north coast, Peru. H. 24 cm. (9.5 in.) 41.2/8022

gold, continuing excavations at the site by Peruvian archaeologist Walter Alva have uncovered three more royal tombs at Sipán's 10-meter-high (33-foot-high) Moche burial platform. The site itself was occupied from Moche to Chimú (A.D. 1350) and Inka (A.D. 1470) times, and the burial platform lies in the shadow of two heavily eroded pyramids, possibly of a different period. The burial platform is a solid adobe construction that underwent six building stages and served from A.D. 100 to 300 as a mausoleum for a succession of local Moche lords (fig. 72).

Judging by the iconography of dozens of metal objects that appeared on the local and international art market, Alva believes that the tombs looted by *huaqueros* in 1987 are earlier than the tomb of the Warrior Priest, or Lord of Sipán. The Warrior Priest, a thirty-year-old man and the first of several major burials excavated by archaeolo-

gists, lay in an elaborate coffin of wooden planks held together by copper straps. Algarrobo-tree beams roofing the funerary chamber have been radiocarbon-dated to A.D. 290. As for the two other tombs excavated by archaeologists, the so-called Old Lord of Sipán's tomb dates to the earliest construction phase, while the tomb of Sipán's priest, another elaborate burial uncovered by Alva and his team, is contemporary with the Warrior Priest's tomb (fig. 71).

Until the discoveries at Sipán, the most elaborate Moche burial to be excavated scientifically was that of the warrior priest of Virú, discovered in the 1940s. But the more recent excavations at Sipán, La Mina, and San José de Moro in the Jequetepeque Valley have revealed even richer burials. These tombs also provide a wealth of information on the nature of regional Moche rule, the organization of Moche society, and, in the case of Sipán, metalworking.

Sipán's skilled metal smiths produced an array of hammered and cast gold, silver, copper, silvered copper, and gilded copper necklaces, backflaps, headdresses, earspools, weapons, and nose ornaments that accompanied the Sipán lords to their graves. Especially ingenious is a silver nose ornament with a tiny golden warrior attached, recovered from the Old Lord of Sipan's tomb. Turquoise armor covers the warrior's body, and in his hands he holds a shield and a club. The outspread wings of an owl perched on the warrior's head form his headdress. He also wears a golden nose ornament and earspools inlaid with turquoise. The miniature warrior may represent the individual buried in the tomb. The top layer of offerings in the Old Lord of Sipán's tomb include a necklace of nine hollow golden bowls, each capped by a gold spider web. A gold figure, half human, half spider, perches on each web, its legs curled around the web (fig. 73).

In contrast to the exquisite artistry and technological excellence of Sipán metallurgy, most ceramics from Sipán were hastily made, and some even have visible mold marks. One thousand of these crudely crafted vessels, which probably held offerings of food and drink, accompanied Sipán's Warrior Priest. His tomb also contained whole Spondylus and Conus shells, native to the warm waters of Ecuador. A retinue of sacrificed retainers including two women, three men, and a dog surrounded the Warrior Priest's coffin.

The Warrior Priest's tomb, as well as that of the Sipán priest, and the more recent discovery of a Moche priestess at San José de Moro, are the first solid evidence that the so-called Sacrifice Ceremony was an actual and not an imaginary Moche ritual. This ceremony is illustrated in a mural at Pañamarca in the Nepeña Valley and several fine-line drawings on ceramics. Donnan, who first identified the scene, describes the Sacrifice Ceremony as a complex tableau that shows unclothed prisoners, some carried on litters, subjected to an elaborate bloodletting ritual. As attendants slit the captives' throats, the blood-filled goblets are presented to richly attired figures and attendants (fig. 74). Archaeologists found similar goblets in the priest's tomb at Sipán and in the burial of the San José de Moro priestess. Because the bodies buried at Sipán and San José de Moro are accompanied by many of the ritual paraphernalia depicted in the

Sacrifice Ceremony, Donnan believes they may represent the individuals shown in painted scenes of the sacrifice ritual.

Although archaeologists found few finely crafted ceramics at Sipán, elsewhere in the Moche realm potters produced elaborately modeled and decorated ceramics painted with fine-line scenes. Many of these fine-line tableaux depict ceremonial events like the Sacrifice Ceremony. Others represent ritual battles, burial ceremonies, and the presentation of offerings. Even scenes showing apparently ordinary events—a deer hunt, for instance, that depicts hunters carrying spear-throwers, spears, clubs, and nets, and accompanied by dogs—are imbued with symbolism and ritual meaning. Thus, although many images shown in Moche art seem to be scenes of daily life, few are

70 Drawing of a late Moche frieze at Huaca Cao Viejo, El Brujo, in the Chicama Valley, northern Peru. Found on a gabled house set into a temple terrace, the frieze portrays fishermen holding nets, crowned figures, and an array of animals.

71 FACING PAGE

A lavish array of funerary objects accompanied the Old Lord of Sipán. From the top, a crescent-shaped gold nose ornament, matching gold and silver earspools, a silver nose ornament topped by a miniature gold warrior wearing an owl headdress and turquoise armor, and four sets of necklaces—two of gold and two of silver.

72 RIGHT

Two heavily eroded adobe pyramids shadow a low-lying, solid adobe Moche burial platform at Sipán, Lambayeque Valley, northern Peru. The platform served as a mausoleum from A.D. 100–300 for a succession of Moche lords. Elaborate gold-filled burials, excavated by archaeologists, point to the wealth of Sipán's elite.

73 The offerings found in the tomb of the Old Lord of Sipán highlight the artistry and skill of Moche metal smiths. Nine hollow gold bowls are capped by gold spiderwebs. Gold figures, half human and half spider, perch on each web, their legs curled around the webs. Suspension holes indicate that they once formed part of a necklace.

74 The Moche Sacrifice Ceremony portrays a complex event with naked prisoners, some carried on litters, in an elaborate bloodletting ceremony. As attendants slit the captives' throats, the blood-filled goblets are presented to individuals seated inside temples. Much of the ritual equipment, such as goblets like the one in this drawing, was found in tombs excavated at Sipán, the first solid evidence that the Sacrifice Ceremony may have been an actual Moche ritual.

shown in domestic contexts. There are no portrayals of routine activities, such as pottery making, weaving, cooking, or washing.

Moche potters are especially famed for their depictions of eroticism. On their ceramics, Moche artists illustrated a variety of sexual practices, including sodomy, masturbation, and fellatio, but none of this art shows any practices that would have led to insemination. Art historians suspect that the activities illustrated in Moche erotic art were ritual practices, distinct from the sexual practices of everyday life.

Because Moche ceremonial and funerary sites have been the focus of attention, we know little of how the lower classes lived. Few Moche dwelling sites have been studied. Excavations just south of the modern fishing village of Huanchaco, near Trujillo, uncovered the remains of a Moche fishing community in which people lived in small, rectangular-roomed houses with walls of beach cobbles set in mud mortar. These people dug storage pits into the floors of their houses and interred their dead in burial chambers within the rooms. The lower classes did not have access to the exquisite objects of Moche art, which were reserved for those at the pinnacle of Moche society.

The archaeological record and recent analyses of ice-core samples from the Quelccaya ice cap in the southern highlands show that throughout the sixth century A.D. a series of severe environmental disturbances rocked the Andes. According to Moseley, who with Carol Mackey directed a multifaceted research project in the Moche Valley in the 1970s, there is evidence of flooding at the Pyramids of the Sun and the Moon, resulting from torrential rains brought on by the El Niño weather system, followed by a thirty-year drought. Ice-core samples from the Quelccaya ice cap near Cuzco indicate that this severe drought began about A.D. 562, ending in A.D. 594. Sand dunes invaded the southern sector of the site, burying fields and cutting off the intakes to irrigation canals. These natural events coincide with the population shift inland to Galindo.

The end of Moche dominion over the north coast was followed by the rise of the Chimú Empire, or Kingdom of Chimor, hundreds of years later. Chapter 8 discusses the Kingdom of Chimor, which controlled an even larger territory than its Moche forebears, and was the largest state to contest Inka expansion in the fifteenth century.

 ## THE NAZCA

Contemporary with the Moche was a south-coast society known as Nazca. The Nazca sphere of influence extended from Cañete to Yauca, a distance of 350 kilometers (217 miles), and into the Ayacucho highlands to the east. The Nazca cultural heartland, however, was restricted to the Ica Valley and Rio Grande de Nazca drainage. These southern valleys are much smaller and more arid than those in the north and offer only some 13,000 hectares (32,000 acres) of available agricultural land, much too small an area to sustain a large population. The Nazca civilization flourished for several centuries, from about 100 B.C. to A.D. 700.

The origins of Nazca civilization can be traced to the Paracas culture that flourished in the Ica, Pisco, and Chincha valleys north of Nazca proper. The most famous manifestation of Paracas culture was discovered at the Paracas site in 1925 by Peruvian archaeologist Julio C. Tello. On the barren and windswept Paracas Peninsula between 300 B.C. and A.D. 200, people lived and buried their dead in elaborate funerary bundles. They wrapped the dead in layer upon layer of stunning woven and embroidered textiles. Many of these bundles contain sheet-gold mouth and face masks.

The earlier Paracas phase, Cavernas, is renowned for incised ceramics that were embellished after firing with resin-based pigments (see fig. 39). Vessel shapes include double-spout and bridge pots. There are some modeled vessels as well as bowls, vases, and figurines. Textile designs depicted interlocking fish and snakelike creatures. During the following phase, known as Necropolis or Topará, Paracas weavers produced the famed colorful textiles embroidered with images of elaborately attired individuals. Images of supernatural beings painted on early Nazca pots recall the richly attired supernaturals embroidered on Necropolis phase Paracas textiles. Ceramics from this phase are elegantly simple and very thin-walled. Shapes echo the forms of gourds and fruits and occasionally animals, such as monkeys (see fig. 38). Some scholars feel that innovations in ceramic technology spurred the Nazca artists to concentrate on producing fine pottery rather than on reproducing the finely woven textiles of their Paracas Necropolis forebears. But the nature of the relationship between

Cavernas-Necropolis and Nazca is still poorly understood.

Nazca weavers produced cloth using many of the techniques developed earlier by the Paracas Necropolis people: plain weaves, double weaves, gauzes, embroidery, and brocade. Nazca textiles include *uncus* (a kind of sleeveless shirt), short skirts, turbans, belts, and mantles. Feathers of tropical birds often were used to decorate cloth.

The Nazca people lived in scattered settlements along rivers. These were built of adobe, wattle and daub, or stone laid in mud. They never built massive adobe pyramids on the scale of the Moche, their northern counterparts. Cahuachi, the most important early Nazca ceremonial center, lies on the south bank of the Nazca River, downriver from the modern town of Nazca. Cahuachi was the dominant ceremonial site through approximately A.D. 200 or 300. It sprawls over forty lowlying hills that were capped by Nazca builders with adobe structures that overlook the river and, in the distance, the famed Pampa, or Plain, of Nazca (fig. 75).

Archaeological research by Helaine Silverman indicates that the site was not a great urban center, as previously believed, but rather assumed a citylike appearance when it filled up with pilgrims from the area who came there to worship. The Great Temple, Cahuachi's largest structure, faces north and is composed of a series of broad terraces and areas of special-purpose storage. Silverman believes that sometime about A.D. 200 or 300 Cahuachi ceased to function as a pilgrimage shrine and almost all construction at the site stopped. Silverman suggests that at this

75 Cahuachi, the dominant Nazca ceremonial center until about A.D. 200 or 300, sprawls over forty low-lying hills, capped by Nazca builders with adobe structures. The site may have been a pilgrimage center that drew hundreds of worshippers from the area. South coast, Peru.

time the focus of Nazca ritual and ceremony moved north to the Pampa itself, where archaeologists have noted an increase in the elaboration of ground markings. Also about this time, the Nazca people abandoned their settlement at Tambo Viejo in the Acari Valley, seventy kilometers (forty-three miles) south.

Perhaps the best-known Nazca monument, and the one that has inspired endless speculation, is the labyrinth of geoglyphs, or markings—large-scale ground drawings of animals, straight lines, and geometric shapes. These markings are concentrated on the Pampa of Nazca and they crisscross the desert in and around the Nazca core area. Some over two thousand years old, the markings have survived because of scant rainfall in the region. Most of the damage to the markings dates from the construction, in this century, of the Pan-American Highway through the Pampa and from vehicle traffic on the fragile Pampa itself. These activities not only have left tracks but also have obliterated some of the markings.

Like the Moche, the Nazca cultivated a vast array of fruits and vegetables, fished and hunted,

and traded with highland peoples to the east for food and for exotic items such as obsidian. Indeed, contact with the highlands may have been extensive throughout the period. Although rare, some Nazca burials contain offerings made of Spondylus shell, obtained ultimately from Ecuador, indicating far-flung trade contacts. Archaeologists are uncertain what the Nazca gave in exchange for these goods.

Although many Nazca burials have been looted for their pottery and textiles, enough have been excavated scientifically to give us an idea of Nazca mortuary practices. The Nazca people continued the Paracas practice of cranial deformation by binding infants' heads between two boards to produce an elongated forehead. At Cahuachi, early Nazca burials faced south and were deposited in pits and chambers. Late Nazca burials from Chaviña, at the mouth of the Acari River, were placed in rectangular chambers with plastered adobe-brick walls. These were roofed with poles made of bundles of reeds and covered with cobbles. Tomb offerings included fine ceramics and pottery figurines, textiles, pyroengraved gourds, beads, and spear-throwers, or atlatls. Gold mouth masks crafted of hammered sheet gold and necklaces of Spondylus shell are among the objects found in richer Nazca tombs. Painted figures on pottery often show people and supernatural beings wearing these objects, perhaps as part of elaborate ceremonial attire.

Max Uhle, excavating in the Ica Valley in 1901, first identified the Nazca pottery style and later traced it to Nazca proper. Some archaeologists divide this pottery style into nine phases, based on stylistic changes in the shapes and decoration of pottery. Pottery forms include double-spouted vessels, bowls, and vases. Most Nazca ceramics are brilliantly colored with mineral-based pigments. The earliest phase, Nazca 1, is characterized by modeled ceramics and pottery decorated with pre-fire slips, and with areas of color separated by incised lines, a technique that recalls the preceding Paracas phase. The next phases, 2, 3, and 4, are distinguished by naturalistic depictions of plants and animals painted sometimes in as many as a dozen shades of mineral pigments that range from off-white, buff, cream, tan, and orange to red ochre and black. The Nazca bestiary included felines, fox, deer, llama, monkey, frog, serpent, lizard, spider, sea birds, condor, hummingbird, fish, and orca (the so-called killer whale); plants and fruits included chili peppers, lima beans, maize, achira, and lucuma. Ceramic musical instruments, related to ritual and ceremony, included panpipes, bone pipes, drums, horns, and rattles. Modeling on ceramics was not as common as it is in Moche. In the early Nazca style, deities combine various human, feline, and avian attributes.

The next two Nazca phases, 5 and 6, depict themes similar to the earlier ones, but the designs become more abstract and angular in outline, with fewer naturalistic images and more geometric patterns. Figures look much more complex as realism gives way to use of symbols. Some scholars believe that the frenetic, abstract, late Nazca designs, often dominated by warriorlike figures carrying human trophy heads, reflect increasing militarism. The iconography of the late Nazca phases—7, 8, and 9—indicates increasing contact with the Ayacucho highlands.

Water is a scarce commodity on the parched south coast. Droughts are frequent, and some rivers behave quite peculiarly. For geological reasons, water in the Nazca River only flows above

76 Two late Nazca figurines carved from killer- or sperm-whale ivory. Headdresses are made of colored shell set in a black resin base. The slanted foreheads result from cranial deformation. South coast, Peru.
H. 7.4 cm. (2.9 in.) 41.2/7854
H. 7.7 cm. (3 in.) 41.2/7983

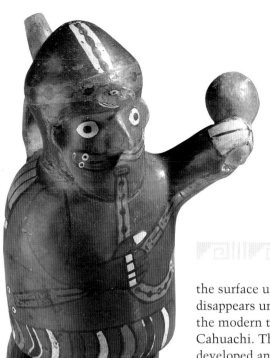

77 Richly painted early Nazca ceramic bottle in the form of a man holding a rattle. Wings on his back and serpents emerging from his mouth may be fertility symbols. South coast, Peru.
H. 25.3 cm. (10 in.) 41.2/8584

78 The long necks of the birds painted on this early Nazca bowl suggest members of the cormorant or heron families. South coast, Peru.
H. 6.6 cm. (2.6 in.) 41.2/5299

the surface upriver from the town of Nazca; then it disappears underground in the mid-valley around the modern town of Nazca and resurfaces below Cahuachi. The ancient people of the Nazca Valley developed an ingenious system for tapping the water table. They constructed underground aqueducts, or filtration galleries, that terminate in reservoirs and irrigation canals. Water levels in the filtration galleries vary according to the season, dropping in November and December before the onset of the rainy season in the mountains to the east. Concentrated around the middle valley, these filtration galleries are similar in concept to the *qanats* of Iran, and some scholars believe that they may have been introduced in the sixteenth century by the Spaniards. But archaeological evidence, based on the distribution of Nazca sites in the area, indicates that the underground aqueducts were a local pre-Hispanic invention, first built in the middle Nazca period.

Archaeological research by Katharina Schreiber and Josue Lancho has shown that before

the construction of the filtration galleries no settlements existed in the mid-valley, although there were settlements in the upper and lower valley. But once the filtration galleries were built, about A.D. 500–600, the previously unoccupied areas were inhabited. Increasing aridity on the coast brought on by drought in the southern highlands may have forced the ancient Nazca people to search for more permanent sources of water. Evidence of rainfall levels recorded in ice cores from the Quelccaya ice cap indicates the onset of a major drought around A.D. 550–600. The construction of the filtration galleries appears to correspond with these climatic conditions.

This ancient preoccupation with water may have led to the creation of certain Pampa markings. Anthony F. Aveni and his colleagues have identified 62 ray centers—lines converging on a specific area—and 750 associated lines among the markings in the Nazca core area. These stretch for over 200 square kilometers (77 square miles) and each ray center contains 10 to 12 spokes. Aveni found ray centers on natural rises overlooking streambeds and along bases of mountains. He concludes that these lines delineate the flow of water across the Pampa, and that they were connected with some sort of ritual to summon up water. Aveni writes that "the Nazca lines and the associated geometry were intended, at least in part, to be walked over in some complex set of rituals that pertained most likely to the bringing of water to the Nazca Valley and perhaps to associated mountain worship" (Aveni, 1990: 112).

Aveni's theory is not the only one that links the markings to a preoccupation with water.

80 An early Nazca jar modeled and painted to represent the head of a whiskered feline wearing a mouth mask. Nazca priests and supernatural figures are often shown wearing elaborate masks like these, perhaps as part of ceremonial attire. Mouth masks of hammered sheet gold are among the objects found in richer Nazca tombs. South coast, Peru.
H. 16.5 cm. (6.5 in.) 41.2/616

81 Nazca artists often portrayed killer whales, or orcas, sometimes carrying human trophy heads. This early Nazca ceramic vessel, modeled and painted in the form of a killer whale or shark, recalls figures etched on the arid Nazca Pampa. Today, orcas are rarely seen in Peruvian waters. South coast, Peru.
L. 35.8 cm. (14.1 in.) 41.2/7979

Anthropologist Johan Reinhard, too, has tied this preoccupation to fertility and mountain worship and has shown that mountain worship is still pervasive in the southern Andes. Rivers on the arid Peruvian coast depend on rainfall in the mountains to the east, and because clouds gather on mountains, mountains were perceived to control weather. Thus mountains were worshipped as the dwellings of mountain gods. Reinhard has also linked some of the Nazca markings, such as spirals, birds, and spiders, to age-old Andean fertility symbols connected with water.

Other explanations for the markings include hypotheses that they formed part of giant textile workshops, irrigation schemes, or landing strips for spaceships from other galaxies. Archaeological and artistic evidence, however, points to the Nazca, and earlier, origins of these markings. Although they are best appreciated from the air, many of the markings can be seen from surrounding hilltops. There is no evidence that they were meant to be viewed from hot-air balloons or primitive gliders. These theories cannot be proven and are based on either totally erroneous information or on non-Andean concepts.

Perhaps the most widely accepted popular view is the one posed in 1941 by the American geographer Paul Kosok. Kosok postulated that the markings formed part of a giant astronomical calendar that signaled the onset of the rainy season in the mountains and marked celestial events in the Nazca skies. Efforts to link certain animal markings to constellations, or to connect lines with solstices, have met with little acceptance among most Nazca scholars, largely because Kosok's disciple, the German mathematician Maria Reiche,

has published little data to support the astronomical theories.

The Nazca markings include geometric forms, such as trapezoids, rectangles, straight lines, spirals, zigzags, and concentric ray systems. There are also animal and human forms: birds (fig. 84), killer whales (fig. 83), a monkey, a spider, and a flower. The largest markings extend over the barren Pampa for several kilometers. Some of the trapezoids are over a kilometer long, while lines often extend for several kilometers. The animal figures, though immense in their own right, are much smaller and are concentrated on a ten-kilometer-square (six-mile-square) strip on the northern edge of the Pampa, overlooking the Ingenio River. They are made up of a single, unbroken line that never crosses itself. The spider, for example, is over 50 meters (164 feet) long and the monkey more than 100 meters (328 feet) across. One bird marking with a prominent zigzag neck, identified as a cormorant, measures just over 300 meters (984 feet) long. Researchers have recorded some fifty animal figures. Human figures, which are rare and usually occur on hillsides, are thought to be earlier than the animal figures. Similarities between certain designs on Nazca ceramics and those etched on the Pampa as well as occasional offerings of Nazca-style ceramic sherds on the Pampa together offer conclusive proof for the Nazca origins of the markings.

The heaviest concentration of Nazca markings is on the Pampa, 50 kilometers (31 miles) inland and 500 meters (1,640 feet) above sea level, sandwiched between the region's three most important water sources: the Grande, Nazca, and Ingenio

83 The ancient Nazca people of southern Peru etched large-scale ground drawings of animals and geometric shapes on the arid desert near the modern town of Nazca. Because of scant rainfall in the region, the markings have been preserved, some for more than 2,000 years. This 25.9-meter (85-foot) ground drawing represents a large marine animal, probably a shark or a killer whale, holding a human head. South coast, Peru.

84 A ground drawing about 91 meters (300 feet) long that probably represents a hummingbird. Nazca Pampa, south coast, Peru.

rivers. Over the millennia, manganese and iron oxides deposited on the Pampa's desert surface by aerobic microorganisms have left a thin patina, known as desert varnish. The Nazca people created the markings by removing this darker surface layer to reveal the lighter-colored soil beneath. They enhanced the outlines by laying the cleared stones along the edge of the marking. The figurative geoglyphs are believed to date to the earlier Nazca phases, while the trapezoids and geometric figures may be later. The work of archaeologist Persis Clarkson and geomorphologist Ronald Dorn has shown that organic materials removed from beneath the surface layer of rock varnish can be dated by accelerator mass spectrometry to 190 B.C.–A.D. 660. Like the pottery offerings, these dates confirm the Nazca cultural affiliation of the geoglyphs.

The markings are not confined to the Pampa, however. Helaine Silverman and David Browne have identified scores of geoglyphs on the hillsides of the Rio Grande de Nazca drainage. Other scholars have spotted Paracas-style markings in the form of catlike creatures on a hillside near Ica and triangular clearings on hilltops south of Ica. Triangles also have been spotted west of Ica and in the Pisco Valley.

By A.D. 700 the once-flourishing Nazca culture was increasingly influenced by peoples from the Ayacucho highlands to the east, the cradle of the Wari Empire. Wari, in turn, owes much of its artistic inspiration to Tiwanaku, the sprawling urban center on the southern shores of Lake Titicaca. Archaeologists have dated the earliest constructions at this famed center to 400 B.C., contemporary with the florescence of Pukará at the northern end of Lake Titicaca. Between A.D. 375 and 600 or 700, Tiwanaku's so-called Classic period, the site reached its apogee to become one of the region's longest-lived empires until its collapse about 1000. Tiwanaku may have served as a pilgrimage center, and its art may have been spread across the Andes by roving missionaries. Wari and Tiwanaku repeated a pattern introduced by the highland Chavín cult several centuries earlier and also heralded the empire of the Inka. Dominating the Andes for several centuries, Wari and Tiwanaku brought together previously independent culture areas with a single, distinctive style.

DEITIES AND CONQUESTS

THE FIRST EMPIRES

About A.D. 400 a new and pivotal epoch began in the Andean region. This was a time of unprecedented political and economic expansion that would bring a shift of both the political and artistic center of gravity from the coastal areas of Moche and Nazca inland to the southern and south-central highlands. Early in the twentieth century Max Uhle recognized that the art of the Bolivian altiplano had influenced large areas of the Andes, including most of the Peruvian coast. By the 1950s it was determined that this influence came from two cities, Tiwanaku, near Lake Titicaca in Bolivia, and Wari, near the modern city of Ayacucho in the south-central highlands of Peru. The origins and natures of these two cities are among the most hotly debated issues in Andean archaeology. These issues include questions of the states that they apparently ruled, of their relations with each other, and of their influence on more distant coastal and northern highland regions. Fortunately, recent research in both Peru and Bolivia is providing a wealth of new information. This new research should soon enable us to write a more definitive chapter on the rise of what most scholars feel were the first truly imperial Andean states.

As we await further results from these investigations, only a tentative picture is possible of this complex and fascinating period. This picture suggests that one of the cities, Tiwanaku, inherited and elaborated a religion that emphasized sky gods. Tiwanaku's religion had roots in Pukará and probably in earlier religions, dating back at least to Chavín times. Slightly later—some would argue at almost the same time—Wari began to grow. Appar-

ently it adopted certain aspects of Tiwanaku's religion combined with features from other areas, particularly the north Peruvian highlands and Nazca. Wari spread its influence even wider than Tiwanaku, further disseminating the Tiwanaku images. Both cities and the states they ruled represented a remarkable new synthesis in Andean culture, politics, and economics. This synthesis coincided with a relative decline in the exuberant cultures of the north and south coast of Peru; but it further honed the political and administrative tactics that laid the groundwork for later cultures, such as Chimú and, ultimately, the Inka.

The single most vexing problem that clouds our understanding of this period is the lack of a precise chronology for tracing the histories of the two states. In spite of the advances in radiocarbon dating and in plotting changes in pottery and textile styles over time, we still cannot measure prehistoric time in units much smaller than blocks of about fifty years. That time unit is not precise enough to coordinate events in two dynamic states. In addition, there has not yet been enough research to produce a reliable group of dates to plot the trajectories of the two states even in fifty-year blocks. The evidence for Tiwanaku is especially problematic. With these caveats, we can suggest that major construction was under way at Tiwanaku by A.D. 200, as indicated in chapter 6. Tiwanaku probably reached its Classic period, called Tiwanaku IV by Bolivian archaeologist Carlos Ponce Sanginés, about 400. The expansion of Tiwanaku out of the Lake Titicaca heartland had probably begun by 550. Wari was established by 600 and declined as an empire about two centuries later, although its

85 The outstretched arms with hands on chest of this painted ceramic figure of a woman suggest an offering pose. Wari style, probably Ica region, south coast, Peru. H. 28.4 cm. (11.3 in.) 41.2/8596

influence in ceramics and other art forms continued for at least another century. In the mid-sixteenth century, Spanish chronicler/soldier Pedro de Cieza de León wrote of Tiwanaku: "It [the site of Tiwanaku] is famous for its great buildings which, without question, are a remarkable thing to behold. Near the main dwellings is a man-made hill, built on great stone foundations. Beyond this hill there are two stone idols of human size and shape, with the features beautifully carved, so much so that they seem the work of great artists or masters. They are so large that they seem small giants" (Cieza, 1959 [1553]: 282–83).

Tiwanaku is one of the most intriguing ancient kingdoms of the New World. Centered on the high plains around Lake Titicaca, with the site of Tiwanaku as its capital, it became the most influential kingdom in the Andes during the fifth century. Elements of its art spread through most of the region considered in this book. Some of this stylistic expansion apparently accompanied political expansion of the boundaries of the Tiwanaku realm; but much of it resulted from the expansion of Wari, which had taken several elements of the Tiwanaku style as its own. Some elements were adopted even by kingdoms on the Peruvian north coast, the descendants of Moche, that almost certainly were independent of any political expansion by either Tiwanaku or Wari.

Unfortunately, the importance of Tiwanaku is not matched by information that tells us how this small regional kingdom was transformed into a major state, with a religion that influenced millions of people and left its stamp on the Andes for a millennium. Given the present status of our knowledge, Tiwanaku still seems like a mysterious kingdom rising in an area that appears inhospitable to major cultural development. But this culture produced a great city with monumental architecture, stone sculpture, and a rich ceremonial life based on a major religion. Then, even more rapidly than it rose, Tiwanaku fell into ruin and dissolution in the early eleventh century. The full publication of ongoing research in the city of Tiwanaku, in the surrounding hinterland, and in far-flung provinces will illustrate much more clearly Tiwanaku's prehistory.

At 3,850 meters (12,630 feet) above sea level, Tiwanaku was one of the highest capitals in the ancient world. Lhasa, in Tibet, lies at about 3,658 meters (12,000 feet) and Kathmandu, in Nepal, is much lower. Ponce Sanginés has plotted the size of the city at 2.8 by 1.6 kilometers (1.7 by 1 mile) based on the area where pottery sherds and other artifacts occur on the surface. New research suggests that at its apogee it was probably even larger. Architectural remains can be seen on sixteen hectares (forty acres) of this area. The area of stone construction probably formed the administrative and ceremonial core of the city, and the balance of the area was devoted primarily to residential structures, probably of adobe. Population estimates have ranged from twenty thousand to forty thousand. By any measure Tiwanaku was large for an ancient city.

City planning in the ceremonial core followed a grid pattern, and the structures that remain are laid out in rather rigid accordance with the cardinal directions. One of its main features is a series of monumental gateways. There has not yet been enough research to outline the construction history of the site precisely. But it is certain that careful planning gave the combination of monumental buildings a sense of harmony and coherence, even though they were built at different times. Nor can we accurately assign specific uses to the various buildings, although the elaborate architecture in Tiwanaku's core was clearly public in nature and probably provided large spaces for religious and civic rites as well as for possible palace buildings.

The two largest and most conspicuous features in Tiwanaku's core are the Akapana and Pumapunku. The Akapana, probably the monument referred to by Cieza in the passage quoted above, is a natural hill transformed by five stone-faced terraces into a truncated pyramid about 200 meters (656 feet) long and 18 meters (59 feet) high. Pumapunku is located southeast of the Akapana pyramid and looks somewhat isolated from the remainder of the ceremonial buildings. It is a T-shaped mound formed by three stone-faced terraces, with a spacious patio in the center. According to Bolivian researcher Jorge Arellano, the upper terrace floor was covered with a layer of reddish ochre about two centimeters thick; the floor of the central patio was composed of compacted white silt and clay. As a result of poor preservation, drawings that interpret and reconstruct the architecture of Tiwanaku vary considerably from investigator to investigator. Indeed, substantial controversy surrounds several aspects

86 The central structures at
Tiwanaku, capital of a
long-lived Andean state.
Southeast of Lake Titicaca,
Bolivia, at 3,870 meters
(12,690 feet) above sea
level, Tiwanaku was the
ancient world's highest
urban center. The Akapana
mound (top right) rises
beside the Kalasasaya, a
large, nearly square
enclosure.

of reconstruction at the site itself. Ancient as well as modern rebuilders apparently moved several of the sculptures to serve new purposes, or to suit their fancies. Some archaeologists and architects, for example, feel that the Gateway of the Sun, presently standing in the Kalasasaya, was originally part of Pumapunku.

Other major construction in the heart of Tiwanaku includes Kerikala, Putuni, Kalasasaya, and the Semisubterranean Temple. These buildings stand north of the Akapana, and most of those with preserved entrances have gateways opening to the east. The westernmost of the buildings is Kerikala. Referred to by Ponce Sanginés as a

"palace," it consists of four wings of small rooms surrounding a central patio. Excavations in the rooms uncovered hearths containing ash and the bones of deer, camelids, and other animals. Among the ceramics in the rooms were remains of vessels that may have been used as lamps. While these finds are consistent with some form of habitation, Arellano feels that this was not the architecture of a residential complex or of a religious order, where "priests" might have lived in small cells. For him the evidence is more consistent with a periodic marketplace that may have been used during rituals regulated by a calendar. The small cells, in his view, may have been storerooms for trade products or perhaps for surplus goods from the rural lands outside the city.

Directly east of Kerikala is Putuni, which Ponce Sanginés also regards as a palace. Putuni has an ingenious system of subterranean canals that incline at a regular gradient of five degrees. The complex consists of a rectangular courtyard enclosed by concentric stone retaining walls with earth fill between them. The combination of walls and fill creates what is essentially a platform surrounding the patio. Stairs in the retaining walls ascend to the platform, and freestanding buildings once may have stood on top of it.

East of Putuni is the great enclosure of Kalasasaya, a platform reached by steps hewn out of stones laid between two huge, vertical monolithic pillars. The retaining wall that forms the platform is composed of large vertical stones separated by horizontal blocks. At the base of the south wall is a series of canals and water catchment basins that probably served ceremonial functions.

87 On the Gateway of the Sun at Tiwanaku the central figure of the gateway god is shown frontally with rays extending out from the head, and eyes shedding tears. The deity is flanked by winged attendants.

88 The head of a Tiwanaku stela known as the Ponce Monolith. The monument has complex etching typical of Tiwanaku monolithic sculpture.

In the eastern part of the Kalasasaya a stela stands in a rectangular patio. The stela is known as the Ponce Monolith (fig. 88) and resembles the much larger Bennett Monolith (fig. 89).

Wendell Bennett found the monolith named for him in excavations sponsored by the American Museum of Natural History in 1932. It had stood in a sunken patio known as the Semisubterranean Temple, east of the Kalasasaya platform. This temple, later excavated by Ponce Sanginés, is about 28.5 meters (94 feet) long by 26 meters (85 feet) wide and 1.7 meters (5.5 feet) deep. The walls of the sunken patio are faced with rectangular sandstone blocks, interrupted at intervals by vertical pillars. A series of stylized human heads attached by tenons projects from the walls. The Bennett Monolith, now moved to a small park in La Paz, is 7.3 meters (24 feet) tall, making it the largest known Andean sculpture. It portrays a richly attired human figure wearing a headdress and holding what appears to be a *kero,* a flared drinking vessel, in one hand. The other hand holds what has been interpreted as a staff or a snuff tablet.

Quarrying and transporting the stone for Tiwanaku's monumental constructions was an enormous investment in labor. The andesite often used in the sculpted monoliths was quarried on the Copacabana Peninsula and brought across Lake Titicaca on reed boats to the port of Iwawe. From Iwawe the blocks of stone were hauled overland using ramps and skids. Other massive stones came from quarries closer at hand. One sandstone block weighing about 130 tons was brought to Pumapunku from a quarry ten kilometers (six miles) south of Tiwanaku. Skid marks between the

89 Carved in red sandstone, the Bennett Monolith is the largest stone sculpture of the ancient Andes. The huge figure carries a decorated beaker and is covered with twenty-nine smaller figures. Discovered during excavation in the Semisubterranean Temple, it now stands in a plaza in La Paz, Bolivia.

90 Gateway God: The Inka god of thunder and lightning was a sky figure who brought rain. The flash of his shining garments was the lightning, and he held a war club and a sling. A similar Tiwanaku god appears most prominently as the central figure on the Gateway of the Sun. He holds a spear-thrower "staff" in his right hand; the stafflike object in his left hand may represent spears in a container. The drawing omits the stepped platform on which this figure typically stands.

quarries and the construction sites can be detected in aerial photographs.

Many of the monuments in the central sector of Tiwanaku were embellished with stone carving. Elaborate carving on some of the gateways, most notably the Gateway of the Sun, was executed mainly on the lintels or architraves below which people passed. Monolithic stelae often were carved in the round and erected in the plazas, although ancient and modern renovators have moved many from their original positions. Many of them may have been ornamented with gold plates and inlays and also painted in bright colors. The designs carved on these monuments almost certainly had religious themes that were intended to impress all who visited the elaborate ceremonial precinct with the power of the gods and by extension the power of the rulers.

Several scholars have studied Tiwanaku religious imagery and compared it with Wari religious images as well as with what Spanish chroniclers wrote about Inka religion a few centuries later. The interpretations here are based largely on the work of archaeologist Dorothy Menzel. The figures seen in full-frontal position, each holding a staff in either hand, are usually thought to represent gods; however, they may have represented humans, probably with divine properties, dressed in ritual regalia. Typically, rays—which may suggest light—project from the heads of the gods and end in animal heads or circles. Each god also wears a necklace of rays. Tiwanaku textiles and pottery are often decorated with the same religious imagery as the stone sculptures, and these images are sometimes engraved on gold plaques.

With its patios, gateways, and sculptures embellished with religious images, the central precinct of Tiwanaku provided large and carefully planned spaces for public ceremonies. Architect William Conklin has pointed out that it was architecture designed to impress. But we lack evidence to reconstruct the public activities framed by this elaborate architecture. Intriguing parallels exist between the public architecture of Tiwanaku and that of the Inka a few centuries later. Both emphasized gateways that marked boundaries between one space and another. The Inka had great concern with such boundaries and with the movement of people across them. The ceremonial passage from one space or one patio to another may have marked important social and political transformations, and the gateways themselves may have symbolized and legitimized such changes. It seems evident that the public architecture of Tiwanaku is ancestral to that of the Inka, and thus it is reasonable to suggest some of the same emphasis on ceremonial paths punctuated by gateways, shrines, and other stopping points along the way. Like the Inka, Tiwanaku rulers had to convince the people of their power and to guide the populace through a transformation establishing a new order of elite whose instructions were to be obeyed.

As in most of the other early civilizations, a major means of legitimizing the elite was to inculcate religious beliefs that equated the power of the rulers with the natural and supernatural order. The imagery employed at Tiwanaku and the rituals performed amid its ceremonial spaces probably served to make the rulers' commands seem part of the natural order. Rule and obedience to that rule

became processes of growth and creation as essential as the sun, earth, and water. Central authority became legitimate, and a new set of institutions grew up. These institutions would ensure labor to support the government and the elite—to build cities, to craft fine objects, to produce an agricultural surplus in order to feed the elite and the artisans. Finally, labor had to be invested in the society's infrastructure, including the creation of a vast system of artificial fields that were needed to increase agricultural production.

Tiwanaku's rulers went beyond impressive imagery and public architecture to support their religious and political ceremonies. Objects related to the use of drugs are a common part of the Tiwanaku archaeological inventory. In the Andes, snuff dates to the Preceramic period, but it seems to have gained increasing social or religious importance in Tiwanaku culture. Snuff, dried and finely ground plant material, may have been prepared from leaves, resin, and seeds of various plants. Objects associated with drug use included snuff trays and inhaling tubes, spatulas, containers, and pouches. Historic and modern data suggest many uses for drugs in the Andes: as preventive medicine, for curing, to alleviate hunger pains, as stimulants for alertness in war and hunting, and to induce trances during curing and fertility ceremonies.

Flared drinking cups, or keros (fig. 96), became common in Tiwanaku times. Goblets of this shape were also found at Wari, continued in general use among the Inka, and a modern version in glass is still used in the Cuzco area. Keros are associated with drinking chicha, and in Inka and

91 Winged Attendants: On the Gateway of the Sun human-headed (top and bottom) and eagle-headed (center) spirits run toward the thunder god from both sides. These smaller winged attendants are seen in profile rather than full face. Like the central figure, each has a rayed headdress and carries a stafflike object.

93 Mother Earth: On the Bennett Monolith a female figure stands on a platform below the sun and moon. Her head rays end in serpents and there are maize symbols on her feet. For many centuries, people of the Andes have offered sacrifices of coca leaves, maize beer, and other items to an earth goddess. The associated symbols and attendant llama figures suggest that this ancient Tiwanaku figure was connected with the fertility of the earth.

92 The Sun and the Moon: The back of the Bennett Monolith is carved with a pair of images that probably correspond to the Inka sun god and moon goddess. For the Inka, the sun god protected crops and was even more important than the thunder god. The Tiwanaku sun image, with head rays ending in feline heads, suggests a link with the Inka sky figure, represented by a golden disk showing a human face surrounded by rays.

94 The Llama: Winged attendants of the earth goddess alternate with mythical llamas carrying plants. The symbol on the goddess as well as on the llama's body and on a stalk behind it probably represents the maize plant.

Colonial times fine keros were used in ceremonies and important political events. Archaeologists have established that chicha consumption was part of the ceremony of rule for the Inka. The artifacts that have been found suggest that both chicha and drugs were central elements of the ceremonial and political life of Tiwanaku. Sharing these substances, in circumstances propitious to forming and maintaining ties of allegiance, was important in archaic societies. They may well have facilitated the acceptance of new levels of cooperation and service to rulers required by the growing Tiwanaku state. The labor involved in building a magnificent capital and artificial field systems might be more easily enlisted with the help of dramatic ceremonies involving the altered states of mind that alcohol and some of the drugs induce. This evidence for the presence of alcohol and drugs does not suggest high rates of alcoholism or drug dependence. When the use of such products is embedded in ritual, they are less likely to be abused than in modern society where control is left to economic and legal mechanisms.

For many years one of the archaeological puzzles of Tiwanaku was its economic base. How was it possible to build a major city and state and maintain them for centuries in a rugged and seemingly barren high-altitude landscape? One misconception, noted earlier, arose because the altiplano landscape looks more barren to European and Euroamerican eyes than to its Andean inhabitants. Research over the past twenty-five years has revealed that people in Tiwanaku times practiced a form of agriculture known to their Pukará predecessors but now practically lost. According to those who have studied it, it could have readily provided food for a city and society the size of Tiwanaku. The evidence has come from a large series of fossil fields, along the edge of Lake Titicaca, that can be easily traced in aerial photographs. These fields and associated provincial administrative centers seem to have been agricultural estates, possibly under state control.

The fields consist of curvilinear earth platforms from 5 to 15 meters (16 to 49 feet) wide and as many as 200 meters (656 feet) long. Used as elevated planting surfaces, the platforms alternated with the lower areas, called swales, into which the lake waters could flow. Such platforms, called raised fields, are known in other areas of the New

95 ABOVE
Wooden tray, carved with a seated human figure and incised with stylized felines, probably used in preparing drugs. Tiwanaku style, San Pedro, Chuquicamata, northern Chile.
L. 15.3 cm. (6 in.) W. 5.5 cm. (2.2 in.) 41.0/8911

96 RIGHT
Two bands of feline-headed figures holding plumed staffs, painted on a ceramic kero, or beaker. Tiwanaku style, Arani, Bolivia.
H. 20.8 cm. (8.2 in.) 41.1/3828

World such as the Maya region. At Pampa Koani, Alan Kolata of the University of Chicago excavated raised fields constructed on a base of cobblestones covered by a layer of dense clay about 10 centimeters (4 inches) thick. Above the stone and clay foundation lay three distinct layers of sorted gravel, capped with a final layer of rich topsoil. The cobblestones served as the basic pedestal, raising the field above the marshy lake shore. The clay layer impeded infiltration of the brackish waters from the lake that would have damaged crops; at the same time it acted as a barrier for fresh water percolating down from nearby hillsides. Like pebbles at the bottom of a flowerpot, the layers of gravel enhanced the platform's drainage.

The water-filled swales that lay between the cultivated ridges also were important in maintaining a productive field system. Water often stood in the swales, encouraging the growth of aquatic plants, animals, and insects. The remains of these organisms produced a supply of natural fertilizer that farmers could use to renew essential soil nutrients. In areas very near the lake shore, water standing almost continuously in the swales could be used during short dry spells for splash irrigation. By absorbing the intense daytime heat of the sun and releasing it slowly at night, the water in the swales acted like miniature lakes in helping to slow nighttime temperature changes, preventing frosts by moderating the stark day-night temperature swings.

As an experimental check on the productivity of raised fields, Clark Erickson of Philadelphia's University Museum constructed fields at the northern end of Lake Titicaca similar to those used by Tiwanaku farmers. His work demonstrated the unusually high output of such systems. These artificial fields supplemented cultivation of potatoes and the Andean grain quinoa, helping to ensure the agricultural basis of Tiwanaku.

Llama and alpaca herding for wool, meat, and carrying burdens provided another important source of subsistence and wealth. In an environment where warm clothing was important and in a cultural setting that had long since assigned textiles a high value, people of the altiplano took advantage of the opportunity to amass wealth in their herds. While the productive base of Tiwanaku is no longer a mystery, many details of how the economy functioned remain unclear. For instance, we still do not know what kind of exchange relationships tied the inhabitants and rulers in the capital to the farmers and herders as well as to people in other ecological zones who supplied important resources from far away. Some researchers, such as David Browman, see periodic markets and llama caravans, for carrying goods long distances, as the means of exchanging goods between specialized producers and different ecological zones. An alternative, suggested by Peruvian archaeologist Elias Mujica and others, is based on a model that involved varying ecologies controlled directly by Tiwanaku colonies. Unfortunately, it is very difficult to extract information from archaeology that would prove one of these models of Tiwanaku exchange a more accurate description than the other. Markets are notoriously hard to detect in the archaeological record, and many aspects of the transport of goods between groups or regions are similar, regardless of the principles that organize them. Further evidence on the form and distribution of Tiwanaku settlements will give us better insight into the Tiwanaku economy.

The most significant archaeological clues to both the economic and the political nature of a state ultimately come from its far-flung provincial regions rather than from its capital. How were peripheral areas controlled? To what extent were labor and other economic resources extracted from them? To what extent were they exploited through a system of trade and taxation, or through the more direct mechanisms of controlled colonies? Were special administrative outposts built where administrators from the heartland oversaw provincial affairs? Around Lake Titicaca, sites such as Lucurmata apparently were related to the management of the economically critical ridged-field systems.

In regions well removed from Lake Titicaca, archaeological evidence suggests two somewhat different manifestations of Tiwanaku art, religion, and, quite probably, political control. One of these involves the dispersion of ritual paraphernalia and its associated ideology. It has been suggested that religious proselytizing accompanied by trade were the mechanisms of this dispersion. The most notable evidence for this kind of dispersion is found in northern Chile. Many years of research by Father Gustavo LePaige and his colleagues in the oasis of San Pedro de Atacama has unearthed Tiwanaku ceramics, apparently imported from the Tiwanaku region. Broken vessels often were carefully repaired in ancient times, a clue to the

scarcity and value of the pottery. Snuff tablets and other items, apparently used with some kinds of drugs, also have been found in these contexts. Many of these objects were decorated with the gateway god and other Tiwanaku religious images. The vessels and ritual items represent a relatively small percentage of the total inventory of Tiwanaku material culture, and the Tiwanaku manifestations in these regions probably did not involve either the resettling of peoples from Tiwanaku or political control from the Lake Titicaca city.

The other manifestation of Tiwanaku appears in architecture as well as in a wide range of other material items from the Lake Titicaca

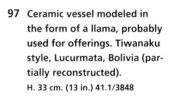

97 Ceramic vessel modeled in the form of a llama, probably used for offerings. Tiwanaku style, Lucurmata, Bolivia (partially reconstructed).
H. 33 cm. (13 in.) 41.1/3848

98 Plan of the ceremonial sector of Omo, a Tiwanaku enclave in the Moquegua River drainage of southern Peru. The site has three stepped platforms on the side of a hill. A square and sunken central patio, contained in the uppermost platform, identifies the architecture as Tiwanaku.

region. Research by Paul Goldstein of the American Museum of Natural History at the Omo site complex in Moquegua, in southern Peru, brought to light the first clear example of Tiwanaku ceremonial architecture distant from the capital. At the Omo complex, Goldstein found a platform mound about 120 meters (394 feet) long. The form of the mound is clearly Tiwanaku, but it is built of adobe rather than the stone-faced earth used to construct platforms found in the capital (fig. 98) The mound consists of three stepped platforms on the side of a hill. A square and sunken central patio contained in the uppermost platform, particularly, reflects the Tiwanaku source of the architecture. Near the central structure lie a sizable residential area and a cemetery. The combination of ceremonial and residential architecture—built in the provinces but in the style of the capital—is a hallmark of political control of outlying areas in the Andes. It will be seen in Tiwanaku's sister state, Wari, and again in fully developed form with the Inka Empire.

While some of the Tiwanaku settlements in Moquegua apparently were occupied during the Tiwanaku IV period, the ceremonial platform seems to have been built during Tiwanaku V. A radiocarbon date puts it near the end of Tiwanaku times. There are some suggestions of a short gap in the archaeological record for the Tiwanaku occupation, just prior to construction of the site with ceremonial architecture excavated by Goldstein. At about this time, a center with definite Wari affiliation was built on Cerro Baúl, within the area occupied by Tiwanaku sites. The apparent break in the Tiwanaku record may have been related to

Wari penetration into the area. Unfortunately, dating is not yet precise enough for us to chart the specific chain of events; but it seems relatively certain that Tiwanaku peoples lived in Moquegua before the Wari site was built and were living there after it was abandoned.

Tiwanaku sites, in general, seem to have been constructed in sparsely occupied areas, and it is very likely that they were built by peoples from the vicinity of Tiwanaku itself. As noted in chapter 2, establishing colonies in lands with different ecological features was central to the way Andean peoples, particularly those from the highlands, dealt with their diverse habitats. It also underlies the kind of direct exchange relationships referred to as an alternative to trade and markets.

More than five centuries after the time of Tiwanaku, Garci Diez de San Miguel made an inspection for the Spanish Crown of the Lupaca, a rich kingdom that had been subjugated by the Inka. The heart of the Lupaca kingdom was also in the high altiplano of what is now Peru, across Lake Titicaca from Tiwanaku. Diez de San Miguel's report revealed that Lupaca peoples had settled in Moquegua to give the kingdom access to lands suitable for growing maize in the warm Osmore Valley. It may be that the system of settling colonies to assure access to goods from lands with new potentials existed at the time of Tiwanaku. That would explain the Tiwanaku remains in Moquegua. There are hints that a similar situation may have existed in the warm Cochabamba region of the eastern Bolivian Andes. Chicha, brewed from maize grown in the warm lower lands, may have been at least one of the drinks that filled the flared kero cups so characteristic of the Tiwanaku culture. Had Tiwanaku modeled the Omo ceremonial complex on those at the capital to help it rule the warm lands so suitable for growing a product important to the state and its religion?

The evidence accumulated to date shows that Tiwanaku was an extensive and powerful state, capable both of influencing other regions with its art and its religious practices and of moving its peoples into provincial areas for direct control. The heavy ceremonial emphasis seen in its architecture, the rich religious imagery incorporated into its art, and the fact that artifacts of ritual paraphernalia were more common than arti-

facts of military control suggest that Tiwanaku's power was based more on religion and economics than on a strong military. One of the most fascinating questions of Andean prehistory is how this rather theocratic form of rule may have contrasted with that of Wari and how these two important states interacted.

 ## WARI

As an archaeological site, Wari looks quite different from Tiwanaku. This stems in part from the contrasting environments in which they are located. Wari covered about two square kilometers (less than one mile) on a plateau of volcanic origin about twenty-five kilometers (fifteen miles) north of the Peruvian city of Ayacucho. Its elevation is about 2,800 meters (9,180 feet) above sea level. Thus it lay in an intermontane valley (described in chapter 2), rather than in the puna environment of Tiwanaku. The difference in rainfall between the two areas is especially marked: at Wari there is arid-looking scrub vegetation, especially in the May-to-September dry season. Instead of the impressive platform mounds and monumental sculptures of Tiwanaku, at Wari there are numerous high walls enclosing rectangular compounds. Many of the walls, made of fieldstone, are preserved to heights of 6 to 12 meters (20 to 40 feet), and some run for hundreds of meters. Stones often project from the walls in positions that suggest supports for multiple floors. As with Tiwanaku, the architecture visible on the surface gives only a very partial picture of what the city was originally like. Excavations are required to reveal the foundations and low walls of buildings beneath the plow zone. As at Tiwanaku, archaeological research has been limited, exposing only a very small part of the remains that lie below the surface. Thus we have only a tentative, incomplete history of the construction of the city and of the nature and uses of its various zones. Nevertheless, research by archaeologists Luis Lumbreras, William Isbell, Mario Benavides, and several of their colleagues has begun to build the outlines of the city's architecture.

As a culture and a city, Wari grew out of a previous local culture known as Huarpa. The people of the Huarpa culture were roughly contemporary with those of the Moche, Nazca, and others. Three separate Huarpa communities existed within the area of what became the city of Wari. One of these settlements became a town and may have been the nucleus from which urban Wari grew.

During the periods that archaeologists call 1A and early 1B, Wari grew rapidly, probably partly through immigration from other areas and settlements. During this time it became both a residential and a ceremonial city. Some of the ceremonial structures were built in dressed stone. An example is the semisubterranean temple in the Moraduchayuq sector, a public building with an open court excavated by Isbell and his colleagues. Other examples of impressive ceremonial compounds from about this time are the Cheqo Wasi architectural group, excavated by Benavides, and the Vegachayoq Moqo temple complex, excavated by Enrique Bragayrac. Both of these areas of the early city contained megalithic stone construction. The technology and, to a lesser extent, the concept of early Wari ceremonial architecture are somehow related to Tiwanaku. There were several of these dressed-stone ceremonial complexes, and their distribution suggests that during this period Wari had become a city covering more than 100 hectares (250 acres). These ceremonial precincts and the religion they served were probably closely related to the rapid growth and florescence of Wari at this time.

Wari reached its peak as a city in the later part of the period archaeologists call 1B (600–700). At least most of the buildings whose remains can now be seen on the surface of the site probably were constructed during that relatively long span of time. Large-walled compounds of rectangular rooms around patios, the basic architectural unit, were surrounded by streets forming an irregular grid. This plan is especially evident in the northern part of the city where compounds were rectangular to trapezoidal in form and typically measured between 150 and 300 meters (492 and 984 feet) on each side. Buildings and compounds in the southern part of the city seem to have been substantially smaller. Not enough research has been done to determine whether these differences between north and south relate to internal differences in the organization of the city or to a process of urban replanning and renewal that was replacing the smaller constructions of the south with larger and more orderly architectural units. Isbell and his colleagues have noted areas near the border between the northern and southern sections where buildings had been razed, possibly for replacement.

Luis Lumbreras excavated in a sector of Wari known as Ushpa Qoto, which occupies an area of about 300 by 500 meters (984 by 1,640 feet) in the northern part of the city. In Ushpa Qoto, large buildings of up to three stories surround a large rectangular plaza. He also reports semicircular buildings around a small plaza and houses probably divided into rooms by partitions of perishable construction. Excavations in one large compound uncovered rooms joined together around a semicircular patio. A pottery workshop along with an apparent storehouse, containing molds and other supplies and equipment for making ceramics, were found in another part of the compound. The Ushpa

99 Gateway God: The Wari version of this deity has especially strong similarities to the Tiwanaku gateway god. This example, from the coast, lacks a fanged mouth and stands on a stepped platform.

Qoto sector also featured a complex system of subterranean channels, some associated with hewn stones and at least one lined with fine clay. Some researchers think that these underground channels, common in other parts of Wari as well, were for supplying water to the city, but thus far no link has been made to a water source. More likely they served as drains. Water and the flow of water were of great religious and ritual importance during Inka times, and some of the canals at Wari, as well as those at Chavín and Tiwanaku, may not have served ordinary utilitarian purposes.

Although they lack an excavated archaeological sequence to confirm it, Isbell and archaeologists working with him have suggested that most of the long, massive walls at Wari date to a late period in the city's history, the period known as 2 (700–800), perhaps even the second part of that period, 2B. Possibly the clearing of areas for reconstruction also dates to this late period. The enormous walls may have been the last stage of city planning, perhaps intended to enclose buildings that were never constructed.

The walls are often several meters thick, very tall, and some of them somewhat curved. Though tall enough for multiple stories, they lack evidence of architectural devices for anchoring upper floors. The spaces they enclose usually take the shapes of trapezoids or elongated triangles. These walls often seem to be related to areas of cleared buildings, ramps, and other features of construction in progress. The rather disorderly picture conveyed by the surface remains of Wari may result at least in part from a process of renovation and growth cut short by events that led to the

100, 101 Sun and Moon: Wari images of the sun (left) and moon (right) resemble those from Tiwanaku, but they have whole bodies and also incorporate the maize symbols and serpent heads seen on the earth goddess.

collapse of the state or empire the city ruled. Whatever else can be said of Wari, its architectural history clearly was complex and dynamic, exactly what we would expect for the capital of an important and far-flung realm.

Stone statues have been found in the Ayacucho region. Although none has been excavated by archaeologists, they relate to the Wari culture regardless of their exact provenience. Most are human figures carved in three dimensions and high relief. One portrays a seated feline, executed with a naturalism unusual in Andean sculpture. The humans wear elaborate headdresses with four points, similar to those of the stone figures of Tiwanaku. Although the Wari statues were once covered with paint, they are simpler than those of Tiwanaku. They depict a single figure without the attendants and rich supplementary decoration typical of Tiwanaku sculpture.

The religious iconography of Wari is expressed primarily in textiles and pottery. Both media reached an unparalleled level of technical excellence. Tapestry bags and tunics were embellished with religious icons. Elaborate pottery was made specifically for religious use. The most famous type was the enormous open vessel that was ritually broken, or "killed." On the coast these large vessels were often painted with paired figures, one wearing a belted tunic and the other an unbelted garment. Menzel has interpreted these figures as male and female. Other vessels take a three-dimensional human form or are decorated with human features in relief. Many of them are jars and bottles painted in several bright colors and made of fine-textured hard paste (figs. 99, 100, 101, 102, 104). The imagery of this apparently religious pottery is similar but not identical to that of Tiwanaku. In Wari images the gods wear rayed necklaces, and human-faced figures and attendants typically have feline fangs, following an ancient northern tradition.

As with Tiwanaku, the agricultural base of Wari depended on technologically advanced methods of cultivation using field systems that required substantial labor. The Wari system seems to have been rather like agricultural systems employed by the Inka on a much larger scale centuries later. It brought terracing and irrigation to steep hillsides, particularly in warm environmental zones. Studies by Enrique González Carré have shown that water was brought to the area of

Wari in a long primary canal from high altitude sources. This canal fed secondary canals linked with terraces. Mastering the technology to make these relatively warm slopes productive enabled Wari to achieve an overall increase in growing food crops. Perhaps even more important than the increased production was the value of the foods grown. The irrigated terraces were suitable for maize, which was important not only for its nutritive value. Easily stored, it was crucial for seeing people through years of scarcity and drought. It was also used to make chicha. Chicha probably had already become an important accompaniment to feasts offered by Wari's political and religious leaders. In Inka times such feasts were an essential element in attaining and maintaining political power as well as in acquiring the labor that made large-scale Andean polities and economies possible.

The most impressive evidence for Wari's political achievements is found not in Wari itself but in numerous installations built, apparently under Wari supervision, in other parts of the Andes. We tend to define the limits of the Inka Empire by the distribution of the hundreds of towns, administrative cities, and other installations built at the

102 Attendants: These feline-headed figures with elongated snouts, attendants to the principal deities, have been called "sacrificers" by archaeologist Anita Cook. They are often seen with a trophy head in one hand and a knife in the other. Sacrifices apparently occurred in both Wari and Tiwanaku religious ceremonies. Today native peoples near Cuzco fear a malevolent cat spirit, possibly a modified form of the ancient sacrificer.

103 A Wari-style polychrome ceramic jar, modeled and painted to represent a figure with a death head, is decorated with flying attendants. South coast, Peru.
H. 17.1 cm. (6.7 in.) 41.2/8594

command of the rulers in Cuzco. These state centers connected by roads were built throughout the empire. Their architecture, and usually their pottery and other portable artifacts, immediately identify the centers as foreign and intrusive into the local system of towns and villages. They counted members of the ruling elite from Cuzco among their population, but they were occupied largely by local people who came to work for the state in various capacities, to participate in rituals and ceremonies, to eat at the Inka's table and drink his maize beer.

Because most of this work and ceremony was scheduled by the ritual calendar, the population of the state centers varied throughout the year, both in the number of people in residence and in the ethnic affiliations of people there at any given time. Large centers such as Huánuco Pampa (described in chapter 9) had a small permanent population of administrators, service personnel, and artisans. Most of the people who used its facilities, however, came for relatively short periods to pay their labor tax while living as guests of the Inka, whose storehouses provided for them during their stay. Thus many people who occasionally occupied the state facilities lived for most of the year in the towns and villages within one or two days' travel distance. The houses that the state maintained for their use mainly stood empty or may have been used by people from other more distant towns and villages.

The system of complementary ecological zones that may have encouraged Tiwanaku to establish colonies in Moquegua is also pertinent for Wari. Spanish administrative documents, like

104 Sky Animals: Birds of prey and felines are most common among the animals that appear as components of mythical Andean sky figures, represented either by stars or by empty black areas in the Milky Way. Light-colored circles representing stars appear on these two Wari sky animals and also as ornaments on the headdress and necklace of the gateway figure.

that of Garci Diez de San Miguel, list the multiple lands held by Andean communities in different ecological zones. John V. Murra's analysis of these documents has shown how people and goods moved back and forth between a core town or village and its satellites, creating a system of "islands" dispersed up and down the vertical Andean landscape. These islands, linked together by caravans, allowed communities to directly exploit a variety of natural resources and climatic zones. In such a system people grew accustomed to envisioning their world as dispersed, as well as to moving at times over great distances between its parts. The system was particularly well adapted to regions of scattered resources and settlements where vacant and barren lands separated areas of important resources. But occasionally peoples from different groups were brought together to exploit a limited and concentrated resource, such as salt. These multiple-group or multiethnic concentrations of people provided a base for developing cooperative social and political skills.

The system of state cities and towns that existed in Inka times was an elaborate extension and amplification, to urban scale, of this Andean vision of communities and resources dispersed over a wide and varied landscape. In the Inka state, some of the "islands" were cities and required management of human as well as natural resources. People moved in order to perform certain kinds of work, to take part in religious and ceremonial activities, or to take advantage of the goods accumulated by the Inka state. That empire was a vast polyglot of peoples, often engaged in the real and symbolic conflicts that assured the main-

tenance of a certain level of difference between groups, while allowing them to coexist and share lands, resources, and ideas.

Although there are no written records for Wari, the archaeological evidence indicates that two of the main features of Inka statecraft also applied to Wari. One of these is the use of string recording devices. William Conklin has described a set of strings wrapped in threads of different colors and attached to a main, or primary, cord. Records of the Museo Amano in Lima show that a string object of this type in its collection was found associated with a Wari mummy. These devices are similar to—and probably precursors of—the Inka knotted-string records known as *khipu*; however, they employ color rather than knots as the primary

105 Dartlike forms, probably symbolizing tears, extend below the eyes of the face painted on this ceramic cup. Wari style, Peru.
H. 8 cm. (3.2 in.) 41.2/8020

means of encoding information (fig. 106). For many purposes the khipu was equivalent to writing, and it was a vital element in the governing of an extensive empire.

The other Inka feature seen during Wari times is the building of state installations in provincial areas. Wari architecture occurs at archaeological sites in these areas, and even more sites contain substantial quantities of Wari pottery. A few are based on the classic planned compounds of rectangular rooms around patios built by Wari at its peak. The distribution of these sites allows us to plot the probable area of Wari control.

One of the most interesting and fully studied of the planned sites outside of Wari is Azángaro, fifteen kilometers (nine miles) northwest of Wari at the lower northern end of the Ayacucho basin. The site is a rectangular enclosure strictly separated into three parts. The northern and central sectors feature rigid internal planning, while the southern sector contains irregular buildings. The site contains Wari ceramics from phase 1B and, primarily, from phase 2 as well as a large percentage of pottery made by local populations. Martha Anders, who studied Azángaro, believed that the architectural patterning in the northern and central sectors related to a calendar similar to the Inka calendar. Basing her view on these clues of site organization, she suggested that a major

function of the settlement was the ceremonial recruitment of labor. In Inka times the ritual calendar was an important device for organizing a rotating tribute of labor. Interestingly, Anders's interpretation of the excavated remains located the settlement's authorities in the sector with the site's most irregular architecture. Furthermore, she felt that these authorities were of local origin, not administrators brought in from Wari itself. The relative proximity of Wari to Azángaro must be considered, however. Was Azángaro part of a system of provincial administration, or is it better seen as an outlying branch of the capital?

Jincamocco, a site in the Carhuarazo Valley, in the southern part of the Department of Ayacucho, has been called a Wari administrative center by its excavator Katharina Schreiber. It also features a rectangular enclosure with three primary divisions. The enclosure covers about 3.5 hectares (8.6 acres), but more irregular and less well-preserved remains outside the enclosure extend the total site to about 17.5 hectares (43 acres). Much of the Carhuarazo Valley was terraced during Wari times, and Schreiber found that local settlements were moved down, below 3,300 meters (10,830 feet) in altitude, into the maize production zone during the period. It seems likely that the terracing and settlement relocations reflect an increasing emphasis on maize production and that Jincamocco was related to the administration of maize agriculture for the Wari state.

The largest of the planned centers in the Wari provinces is Pikillacta in the Valley of Cuzco (fig. 107). The settlement consists of enormous rectangular compounds, some of them crammed with small structures, and it rivals in size the core area of Inka Cuzco. The settlement plan offers one of the clearest and most remarkable examples of Wari architectural planning. Its walled compounds are rigid in form, essentially ignoring topography to maintain straight walls. Communication within the site is strictly limited. The paucity of avenues, streets, and gateways implies an almost unprecedented control of internal access and movement.

The limitations on access implied by the architecture and the scarcity of artifacts on the surface led archaeologists to believe for many years that Pikillacta was a large Wari storage center, used more for goods than for people. Excavations by Gordon McEwan, however, have shown that it

106 Wari khipu have a color pattern system to code information. The red and purple yarns, mostly cotton with some camelid-fiber yarn, are wrapped about the pendant and subsidiary cords. Provenience unknown.
L. (main cord) 21.5 cm. (8.5 in.) L. (average pendant cord) 10.5 cm. (4.1 in.) 41.2/7679

107 Aerial view of Pikillacta, a
Wari settlement in the highlands, near its southern
frontier. Composed of many
walled rectangular com-
pounds, the site layout is
rigid in form, ignoring topo-
graphic features.

was heavily occupied and constituted a major residential, ceremonial, and administrative center for the southern highland part of a Wari empire. Highly decorated Wari pottery is rather limited at Pikillacta, but existing material seems to date occupation there to late 1B and 2.

Two large highland installations built in Wari times serve to show the complexity of Wari's sociopolitical nature and the difficulty of reconstructing it through limited archaeological evidence. These two examples come from near the northern and southern extremes of what seems to have been the Wari Empire. The two sites and their contexts underline the complexity of Andean social structures, in general, during the times of Wari and Tiwanaku. Frontiers were not simple lines separating one state's land from that of another. These states or empires do not fit modern definitions of nation-states and empires.

The site of Viracochapampa lies about two-and-a-half kilometers (one-and-a-half miles) north of the modern town of Huamachuco in the northern highlands of Peru. Many of the features of Wari architecture are present here: great enclosing walls, rectangular buildings around patios, limited patterns of access. Other features, such as numerous halls with large numbers of wall niches, seem more related to local architecture of the Huamachuco area, particularly at Marca Huamachuco, a nearby site continuously occupied during Wari times. Curiously, too, construction of Viracochapampa seems to have begun relatively early in the Wari sequence, in period 1B, and then never finished. Exactly when this site was abandoned is uncertain, but there is no evidence so far that con-

struction continued into period 2. Some of the ceramics from a nearby site date to 2A, suggesting a continuing relationship between Wari and the Huamachuco region relatively late into Wari times. John and Teresa Topic, who have directed most of the modern research in the Huamachuco region, believe that the relationships between Wari and Huamachuco were not simply that of conqueror and conquered. Influence flowed in both directions with control of the area probably never passing completely from local hands. At some point a break occurred in relations with the outside, and the connections between Huamachuco and Wari came to an end.

At the southern end of the geographic extension of the Wari Empire is the site of Cerro Baúl, in the Moquegua Valley. Studied by Robert Feldman and Luis Watanabe, the site stands at the top of Cerro Baúl, a sheer-sided mesa towering 600 meters (1,970 feet) above a wide base (fig. 109). As its Spanish name, meaning "Trunk Hill," implies, the hill looks like a gigantic trunk from a distance, commanding the main affluents of the Osmore River. Its steep sides made Cerro Baúl a natural fortress, and multiple walls were constructed across its only access path. The ruins of more than ten hectares (twenty-five acres) of masonry architecture stand on the summit of the massive hill. Single and multistory structures surround patios in typical Wari fashion; there are also circular and D-shaped structures. It lacks, however, the great walled enclosures seen at Pikillacta, Azángaro, Jincamocco, and other Wari sites. Nonetheless, the architecture of Cerro Baúl is closer than these walled sites to that of Wari itself. Possibly a rela-

108 Wari-style double-spout bottle with a painted animal and geometric designs. Peru.
H. 15 cm. (5.9 in.) 41.2/625

tively early construction date explains this character. Pottery at Cerro Baúl dates to 1 and the beginning of 2A.

The most significant feature of Cerro Baúl for understanding the Wari and Tiwanaku states is explained by overlap. Peoples from, or at least closely associated with, Wari built Cerro Baúl inside territory occupied by peoples closely associated with Tiwanaku. Research in this fascinating area of overlap between the two states is still under way. Some questions, in particular, remain on the dating of various occupations. Archaeologists currently working in the region postulate that Wari peoples built their intrusive and highly fortified site well after the area was settled by Tiwanaku (or local peoples closely connected with Tiwanaku, as we saw above). The site was used for a century or so and then abandoned, while Tiwanaku occupation of other parts of the region continued. The concern for defense signaled by the location of Cerro Baúl suggests that relations between the two groups may not have been peaceful. Several of the Tiwanaku sites also show evidence of destruction, but this may have been partly a deliberate destruction of ceremonial centers.

One interpretation of the intermeshing of settlements and peoples from these two important states is that both were attempting to exploit the warm valley lands. They could not do so peacefully, and Wari apparently retreated in favor of its rival from the southern altiplano. The earlier presence of Tiwanaku peoples and the closer proximity of their capital may have been factors in Tiwanaku's ultimate domination of the area. However,

109 Cerro Baúl is a mesa rising 600 meters (1,970 feet) above its base. A natural fortress, the mesa supports at least ten hectares (twenty-five acres) of masonry architecture on its top. This Wari settlement rests within territory (now the Moquegua Valley) thought to have been controlled by Tiwanaku peoples.

110 Hat of camelid fiber with cut pile introduced into a knotted network. Designs represent stylized human faces and feather head-dresses. Wari style, south coast, Peru.
H. 14 cm. (5.5 in.) 41.2/7143

if the Omo ceremonial complex, discussed above, proves to have been built after Cerro Baúl, we might speculate that Tiwanaku was now following the Wari pattern of building distant centers to administer the provinces of its realm. Taken together, the evidence from Viracochapampa and Cerro Baúl implies that Wari's strategy for controlling foreign lands was not always successful, even in the highlands.

TIWANAKU AND WARI ON THE COAST

Archaeologists have devoted much more time to studying the desert coast than the highlands. Yet there is no clear record of events and relationships for the complicated period when Tiwanaku and Wari were the dominant kingdoms of the highlands. The greatest amount of work has focused on the north coast of Peru, an area distant from the

heartlands of Tiwanaku and Wari. Not surprisingly, the influence there of the two highland kingdoms appears to have been relatively indirect and minor. Farther south, in the regions to the west of the imperial heartlands, this influence was stronger; but we have not been able to grasp its religious, political, and economic structures.

Max Uhle uncovered the imprint of the highland kingdoms on coastal cultures very early in his work on the Peruvian central coast. A cemetery apparently linked with the site of Cajamarquilla, in the suburbs east of Lima, yielded ceramics in the Wari style as well as vessels in a local style. Cajamarquilla, in constant threat of being overrun by expanding Lima, has not received the research it deserves. An enormous city of rectangular houses and narrow streets, it contains numerous plazas enclosed by coursed adobe walls. Lumbreras refers to Cajamarquilla architecture as typical of the Wari coastal style. Menzel, who has studied Uhle's various central-coast archaeological collections, believes that the period of Wari influence at Cajamarquilla dates to period 1 and that later, in 2, the focus of Wari associations shifted southward to Pachacamac, in the nearby Lurín Valley. Pachacamac is a monumental site of coursed adobe houses, storage chambers, and temples overlooking the Pacific Ocean. In immediately pre-Hispanic times it was the seat of an important oracle and a major site for religious pilgrimages. It has been continuously occupied from pre-Wari times onward, and sorting out the part of its construction that dates to Wari times, or its relationship to the Ayacucho-based empire, is still difficult. We may safely suggest, however, that its

111 Feline star animals appear on front panels of this ceramic jar. The neck is modeled and painted as a human face with ears of maize extending below the eyes. Wari style, probably south coast, Peru. H. 51.7 cm. (20.4 in.) 41.2/7840

association with Wari deeply involved religion, and we may even speculate that the importance of Pachacamac as a shrine in Inka times had its origins with Wari (fig. 112).

Still farther south, Wari materials have been found at Pacheco near Nazca. Most notably these consist of large urns decorated with the gateway god. The urns, some reaching almost a meter in diameter, had been deliberately broken. Ann Peters's discovery of Maymi, a site with Wari pottery in the lower Pisco Valley, has provided a major opportunity for improving our understanding of the relationships of Wari with the coastal region directly below it. Tragically, an excavation project of the site was interrupted by the death of its director, archaeologist Martha Anders, who was killed in an accident on the Pan-American Highway. The excavations had uncovered both Wari and late Nazca pottery as well as evidence for both ceramic manufacture and religious ritual. Further study is needed to follow up on the evidence that both highland Wari people and those associated with the final phases of Nazca culture lived contemporaneously at Maymi.

During the period when Wari prospered in the Peruvian south-central highlands, marked changes also took place on the north coast. The Moche state, which had brought such a spectacular outpouring of art and metallurgy, apparently underwent important transformations by the time of Moche V (A.D. 500–c. 700). Changes in architecture and iconography point to profound shifts in religion, the economy, and the organization of society.

Michael Moseley believes that an episode of earthquakes and extreme climatic instability, involving floods and drought, may have been a factor in the changes. As noted in chapter 6, he cites the evidence for extensive flood damage at Huaca del Sol and Huaca de la Luna shortly before they were abandoned. Repairs were made at the two sites after the flood, but a mural at one of the courts at Huaca de la Luna depicts a frontal human figure holding a staff in either hand. Though not completely preserved, the figure shows notable similarities to the Tiwanaku gateway god. Although the mural was executed by local artists, its inspiration came from the highlands. Highland influences are also seen in the pottery and textiles of the period. Highland elements, however, never seem to dominate late Moche iconography and religion. During Moche V a powerful emphasis on marine images emerged. New ritual characters, such as an iguana with human features and an old man known as "wrinkle face," travel in reed boats and are shown with Strombus shells.

The late Moche site of Pampa Grande, studied by Izumi Shimada, was discussed in chapter 6. Its central feature is a gigantic adobe pyramid known as La Fortaleza. Rising 55 meters (180 feet), it is one of the largest adobe pyramids ever built in the Andes. While La Fortaleza clearly shows the heritage of earlier Moche architecture, other aspects demonstrate the profound changes

that had taken place. One notable new architectural emphasis was the rectangular enclosure, like the huge one surrounding La Fortaleza. Another was the construction of large numbers of storehouses at Pampa Grande and sites such as the Moche V site of Galindo, studied by Garth Bawden, in the Moche Valley.

The new architectural emphases and some of the iconographic changes hint at affinities with the highlands, especially with Wari. The exact nature of the relationship between Wari and the final, transformed phase of Moche is still unknown, but few archaeologists believe that the north coast actually formed part of a highland empire at this time. The end of Moche came with the burning of Pampa Grande. It was replaced by the new north-coast kingdoms of Sicán and Chimor (see chapter 8).

Tiwanaku and Wari both collapsed as states, but the changes they made in the ways the Andean region was managed became part of a heritage of special strategies to exploit rich but widely dispersed resources. Based on moving people to directly exploit resources, these strategies almost certainly were not new, but they represented an evolution in the ways highland communities had probably exploited their world for centuries. Tiwanaku and Wari added two new elements to these old and fundamental principles. On the one

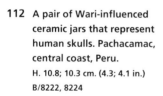

112 A pair of Wari-influenced ceramic jars that represent human skulls. Pachacamac, central coast, Peru.
H. 10.8; 10.3 cm. (4.3; 4.1 in.)
B/8222, 8224

hand, new or greatly expanded technologies of land reclamation allowed previously underutilized regions to become increasingly productive. On the other hand, a set of social mechanisms allowed the states to mobilize and invest ever-larger numbers of laborers in projects of reclamation and production for the states. Earlier religious ideas and the traditional patterns of human relations in small communities were recast to channel human energy into the economic and political support of the new multiregional states. For decades, many archaeologists have attributed the expansion of Tiwanaku, and especially Wari, to military conquest. While conflicts and military skirmishes were undertaken by both states, the fundamental factors were economic, backed by new and more sophisticated religious and political ideologies.

The processes of growth of Tiwanaku and Wari shared common features, but, as we have seen, they differed in many basic aspects. Although both relied significantly on advances in agricultural technology, the different ecological circumstances of their homelands brought quite different techniques: the raised fields around Lake Titicaca, contrasted with the irrigated terraces of lower Andean slopes and intermontane valleys. The two states shared religious symbols and presumably many features of religious ideology. However, the architecture and the excavated evidence for religious ritual show that the organization and ceremonies of religion also were quite different.

In Tiwanaku, religious expression was grandiloquent and public. A religion of public ceremony, it almost seems to have been the essence of the political arena. The state as a separate and secular set of ideas and practices was obscured by the state conceived in terms of religious ritual. The sites remind us of the term "theater state," used by anthropologist Clifford Geertz to describe Balinese states, where architecture and religious icons are related to ritual movement by a large participatory public.

Wari's use of similar religious iconography contrasts starkly with Tiwanaku and its great temples. Wari incorporated religious icons mainly into more portable items of cloth and ceramics. Its architecture was an architecture of division more than of public assembly, ritual movement, and participation. Its ceremonies and its use of religion

appear to be more private and aimed at smaller groups. There are more suggestions of the preeminence of secular concerns, of breaking the society into smaller social units in order to organize and manage it more effectively for economic and political purposes.

Some of our problems in comprehending this complex chapter in Andean prehistory derive from our own experience, which tells us that the boundaries of states are continuous and that their control over the area within those boundaries is bureaucratic and relatively uniform. What we have seen of the first Andean empires does not fit such a pattern. In part this is because the times were very dynamic, as new states were growing and political and economic strategies were still being introduced. In part it is because the highland Andean traditions from which the states grew emphasized discontinuous communities and the management of dispersed resources. The interplay of peoples and ideas—borrowing, interacting, cooperating, sometimes fighting—are characteristics of societies everywhere. But the constant mixing and intermeshing in the Andes was special. A more balanced combination of the public and private features of politics, religion, and society emerges a few centuries later in the Inka Empire. The experience gained by the two great cities of Tiwanaku and Wari, and the states they ruled, was not lost.

BETWEEN THE HIGHLAND EMPIRES

PERIOD OF POWER AND CONFLICT

With the decline of Wari and Tiwanaku, the cultural initiative shifted once again to the desert coast. The center of development was the north coast. Its great wealth in water for irrigation gave it a strong economic potential for political and artistic achievement. In the south, too, important states developed. One of these became a famous kingdom of maritime traders and major allies of the Inka. But the most notable successor to Wari and Tiwanaku was the north-coast kingdom of Chimor. Chimor was the home of the people and culture popularly known as Chimú, with its capital at Chan Chan in the Moche Valley, near the modern city of Trujillo. But once again the picture is complicated, and it is important to mention other kingdoms that flourished at about the same time as Chimor. As archaeological research advances, more and more regions emerge as scenes of notable growth, each with its own contributions to an ever-richer set of indigenous accomplishments.

 SICAN

On the Peruvian north coast the late Moche center at Pampa Grande in the Lambayeque region was burned and abandoned about A.D. 700. But the area that had produced some of the most extraordinary gold work in all of human history continued its enormous metallurgical output in the centuries that followed. Political circumstances changed, however, as did the cultural identities of the lords who went to their tombs accompanied by incalculable treasure. The descendants of Moche in the Lambayeque region belonged to a culture now called Sicán, not to be confused with the nearby Moche site of Sipán, where Walter Alva excavated the tombs associated with the Lord of Sipán (described in chapter 6). Batán Grande, the most important center of Sicán, has been studied for several years by archaeologist Izumi Shimada.

Sicán's beginnings apparently correspond to an era of political confusion in the Lambayeque region, following the burning of Pampa Grande. The period defined by Shimada as Early Sicán spanned the two centuries from 700 to 900, an era of outside influence and stylistic synthesis as well as of strictly local growth and development. The finely burnished blackware vessels characteristic of Sicán ceramics appeared in this early phase. In shape and iconography this pottery borrows both from the early Moche V ceramics of the region and from Wari ceramic style, perhaps via Pachacamac. There are also hints of incursions and influence from the highland Cajamarca region. The long, tapering spout connected by a wide, flattened bridge and the presence of figures wearing four-cornered hats illustrate influences from the still-popular Wari style. So far only limited evidence exists for monumental construction during Early Sicán, but there are suggestions that during this period construction began on the Huaca La Merced pyramid, in the Sicán Religious Funerary Precinct of Batán Grande (fig. 115).

Sicán culture reached its height during the Middle Sicán Period (900–1100). The iconographic centerpiece of Middle Sicán style is a commonly seen figure known as the Sicán Lord, a richly attired male figure whose flat, semicircular face

114 Painted wood carving of an individual holding a cup resembles those installed in niches of elite structures at Chan Chan. Cups like this often held maize beer, drunk on important political and ceremonial occasions. Chimú, north coast, Peru. H. 90.5 cm. (35.6 in.) 41.0/7359

115 The site of Batán Grande in the Lambayeque region has many pyramidal platforms. Occupied for more than a thousand years, it seems to have been the center for pilgrimages and religious activities. Replaced as a major ceremonial settlement around A.D. 1100, it was later abandoned after a massive flood followed by fire. Few sites have been as heavily looted, a testimony to the many rich graves once found there. North coast, Peru.

has distinctive upward-pointing, comma-shaped eyes (fig. 116). The figure usually occupies a central position on ceramic vessels. He is modeled on the spout of single-spout jars and on the handle bridging the two spouts of double-spout vessels. The Sicán Lord also appears often in painted murals, textiles, and metal objects. Sometimes the figure has avian features, such as wings, particularly on gold or silver ceremonial *tumi* knives and on painted murals. Often he is flanked by other figures, such as serpents or small humans. Several features of posture and presentation suggest that the Sicán Lord may have been inspired by the gateway god of Tiwanaku and Wari. But the inspiration is very indirect, and several scholars have suggested that he may represent the mythical Naymlap of north-coast oral tradition recorded by Spanish chroniclers. In 1586, Miguel Cabello de Balboa wrote:

The people of Lambayeque say that in times so very ancient that they do not know how to express them, a man of much valor and quality came to that valley on a fleet of balsa rafts. His name was Naymlap. With him he brought many concubines and a chief wife named Ceterni. He also brought many people who followed him as their captain and leader. Among these people were forty officials, including Pita Zofi, Blower of the Shell Trumpet; Ninacola, Master of the Litter and Throne; Ninagintue, Royal Cellarer (he was in charge of the Lord's drink); Fonga Sigde, Preparer of the Way (he scattered seashell dust where his lord was about to walk); Occhocalo, Royal Cook: Zam Muchec, Steward of the Face Paint; Ollopcopoc, Master of the Bath; and Llapchillulli, Purveyor of Feathercloth Garments. With this retinue, and with an infinite number of other officials and men of importance, Naymlap established a settlement and built his palace at Chot (Miguel Cabello de Balboa [1586]; quoted from Donnan, 1990:243–44).

Scholars disagree on the extent to which the Naymlap myth recounts actual events in the Lambayeque region, but most feel that at least it hints at a blueprint for the way this society was structured and refers to some real places, now archaeological sites. Chot, for example, is probably the site of Chotuna, excavated by Donnan.

Although the relationships between Chotuna and other Sicán sites remain to be worked out, the political and religious capital of Sicán apparently

116 Ceramic bottle representing a masked figure, known as the Sicán lord, carried on a litter by four bearers. Middle Sicán style, north coast, Peru.
H. 21.7 cm. (8.5 in.) 41.2/8569

was located not at Chotuna but at the more lavish Sicán Precinct in Batán Grande, where a series of pyramids rise above that site's abundant trees. The Sicán Precinct is truly monumental, in the tradition of the Moche pyramids and the La Fortaleza pyramid at Pampa Grande. One of the most impressive pyramids is the T-shaped Huaca El Corte near the site's eastern edge. A series of construction phases culminated in a colonnade of forty-eight painted columns with a mural-decorated backdrop wall at the top of the pyramid. Columns also appear at other pyramids, such as El Moscón, and Rodillona. All the Sicán pyramids show a more sophisticated and substantial version of the chamber-and-fill building technique, introduced in Moche V times at Pampa Grande.

The most impressive aspect of the Sicán Precinct is the outpouring of gold and gilded objects it yielded. These include the famous sheet-metal funerary masks of gold or alloy with gilded surfaces. The masks are usually coated with cinnabar over much of their surface and feature the Sicán comma-shaped eyes. Another category of gold or gilded objects common in Sicán is the flared kero, or drinking goblet (see chapter 7; figs. 117, 204). Since at least the time of Tiwanaku, such objects had specific ritual and political importance. (Sicán metallurgy, including examples recovered from an important tomb of a Sicán lord or ruler excavated by Shimada and his colleagues in 1991, is described in chapter 12.)

At Sicán, as in other coastal kingdoms, the agricultural economy depended on a massive irrigation system. There is also evidence that trade was important to the economy. Shimada and his colleagues found substantial quantities of Spondylus shell, both whole and as a material used in the manufacture of objects. This shell was imported from the warm waters off the coast of Ecuador. The coral-colored shell of Spondylus, the spiny oyster, had become sacred in the Andes. In some areas people regarded it as food for the gods. The belief that the shell brought rain may have come from the association of the spiny oyster with the rare rainy years on the Peruvian coast, now referred to as Niños (see chapter 2). When the warm waters of El Niño flowed south into the normally cold water off the coast of Peru bringing rain, it also brought marine species, including the spiny oyster, from Ecuadorian waters.

Thin, I-shaped plates of arsenical copper alloy also indicate links with the north. These plates, called *naipes,* are often found in neat stacks. Similar plates have often been found in Ecuador, where they are called *acha moneda,* axe money. Because of their standardized form and occurrence in stacks, archaeologists believe that naipes and achas monedas were used by specialized traders as a medium of exchange. The existence of groups of specialized traders is documented for historic times in Ecuador and also in the Chincha kingdom on the south coast of Peru. Chincha merchants conducted long-distance trade along two axes: traveling by sea to what is now Ecuador—possibly returning with Spondylus—and overland to the southern highlands—probably trading for metal ores. Copper is very rare in Ecuador, and Shimada has suggested that Sicán may have been at least one source of the metal, and perhaps of the axe money itself.

117 Gold and silver kero with a hammered facial design and an openwork rattle base. The face appears upside down when the kero is used for drinking. Sicán style, north coast, Peru. H. 13.7 cm. (5.4 in.) 41.2/8683

Because of its spectacular metallurgical technology, Sicán also may have been a mint for axe money to trade with the north.

The excavators of both Chotuna and Batán Grande found evidence for major flooding that seriously damaged the sites' architecture. Donnan detected a break in the occupation of Chotuna that probably followed the flooding. At Batán Grande, Shimada found evidence of a great fire started deliberately by igniting wood piled against walls in the Sicán Precinct; the Precinct was abandoned after the fire. The flood probably accompanied an El Niño cycle about 1100, and evidence for this has also been noted at other north-coast sites. The myth of the Naymlap dynasty ties its tragic end to a flood. While we cannot firmly link the myth with prehistoric events or the Sicán center of power, the correspondences are intriguing. Cabello de Balboa relates this story:

Fempellec, the last and most unfortunate member of the dynasty [,]. . . decided to move the idol that Naymlap had placed at Chot. After several unsuccessful attempts to do this, the devil appeared to him in the form of a beautiful woman. He slept with her and as soon as the union had been consummated the rains began to fall, a thing which had never been seen upon those plains. These floods lasted for thirty days, after which followed a year of much sterility and famine. Because the priests knew that their lord had committed this grave crime, they understood that it was punishment for his fault that his people were suffering with hunger, rain, and want. In order to take vengeance upon him, forgetful of the fidelity that is owed by vassals, they took him prisoner and, tying his feet and hands, threw him into the deep sea. With his death was ended the lineage of the native lords of the valley of Lambayeque, and the country surrounding remained without patron or native lord during many days (Cabello de Balboa [1580]; quoted from Donnan, 1990:243–44).

The Sicán pyramids with their rich, gold-filled tombs are striking reminders of the golden hoards in the Moche tombs of Sipán a few centuries earlier. Sipán and Sicán obviously share more than their nearly identical modern names. Following a common tradition in the Lambayeque region, perhaps derived in part from the Moche Valley, rich lords went to their pyramidal tombs accompanied by retainers, women, who were perhaps their wives, and especially by the great treasures that the rich mines and skilled artisans of the region made possible. It was apparently a tradition of wealth and power, justified in part by religion, made palatable by ceremonial ritual, and supported by an advanced technology in metallurgy and irrigation agriculture.

119 Ceramic whistling bottle molded and painted to represent a Muscovy duck, a South American domesticate. Late Sicán style, north coast, Peru.
H. 21.8 cm. (8.6 in.) 41.2/8570

118 A heavily eroded pyramidal platform at the site of Túcume, also known as El Purgatorio. Located south of the Leche River in the Lambayeque Valley, Túcume may have been the largest coastal site in ancient Peru. It was occupied into Inka times by a large and prosperous population and seems to have replaced Batán Grande as the leading center of the region. North coast, Peru.

The period between the abandonment of the Sicán Precinct at Batán Grande and the incorporation of the Lambayeque region into the kingdom of Chimor, about 1375, is known as Late Sicán. Limited research leaves this period less known than Middle Sicán. Perhaps its most notable marker is the Sicán Lord's near disappearance from the iconography. The forms of ceramic bottles continued to evolve in directions established earlier: spouts became increasingly tall, for example. Decoration became more abstract and geometric than before, and if there was ideological meaning, the symbols for it had become much more abstract. The new styles almost seem to signal a purge of Middle Sicán religious and political ideology. Whether or not it was related to floods and other natural disasters, the previous base of power and authority seems to have been dissolved. The seat of authority probably moved westward to Túcume, also known as El Purgatorio. That vast site, with its huge eroded mounds, and others that were apparently built in Late Sicán times, implies that populations continued to be large and relatively prosperous. Early Colonial written sources studied by Patricia Netherly and others speak of a late pre-Hispanic political center, Túcume, that controlled the southern part of the area and another, Jayanca, that controlled the northern part. Both probably existed independently during the Late Sicán period, before they were incorporated into the Chimú and Inka empires. The great periods of the Lambayeque region that produced the treasures of Sipán during Moche times and later gave rise to Middle Sicán were over.

THE KINGDOM OF CHIMOR

As Sicán power developed in the Lambayeque region, a new state was taking shape in the Moche Valley that eventually became the largest kingdom on the Andean desert coast. It was to conquer most of what is now the northern coast of Peru, extending its domain from Tumbes to the Chillón Valley, 1300 kilometers (806 miles) down the desert coast. As with other early kingdoms, the origins of Chimor—the kingdom of the people and culture generally known as Chimú—is celebrated in myths that may have little relation to actual events. Typically, its mythical founder, Taycanamu, was an outsider, sent from afar to govern. Construction at Chan Chan, the Chimú capital, is thought to have begun about 850 or 900.

The transition from the Moche kingdom to Chimor is still poorly understood. During Moche V, the final Moche phase, the Moche focus of power in Lambayeque moved to Pampa Grande. During that same period the site of Galindo became the principal center in the Moche Valley. But the period between the fall and destruction of Pampa Grande about 700 and the beginnings of Chan Chan is especially obscure.

As a city, Chan Chan was clearly one of the most spectacular in the ancient New World—a vast labyrinth of adobe walls stretching across the desert. Its walls defined limits of about 20 square

120 Aerial view of Chan Chan, once the capital of the Chimú state. The city walls enclose about 6 square kilometers (2.3 square miles). Nine to eleven enormous rectangular enclosures, or *ciudadelas,* may have been palace compounds. Located by the sea in the Moche Valley near Trujillo, much of the city seems to have been abandoned at the time of the Inka conquest in the fifteenth century. North coast, Peru.

kilometers (8 square miles) at the mouth of the Moche Valley, although much of this area was open, probably designated for further expansion. The central part of the city, with the bulk of its adobe brick architecture, covers about 6 square kilometers (2.3 square miles). Archaeologists have divided its impressive remains into three major categories. First, many thousands of small, irregular, attached rooms built of cane provided living and working quarters for workers, mainly artisans. Second, more substantial adobe-walled enclosures, called "intermediate architecture," are thought to have been the residences of minor nobility and state functionaries. Third, a group of enormous rectangular enclosure walls circling a maze of rooms and patios, called *ciudadelas*, are interpreted as palace compounds.

Ciudadelas are the most striking visual feature of Chan Chan and were probably the central element in its planning and organization. There are nine to eleven ciudadelas, depending on how strictly they are defined and how some of their seriously destroyed features are interpreted. The ciudadelas were built more or less sequentially, thereby charting the city's growth, and some of the differences between the compounds probably resulted from chronological trends. Netherly and others have pointed out that early Spanish written sources on Chimor suggest a dual pattern of organization, and some archaeologists believe that ciudadelas may have been paired. Each ciudadela is believed to have been the residence of a local lord, who was head of a group sharing common ancestors. Most of the complexes were the seat of the paramount ruler of Chimor at some time during the state's history. In effect they were palaces that served for a period as the primary seats of government and the centers for redistributing the kingdom's wealth. The archaeologists who have studied Chan Chan believe that during the late part of the kingdom, when rulership passed to a new lord, he established his own palace. However, the descendants of previous ruling lords continued to use earlier ciudadelas, which retained some of their political and, especially, economic functions. At any point in time the city was composed of ciudadelas, areas of intermediate architecture, and single, irregular attached rooms for housing retainers and artisans.

Most of the ciudadelas are divided into three main areas and are surrounded by high enclosure walls. Their orientation is in a north-south direction. Within the enclosure walls was a series of structures, relatively standardized both in form and distribution among the three areas: numerous storerooms housed the wealth of the group and its leader; U-shaped structures, known as *audiencias*, probably were administrative offices; shallow walk-in wells were the source of water for the ciudadela; a burial platform provided the resting place for the members of the social group centered at the ciudadela. Courtyards and corridors provided space for movement and perhaps group activities. Typically, the compounds are entered through the north wall, and the north sector seems to have been the most public, with its large courtyard as well as numerous storerooms and audiencias. The central sector also features a courtyard, storerooms, and offices, but its primary feature is the burial platform. This is the most private part of the complex and probably was the part associated with the leader or founder of the descent group. The southern sector was generally a courtyard with a walk-in well and less formal cane architecture thought to have housed service personnel. Some of the ciudadelas, especially those built late

121 Aerial view of a ciudadela compound at Chan Chan. The compound includes a large array of administrative structures, possible storage areas, a burial platform, and a large, shallow walk-in well. North coast, Peru.

122 An unusual collar or chest ornament made from drilled beads of Spondylus, mussel, or clam shell, and malachite on cotton cord. Seven male figures wear crescent-shaped headdresses and earspools. A pillow, a bag, and a second neck ornament, all of extraordinarily fine workmanship, are said to have been found with the piece. Possibly made during the Inka period, north coast, Peru. L. 43 cm. (16.9 in.) W. 34 cm. (13.4 in.) B/3174

in the city's history, have wings and annexes containing audiencias and storehouses. These probably housed supplementary storage and administrative activities.

Gordon McEwan and other archaeologists have suggested that the general concept of the ciudadela shares elements with the walled compounds in provincial centers of the Wari empire, such as Pikillacta and Azángaro (described in chapter 7). These walled compounds, however, bear the strongest resemblance to the late ciudadelas, built long after the Wari collapse. The ciudadelas are perhaps best seen as part of a developing tradition in administrative organization, and the architecture that housed and helped define it. Although they may well have taken advantage of some earlier highland patterns, they drew heavily on local traditions; for example, they melded much smaller versions of the Moche period burial mounds into the ciudadelas. About two centuries later the Inka would take up and further refine the idea of palace compounds in Cuzco and in their administrative centers.

While the ciudadelas were the political focus of Chan Chan's urban plan, the city's productive economy was based in other quarters. Extensive excavations by John Topic in areas of the city's poorest architecture—the small, irregular, attached rooms built of cane—uncovered substantial evidence for craft production. Artisans made some objects of wood and shell, but the crowning technological and artistic triumphs in the Andes were in metallurgy and textiles. Most of the evidence for craft and artistic production at Chan Chan is in these last two fields. Topic suggests that at the

height of the city's prosperity more than twenty-five thousand people lived in the small Chan Chan rooms, and that more than ten thousand of them were adult specialists in the arts and crafts. Men made thousands of metal objects, and women spinners and weavers turned out massive amounts of cloth.

Two caravansaries near the center of the city apparently were places where raw materials, such as skeins of camelid fiber and metal ores, were brought by llama caravans. Llama burials were found in platforms in these transport terminals,

123 ABOVE
Earspools of hollow gourd sections inlaid in black resin with cut and polished shell depict standing figures wearing earspools. Chimú style, north coast, Peru. D. 7.1 cm. (2.8 in.) 41.2/8573 a, b

124 LEFT
A modeled figure of a man sits inside the open-fronted structure of this ceramic bottle. Chimú style, north coast, Peru. H. 17.7 cm. (7 in.) 41.2/608

125 A modeled llama with its legs bound, probably for sacrifice, lies on the top plane of a stirrup-spout ceramic bottle. Llama burials have been found in elite compounds at Chan Chan. North coast, Peru. H. 15.5 cm. (6.1 in.) 41.2/8907

Chan Chan's population was supported by irrigation agriculture. Most crops came from the Moche Valley itself. However, Moseley, who co-directed the large Chan Chan research team, thinks that the irrigation system suffered periodic crises brought on by both natural and human causes. Canals could be seriously damaged by floods or earthquakes, and land irrigated for long periods builds up salts that reduce its productivity. These factors may have been involved in Chimú attempts to bring water from adjoining valleys and to conquer other regions in order to integrate new sources of land, water, labor, and skills into the imperial economy of Chimor.

The evidence suggests two main episodes of Chimú expansion. One of these probably occurred about 1200 and extended from the Zaña Valley in the north to the Santa Valley in the south. The other, thought to have taken place by 1400, brought the valleys between Tumbes and Zaña in the north and between Santa and Chillón in the south into Chimor. Archaeological evidence suggests that the Chimú may have exercised little administrative control over some of this large area that historical sources include in Chimor.

The kind and degree of control Chan Chan exercised over its conquered provinces is not yet clear. Military force may have been an element in both the expansion and control of incorporated peoples. Like the Inka after them, the Chimú were probably capable of using force to put down rebellions or to conquer resisting regions that had a high priority in their imperial rule. But military force was probably not the overwhelmingly predominant strategy of either conquest or control, as some writers have suggested. Instead, the emphasis seems to have been on economic control: control of hydraulic systems for agriculture and production management of sumptuary goods.

As with Wari and Tiwanaku, some of the most critical evidence on the nature of Chimú rule comes from its provincial areas. There seem to have been two major provincial Chimú administrative capitals. One was Farfán, built in the Jequetepeque Valley during the first wave of expansion. The other, Manchán, was built in the Casma Valley as part of the second expansion of Chimor. There were also other smaller centers related to the management of irrigation systems. While the provincial centers of Chimor show recognizable elements of Chimú architecture—such

which also had communal kitchens, large corral-like spaces, and rooms with sleeping benches. John Topic believes that the caravansaries could have housed six hundred people and that the installations were operated by exchange specialists.

Craft production seems to have been divided into preliminary processing and manufacturing operations, such as hammering thin sheets of metal from ingots and the production of fine, finished objects. In Topic's view the less-skilled workers were organized into four *barrios*, or neighborhoods, reflecting Andean principles of dual organization. Evidence of this form of organization is common in both the historical and archaeological records for the Inka period. In contrast, the more skilled production of fine goods was carried out by retainers related to the groups whose lords lived in the ciudadelas. These retainers lived and worked near the ciudadelas and the objects they made presumably found their way into the storage complexes within the walls of great compounds, to be redistributed by or for their individual lords.

126 A standing figure in ceremonial attire adorns this mold-made stirrup-spout blackware bottle with two frogs on its shoulder. Chan Chan, north coast, Peru.
H. 26.5 cm. (10.4 in.) B/3975

127 Pacatnamu sprawls on cliffs above the sea in Peru's Jequetepeque Valley. Construction at this site, named in modern times after a Chimú general, began centuries before its conquest by the Chimú. The aerial photo depicts the largest and most intact of the site's pyramidal compounds. North coast, Peru.

as the audiencia structures that are considered the definitive sign of Chimú administration—all but Farfán lack the monumental ciudadelas. This absence may suggest that the Chan Chan ruling nobility played only an indirect role in provincial administration, leaving control in the hands of lower-level nobility and local authorities.

The two major provincial capitals, Farfán and Manchán, seem to differ from each other rather substantially. Part of this difference may be attributable to the fact that Farfán was founded during the first phase of the expansion of Chimor, while Manchán rose about 150 years later, during the second. During the first phase, the main concern was shipment of raw materials to Chan Chan. By the time of the second phase, Chimor was extending its management of craft production beyond the workshops of Chan Chan itself. In their studies of Manchán, Carol Mackey and Ulana Klymyshyn uncovered evidence of the production of Chimú goods for local consumption. This shift to state-managed craft production in the provinces seems to reflect a major change in the Chimor economy in the later phases of the state.

Studies of Chimú irrigation by Thomas Pozorski and others suggest that the apex of irrigation agriculture in the Chimú heartland occurred well before the state of Chimor reached its greatest extent. During its final phase, many marginal canals in the Moche and Chicama valleys were not maintained, which suggests that the state may have looked to the conquest of other areas for its continued economic and political growth. Apparently the state sought economic expansion by incorporating other areas, rather than by main-

taining canals that brought only very limited increases in productivity.

Whatever the relationship between increased craft production and the abandonment of some canals, there seems little doubt that striking increases occurred in producing fine craft objects during the final phase of Chimor. John Topic has demonstrated this increase in his studies of craft and artistic production at Chan Chan, as has Alan Kolata in his work on architectural and institutional changes in the capital. Manchán may not have been the only site where the Chimú managed craft production outside their own capital. Production at sites in the recently conquered Lambayeque region may have been managed by and for Chimor. Several archaeologists have indicated that a correspondence between the incorporation of Sicán into the Chimú state, and an expansion of fine production, especially in metals, is no coincidence. The Lambayeque area had been an important center of metallurgy since Moche times or earlier, and it has been suggested that some Sicán craftspeople were moved to Chan Chan (see chapter 12). Capturing the skilled work of Sicán smiths for the Chimú redistributive network would have offered a substantial boost to the Moche Valley state, politically as well as economically. The ability to dispense valued prestige goods was a major source of the political power of leaders. At its height, Chimor seems to have been able to command enormous quantities of high-status goods through its state-managed production. Chimú rulers probably redistributed these goods effectively to enhance their power. While they, like the Inka who followed them, claimed to have divine

128 In this ceremonial headdress, feathers are applied to a plain-weave cotton cloth with paired warps, a Chimú feature. The feathers, from both local and exotic birds, include flamingo, macaw, Muscovy duck, Amazonian parrot, razor-billed curassow, and tanager. Probably dating from the late Chimú or Inka periods, the headdress is said to have been found in the Chancay region, central coast, Peru. H. 92 cm. (36.2 in.) 41.0/7306

129 Double-bodied ceramic whistling bottle shows a couple engaged in fellatio. Chimú, north coast, Peru. H. 20.3 cm. (8 in.) 41.2/591

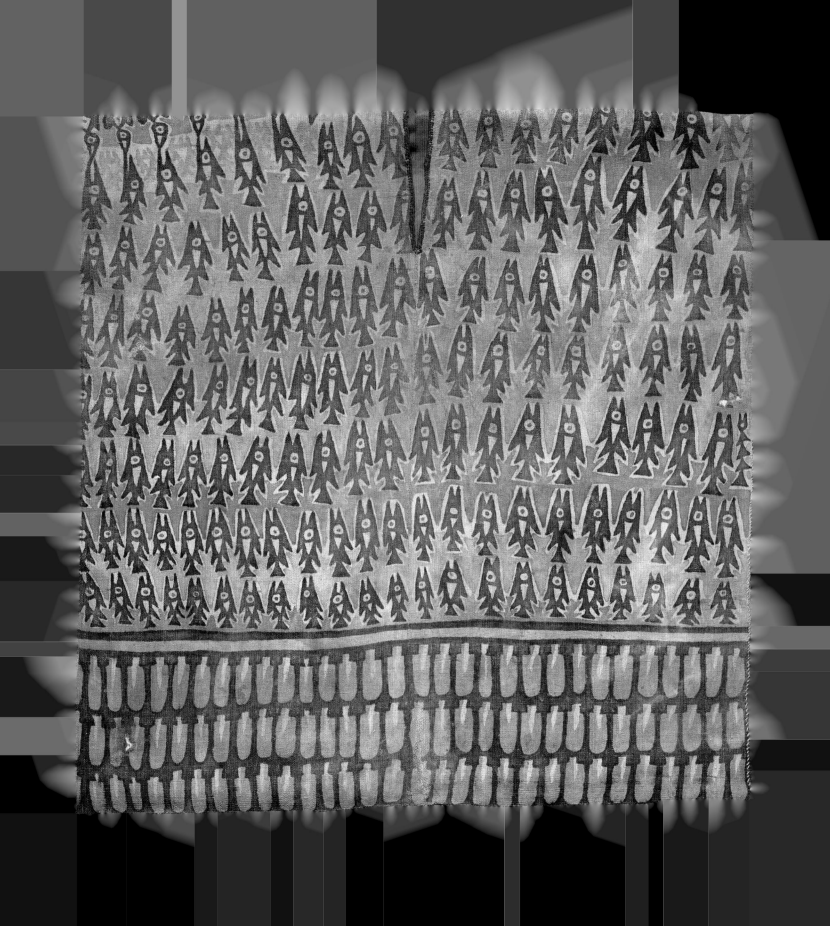

131 Beaded necklace of
Spondylus shell, mussel
shell, and stone beads with
mother-of-pearl tabs on
cotton strings. Chimú style,
probably Chan Chan, Peru.
H. 35 cm. (13.8 in.) B/3172

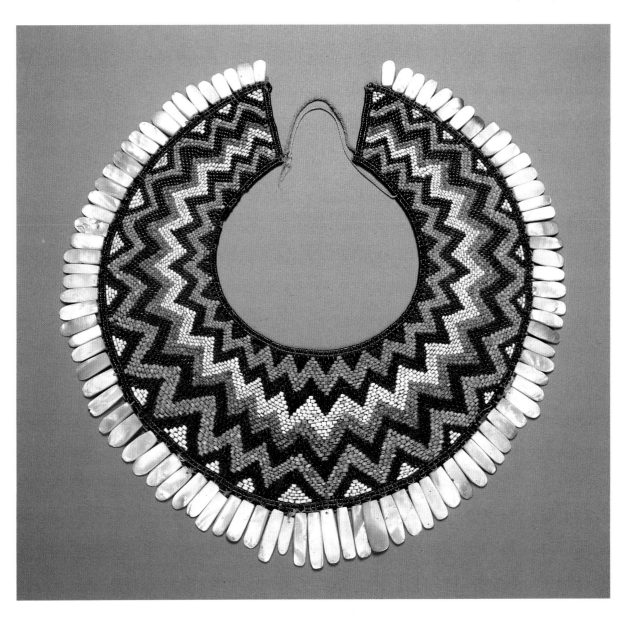

130 FACING PAGE
Plain-weave tunic of cotton
with paired warps and
wefts. On the side of the
tunic shown here, rows of
painted birds fly up toward
the shoulder line, where
they catch the fish represented on the other side.
Typically coastal subject
matter and the use of
threads spun in both Z and
S directions in the weave
point to a central coast
origin. Peru.
79 x 78 cm. (31.1 x 30.7 in.)
41.0/1194

132 Located near the mouth of
the Fortaleza River on
Peru's north coast, Para-
monga is a somewhat enig-
matic site. Possibly
constructed by the Chimú, it
was used into the time of
the Inka Empire. It has five
tiers of high terrace walls
and only four small rooms
on its summit. At one time,
painted friezes covered
much of the adobe brick
architecture.

133 Cut feathers covering this
pair of wooden earspools
include parrot (green),
macaw (yellow, red), and
tanager or honey creeper
(purple). Such exotically decorated ear ornaments were
probably used by the elite.
Chimú style, possibly made
during the Inka period. North
coast, Peru.
D. 5.5 cm. (2.2 in.) 41.2/8015

powers, the role of religion in Chimor probably was becoming secondary to economic, political, and military considerations. Some of the artisans who were central to this aspect of Chimú strategy eventually found themselves decorating many of their finest products with the symbols of a new set of rulers. Spanish sources tell us how some Chimú artisans were moved to Cuzco to work for the Inka after Chimor became part of the Inka Empire in the mid-1460s.

CHANCAY, PACHACAMAC, AND CHINCHA

During the period of the Chimor kingdom, the central coast, just north and south of what is now Lima, was the scene of two important cultural and probably political centers. One of these was Chancay, located in the Chancay Valley. The other was the famous oracle center of Pachacamac, in the Lurín Valley (mentioned in chapters 5 and 7), which continued to grow during this period.

Chancay is known primarily for its ceramic style of black painted designs over a thick, often rather crude, off-white slip. The proximity of the Chancay cemeteries to Lima has made them favorite sites for tomb robbing, and the antiquities market has been flooded with this now well-known style. Unfortunately, there have been few archaeological studies of the area to illuminate the working contexts of the prolific Chancay potters. Chancay

culture is famous for ceramic standing figurines, often produced in male and female pairs (fig. 135), and for mummy bundles with painted or wooden masks (fig. 134). The area probably corresponded to the small kingdom of Collique, studied by Maria Rostworowski using early Colonial documents.

Pachacamac was one of the principal religious sites in the Andes. It maintained important ties to both the Wari and Inka empires, which probably used its religious prestige as part of their own strategies of conquest and domination of other Andean groups. Substantial archaeological work at the site of Pachacamac includes the landmark excavations by Uhle in 1896–97 and studies under

134 The wooden facial mask of this false mummy-bundle head is attached to a cotton cloth filled with a core of plant material, dried reeds, and several shells, which give it the shape of a head. The mask probably once had shell inlays for the eyes. The wig is made of plant fiber. Such heads were placed on top of mummy bundles. Pacha-camac, central coast, Peru. H. 24 cm. (9.5 in.) B/628

135 Perforations on the heads of these male and female ceramic figurines once held feathers. In addition to garments painted on the surface, figurines often were elaborately dressed in actual cloth garments. Chancay style, central coast, Peru.
H. 50.5; 49.6 cm. (19.9; 19.5 in.)
41.2/7545, 7546

136 Pyramid with Ramps at Pachacamac, on the coast just south of Lima. The site was the leading religious center on Peru's central coast for hundreds of years. The Pyramids with Ramps may have been used by political and religious groups who venerated the Pachacamac cult.

the direction of Tello in the 1940s. More recent work has been carried out by Arturo Jiménez Borja, Alberto Bueno, and Ponciano Paredes. The renown of Pachacamac in the archaeological and historical literature relates primarily to its importance in Wari and Inka times. But most of its monumental construction probably dates to the period between the two empires, when it grew unfettered by imperial highland political centers. Rostworowski has suggested that Pachacamac was the center of the loosely organized kingdom of Ichma (also recorded as Ychma and Ichimay), which brought together the small political units of the Lurín and Rimac valleys. She believes that the basis of Pachacamac's authority was religious. Control of earthquakes was among the attributes of the deity associated with Pachacamac, and its priests could use threats of these natural disasters to encourage the political and economic collaboration of neighboring groups. Indeed, the fame of this power may have been part of Pachacamac's resilience in the face of the expansion of highland states.

The most important monuments built at Pachacamac during the Ichma period are known as Pyramids with Ramps (fig. 136). They stand at a lower elevation than the main Temple of Pachacamac, which was probably constructed earlier. More than pyramids, they are terraced mounds with platforms surrounded by walls or cell-like rooms and linked together by access ramps to create large compounds. Jiménez Borja and Bueno have interpreted these compounds as the centers of the various small political units that venerated the Pachacamac cult. This architecture served primarily to control movement of ritual celebrants as they moved up and down the ramps from one platform to another. The large open forecourts offered spaces where groups of different sizes could assemble. In most cases the lowest court was also the largest, suggesting perhaps its use by the larger, less privileged groups in terms of political, economic, and religious status. Corridors, rooms, passageways, and other architectural features supplemented the platforms and their ramps by providing storage, service quarters, and auxiliary access to the platforms for the personnel who attended them.

While the excavators have emphasized the local, Ichma associations of these Pyramids with Ramps, Shimada has noted the similarities between the Pachacamac compounds and those in the Sicán Precinct at Batán Grande. He suggests that construction of the Pyramids with Ramps may predate 1200–1470, the time span usually thought of as the Ichma period at Pachacamac. He also thinks that both the architecture and some of the artifacts found here suggest a connection between Pachacamac and the classic Middle Sicán kingdom (see chapter 7). In any case, Pachacamac's importance in the overall sweep of Andean history and prehistory is its continuity. Probably no other major center played such a significant role for such a long time and in such a variety of political and economic circumstances.

Several small and medium-sized kingdoms controlled the valleys of the south and south-central coast during the centuries separating the highland empires of Wari and the Inka. Perhaps the best known was the wealthy kingdom that dominated the Chincha Valley, about 200 kilometers (124 miles) south of Lima. Studies of early documents by Rostworowski have provided evidence of a population divided into specialized economic groups of farmers, fishermen, and long-distance traders (see chapter 9). The massive compounds of the Chincha capital, now the archaeological site of La Centinela (fig. 137), provided the focus for public activities of the groups, probably based on descent, that made up the Chincha kingdom. Constructed of poured adobe known as *tapia*, these compounds featured multi-level pyramids with large public forecourts. The valley contains many other sites built at about the same time as La Centinela, several of them large and with similar ceremonial compounds. Ancient roads leading in straight lines to La Centinela connect several of the sites and seem to suggest organization and planning that involved the entire valley. Current archaeological research in the valley aims to validate the documentary evidence for specialized economic groups and long-distance trade, but the monumental sites from the time of the Chincha kingdom testify to the valley's enormous wealth at the time it was brought into the Inka Empire.

 ## THE HIGHLANDS

During the time of the great coastal states, new political developments also were taking place in the highlands. Neither monumental architecture nor the other arts of these new political units equaled those of their coastal contemporaries or their highland Wari or Tiwanaku predecessors. Nevertheless, several very large settlements were built, and in the Cuzco region the stage was being set for the rapid expansion of one of these units into the Inka Empire. Substantial archaeological research has been done on only a few of these highland groups. Two that have received recent attention characterize the highland cultures during the period from about 1200 to 1400, when many groups, small and large, reigned in this region.

One of these groups, the Wanka, occupied the upper Yanamarca Valley, not far from the modern Peruvian city of Jauja in the central highlands. Excavations during the 1980s by a team that included Timothy Earle, Terence D'Altroy, and

Christine Hastorf have sketched a picture of loosely linked groups without marked differences in wealth or class. The Wanka were probably not a single political unit, but rather an ethnic group with considerable internal conflict. Though they built some large settlements, they constructed very little public and ceremonial architecture so typical of coastal states. Earle and his colleagues estimate the population of Tunanmarca (fig. 138), the largest Wanka town, at between eight thousand and thirteen thousand. Like other sites in the area, it was surrounded by defensive walls. While the archaeologists can distinguish between house and patio groups occupied by the elite and the common people, neither the architecture nor the objects found in the site demonstrate the kind of status difference or evidence for centralized authority found on the coast.

Farther to the south Garci Diez de San Miguel inspected part of the region around Lake Titicaca in 1567 (see chapter 7). His report shows the region's principal kingdom, the Lupaca, to have amassed great wealth, particularly in herds of llama and alpaca. Murra, in his study of the report, estimated that the lords of the Lupaca kingdom controlled herds of more than eighty thousand animals. The continuing wealth of the region during Colonial times is still clearly evident from the large number of fine churches built during the early years of Spanish domination. They stand today in relatively small towns and villages, like Juli and Pomata, indicating a past far richer than the present.

An archaeological survey by John Hyslop in the 1970s suggested that during the period between Tiwanaku and the Inka the Lake Titicaca region was marked by hilltop habitation sites surrounded by walls. Several larger sites were essentially fortresses that may not have been permanently occupied, but were temporary places to gather for refuge. The dead were buried above ground in towers called *chulpa* (fig. 139). It seems possible that the centralization of power under the Lupaca lords, documented in the report by Garci Diez, may have resulted at least in part from the policies of the Inka, who preferred to have friendly but relatively centralized authority in the areas they ruled. New studies will show the extent to which the enormous sixteenth-century wealth of the Lake Titicaca region in food production and the accumulation of herds had been encouraged by

137 Aerial view of La Centinela complex in the Chincha Valley, about 200 kilometers (124 miles) south of Lima, photographed in 1931. The central Chincha-period pyramid is near the center. There is a large mound of earth from looters to the right of it. The square compound in the lower right was an Inka palace, built 50–100 years later.

138 View over the town of Tunanmarca, the largest of the Wanka settlements. Located in the Yanamarca Valley, in the northern upper Mantaro, the site had an estimated population of 8,000–13,000 in pre-Inka times. Tunanmarca has patio groups and houses for the elite (seen here) and for commoners.

the Inka. Future research in places well north of Lake Titicaca will also tell us how another little-known (and apparently not very powerful) people, who made the pottery that archaeologists call Killke, consolidated their hold over what is now the Cuzco area. This region became the base of the enormous empire discussed in chapter 9.

The period between the fall of Tiwanaku and Wari and the rise of the Inka is frequently referred to as a period of conflict and fragmentation. This picture results in part from comments in the early Spanish sources that were based on Inka accounts about the lands they conquered. Obviously the Inka wanted to present a positive picture of their own accomplishments in bestowing peace and prosperity on an uncivilized and brutish land. Such reports were seriously exaggerated, especially for the coast. Chimor was in many respects an empire in its own right, probably sharing many of the features of Wari before it and the Inka Empire that followed. Certainly, few native New World kingdoms surpassed it in accumulated wealth.

Our very limited archaeological evidence from the highlands suggests that the model of small warring groups in the years after the fall of Tiwanaku and Wari, as described by Spanish chroniclers, was essentially accurate. Coastal kingdoms, in contrast, were based on highly concentrated food resources, with lush irrigated valleys on one side and rich coastal waters on the other. Except in times of environmental stress, they could prosper and achieve powerful central governments with only limited connections to other regions. The resources of the highlands were much more dispersed. Subsistence there was based on herding as well as agriculture, and the people depended on the coordination of a wide range of ecological zones. Their economic net had to be cast wide in order to concentrate the quantity and variety of resources needed to support a large-scale, centralized political system.

Somewhat ironically, the centuries of experience in managing these rich but scattered resources probably gave the highlanders a political advantage in the creation of large states and empires. Even relatively small communities were dispersed, with their members controlling resources in more than one zone. If the political umbrella that made these small-scale systems possible could be expanded to include ever larger areas and kinds of resources, the results would be ever larger and richer states. A tradition had grown up whereby groups gave a better way of life to their members by moving and expanding into new zones, sometimes jumping across long stretches of barren land, or even across territories occupied by others. Political units became "archipelagos," to use Murra's term. Political or ethnic groups were spread over the land like a group of islands, each surrounded by unused land or the territory of others.

Some of these "islands" were actually shared by more than one group. This was apparently the system of the Lupaca, for example, who controlled agricultural lands in the warm Moquegua regions to complement their herding in the high grasslands. This also had probably been the case for Tiwanaku and Wari (see chapter 7). We can see that these systems with intermeshed peoples and multiple boundaries carried with them a tendency to create friction and conflict. But they also carried mechanisms to control that conflict, at first, by means of traditional hospitality and gift giving. Later, as groups became more powerful, control could be imposed by threat or use of force. With peace and order established and competent managers in power, rule could be very effective in the large-scale management of dispersed goods.

Perhaps this experience with management of dispersed resources and dispersed rule partly explains why the really large empires, encompassing substantial areas of both the highlands and the coast, originated in the highlands. The relatively short life span of the same empires probably is also explained in part by the internal conflicts inherent in their diversity and by the difficulty in financing the gifts and hospitality to maintain them over the long term. The stress of long droughts might have depleted the storehouses, and political expansion may have been an important mechanism of economic support. Immediate gains from incorporating part of the land and accumulated wealth from conquered regions were easier to

achieve than long-range gains. More difficult to accomplish were the permanent mechanisms for producing sufficient goods to assure the stability of a large region and provide for an increasingly large and multilayered local and imperial elite. The Inka with their terracing systems, roads, warehouses, and network of production and supply centers were attempting to lay the groundwork for an empire, with a more permanent infrastructure as chapter 9 explains. Also, like earlier kingdoms and empires, they were addressing the need for a complex, effective set of symbols for a new, imperial art. The symbols were expressed in architecture, textiles, ceramics, music, and dance as well as in social organization and ritual. The Inka would spread these symbols virtually throughout the Andean region.

139 A *chulpa*, an above-ground burial structure, in the altiplano, at the south end of Lake Titicaca. The mummies of important members of altiplano society were buried in these structures. Chulpas were built for centuries, from the decline of Tiwanaku until shortly after the Spanish conquest, and they show a surprising number of building styles.

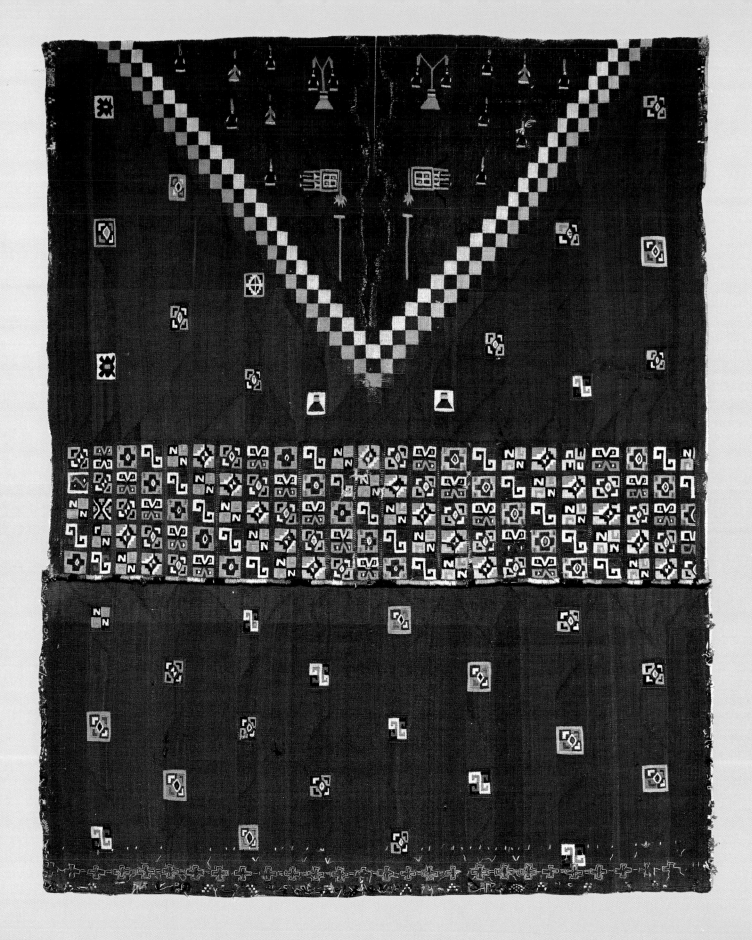

THE INKA EMPIRE

FOUR PARTS UNITED

In the mid-fifteenth century, a small kingdom in the region of Cuzco began to expand. By about 1500 it had become the Inka Empire, the largest empire in the New World. On November 16, 1532, a small band of Spanish conquistadors under Francisco Pizarro arrived in what is now northern Peru, and the course of Andean civilization was changed forever.

Our knowledge of this last, culminating period in the history of native, independent Andean civilization is more complete than that of preceding periods. The many accomplishments of Andean people did not include a system of writing. Only after the European invasion were events and customs recorded. The documents left us by the Spaniards are colored by their interests and biases, and by those of the informants whose accounts they recorded. It is in no sense equivalent to the analytic and objective accounts of a culture that a skilled historian or ethnographer might provide. Nevertheless, it supplements the material record of archaeology, allowing us to understand the meanings of many of the objects, settlements, and other remains.

A few of the written accounts convey a feeling of visual immediacy. One of these is the description by Francisco de Jérez of the last, fatal moments of the ruling Inka and his retinue as they came from the thermal baths just outside the city of Cajamarca, where they had been camped, to greet Pizarro in the city's main plaza.

Soon the first people began to enter the plaza; in front came a group of Indians in colored uniforms with checks. They came removing straw from the ground and sweeping the road. Another three groups came after them, all singing and dancing, dressed in a different way. Then many people advanced with armor, medallions, and crowns of gold and silver. Among them Atawalpa entered in a litter covered with colorful parrot feathers and decorated with gold and silver plaques.

Many Indians carried him up high on their shoulders, and after this came two other litters and two hammocks in which two other important people rode. Then many groups of people entered with gold and silver crowns. As soon as the first entered the plaza, they went to the side and made room for the others. Upon arriving in the middle of the plaza, Atawalpa made a sign for silence (Jérez, 1917 [1535]:56).

This picture of the wealth and splendor of the Inka court contrasts sharply with the events of brutality and destruction that the European invaders visited on the Andes in the months and years that followed. After paying one of the most valuable ransoms ever assembled, the Inka ruler Atawalpa was garroted. The invaders created a puppet government under a member of the ruling Inka group and lived at the expense of the land and the rich stores accumulated by the Inka state. As the Europeans' intention to loot the land and exploit its inhabitants' labor became clear, rebellions had to be put down. Eventually survivors of the Inka leadership escaped into the jungle near Cuzco and founded a neo-Inka state at Vilcabamba. Set in a marginal environment, that attempt to salvage something of the glory of native civilization was doomed to failure.

140 One side of an interlocked tapestry tunic made with camelid-fiber weft and cotton warp. The V-shaped neck area outlined by a checkerboard motif and the *t'okapu* band at the waist, containing important symbols, are typical Inka elements. According to textile expert Ann Pollard Rowe, certain technical features, such as the elaborate embroidery near the bottom edge, seem to indicate that this tunic dates from the Colonial period. Inka style, early Colonial period, Island of Titicaca, Bolivia.
96.5 x 76 cm. (38 x 30 in.) B/1503

The defeat of a large and powerful empire at the hands of a few dozen European adventurers led by an illiterate swineherd turned soldier has always seemed incongruous. European superiority in weapons and military tactics is, of course, part of the explanation. The horses and guns of Pizarro's men increased their mobility and ability to kill. They also caused fright and confusion among a populace who could not have imagined such a way of fighting.

He [Pizarro] ordered a gun to be fired, and the horsemen attacked the Indians from three sides. The Governor himself advanced with his infantry in the direction from which Atahuallpa was coming, and on reaching his litter they began to kill the bearers. But as fast as one fell several more came with great resolution to take his place. . . . seizing Atahuallpa by the hair (which he wore very long) and dragging him roughly towards him till he fell out. Meanwhile the Christians were slashing the litter— which was of gold—so fiercely with their swords that they wounded the Governor in the hand and, though many Indians rushed forward to rescue him, took him prisoner.

When the Indians saw their lord lying on the ground a prisoner, and themselves attacked from so many sides and so furiously by the horses they so feared, they turned round and began to flee in panic (Zárate, 1968 [1555]: 104–05).

Differences in the technology and tactics of war, however, were only part of the explanation for the disaster that befell the Inka in Cajamarca. Why did a people so superior in numbers quickly dis-

perse in disorder once their leader was in captivity? Why was there no rapid counter-response? One interpretation is that the court and the army of the Inka refrained from attacking the invaders to protect the life of the hostage king. Another is that Inka rule was so centralized that others were incapable of acting without the king's orders. The previous Inka ruler, Huayna Capac, and the son he had designated successor had both died, apparently of European-introduced smallpox, just before the arrival of Pizarro. Confusion over the succession led to deep divisions and conflicts within the empire that the Spanish were able to exploit.

Beyond the shock of new weapons and tactics, and the obligation to protect the captured ruler, the cause of the Inka defeat lay in the political principles on which the empire was built. The lack of complete and reliable historical records makes any reconstruction of Inka political organization somewhat speculative. There are clues, however, that allow us to begin to piece together a picture of a state so different from modern nation-states or even sixteenth-century European states that the Inka collapse in the wake of foreign invasion became almost predictable. The first of these clues is the Inka name for their state, Tawantinsuyu, the four divisions. Immediately this suggests a collection of parts rather than a sociopolitical unit built on a single identity or set of traditions. Tawantinsuyu was close to our idea of a loose empire, in which constituent units maintained substantial independence and the threat of rebellion always existed.

A second clue is the rapidity with which the state had been assembled. Evidence suggests that most of the expansion took place in a few decades. Traditionally, this rapid spread of Inka rule has been attributed mainly to military successes. While military force was certainly a factor, especially late in the expansion, it is difficult to see how such a powerful military, along with its necessary economic base, could have been built up so quickly in the early years of the empire. Inka myths and legends were carefully fostered to create an image of power. As they magnified and embellished military power, the myths concurrently connected it with gods and supernatural forces—giving the rulers an element of divine right and their expansion a quality of inevitability. This mythic history had an effect on the people they ruled or sought to rule. It has also affected our interpretation of the nature of Tawantinsuyu. Whatever the ultimate explanation of the rapid Inka expansion, previous chapters have shown that it was not the first instance of a state spreading rapidly in the Andes, to rule and prosper for a few centuries and then quite rapidly decline. One of the defining patterns of Andean sociopolitical growth, especially in the highlands, was the rapid appearance and disappearance of polities. Sites were often built on virgin land and then abandoned after relatively short occupations.

The two immediate predecessors of Tawantinsuyu, the states of Wari and Chimor, had both expanded their control over wide areas, only to decline rather rapidly in the span of about two centuries. Chimor met its end in conflict with the expanding Inka; the dissolution of Wari is much more mysterious, since it was not immediately succeeded by another powerful empire. The events of 1532 preclude the possibility of knowing whether the elaborate infrastructure of roads, warehouses, and administrative cities built by the Inka would have given their empire greater longevity.

 ## CUZCO AND THE URUBAMBA VALLEY

Further clues to understanding the rapid rise and fall of the Inka Empire, and perhaps of other Andean states, come from closer looks at how Tawantinsuyu functioned. Cuzco, the Inka capital, was built around a central sector of palaces, temples, and public buildings. This monumental zone contained many structures built with fine-dressed stone masonry, and some sources suggest that it was laid out in the form of a puma. According to this iconographic version of city planning, the temple/fortress of Saqsawaman (fig. 142) formed the puma's head, and the area between the rechanneled Tullumayo and Saphy rivers formed its tail. That area was known as *puma chupan*, tail of the puma. According to several chroniclers, the great central sector of Cuzco was redesigned and rebuilt by Pachakuti, the ruler credited with expanding the Inka Empire. The city's large central plaza, surrounded by elegant, well-constructed buildings, offered an important public space, designed as both an active political and administrative center and a

141 A 1930s aerial view of Cuzco, once the Inka capital. Fine Inka masonry walls still line some of the city's streets. The modern city now covers the slopes of the surrounding valley.

142 The most notable feature of Saqsawaman, the great Inka monument on a hill north of Cuzco, is its three levels of polygonal masonry walls. Europeans first thought the site was a fortress, but it seems to have been mainly a Sun Temple, storage facility, and area for ritual activity. Although many thousands of workers toiled for decades to build Saqsawaman, it may never have been completed.

143 This masonry wall of the Sun Temple at Cuzco, one of the finest examples of Inka stonework, remains undamaged after nearly five hundred years. The three holes are part of the building's drainage system.

144 A human head tops a ceramic ceremonial vessel (*paccha*) modeled in the form of a pointed digging implement. Liquid, presumably chicha, was poured into the bottle and flowed out through the tool's pointed tip. Pacchas were used during fertility ceremonies. Chimú-Inka style, Peru.

H. 43 cm. (16.9 in.) 41.2/7526

place of power for impressing the privileged from all of Tawantinsuyu. Its central feature, the plaza, stretched across a river, dividing the city and the plaza into two parts. In the two-part plaza was a sacred stone, the *ushnu*, covered with gold. Chicha poured over the stone as an offering was carried away by an underground canal that ran to the Korikancha, or Temple of the Sun. A tall round building, called *sunturwasi*, also stood in this divided plaza.

A series of compounds surrounding the plaza were built in the famous dressed-stone masonry, the stones fitted together without mortar. These compounds included *hatunkancha*, a walled building group with housing for the *mamakuna*, or chosen women, who served the religion, brewed chicha, and made cloth. They also included a temple to Wirakocha, the creator deity, and the Qasana compound. According to John H. Rowe, the Qasana was the palace of Huayna Capac. Some archaeologists and ethnohistorians believe it was the palace of each successive reigning Inka. In addition to the compounds there were great halls, sometimes called *kallanka*, probably similar to those at Huánuco Pampa and several other provincial capitals that served a variety of official and religious functions.

Around this administrative and ceremonial core of the capital lay a much larger area of less dense construction where most of the city's population lived. These dwellings were scattered among cultivated fields, storehouses, terraces, and irrigation canals.

Most of Cuzco's inhabitants belonged to social groups known as *panaqa*, and most of the panaqa were Inka, the ruling group of Tawantinsuyu. The non-Inka apparently were local groups who had lived in the area before the Inka settled there. The capital also housed numerous people from the far-flung provinces. Exactly where and how they lived is unclear, but important local leaders and their heirs were often brought to Cuzco. Sometimes they came as administrative officials, sometimes as guests to be schooled in the policies of the Inka, sometimes almost as hostages—a strategy for ruling their home provinces. Cuzco was also the ritual center of the empire, host to the important ceremonies of the realm. Many of the ceremonies involved people from the provinces, who swelled the city's population during certain periods of the ritual calendar.

Some of the most important and visually striking towns in Tawantinsuyu line the sides of the Urubamba Valley north of Cuzco. The Urubamba was both the breadbasket of the capital and a showcase of Inka land management. This deep valley runs from the high altitude (3,400 meters; 11,150 feet) of the capital to low, almost impenetrable jungle. Because of its lower altitude the Urubamba enjoys a warm climate, well suited for growing maize. Important for its nutritive value, maize also keeps well when stored. Its most crucial use was for making chicha, the maize beer consumed in vast quantities on ceremonial occasions. Sponsorship of ceremonies, essential to achieving and maintaining power in the Andes, was feasible only if access to substantial amounts of maize was assured. The Urubamba Valley was the nearby source of maize for the rich ceremonial life of Cuzco. To increase

145 The concentric terraces of Moray, northwest of Cuzco, are a unique example of Inka terrace building.

146 Machu`Picchu, on the eastern slopes of the Andes, was discovered in 1911 by the explorer Hiram Bingham. The uniqueness of its design and the beauty of its fine masonry make it the most famous of Inka settlements.

maize production in this valley, the Inka completed some of the most remarkable public works projects of the ancient Americas. Systems of irrigation made water supplies for growing the crop more reliable and shortened its growing season. Irrigation canals often flowed through newly built terraces that brought steep slopes into cultivation, greatly increasing tillable land in this warm climatic zone.

The Inka matched the transformation of the Urubamba Valley landscape with equally remarkable sociopolitical transformations. As we have seen on several occasions, Andean groups sometimes deployed colonies of their members to exploit resources of ecological zones at some distance from their primary living area. Expanding this custom, the Inka often moved people to faraway locations convenient for the aims of the state and its rulers. Under this policy, known as *mitmaq*, they were able to move people for strategic reasons, locating rebellious or uncooperative groups among more loyal peoples, or placing loyal groups in unstable regions. Many of the population movements had economic reasons as well. Newly claimed lands, such as those in the Urubamba Valley, were populated by experienced maize farmers, while other groups, such as herders, went to grassland regions where state herds were being developed to increase cloth production.

Transformations brought about by the Inka changed the landscape of the Urubamba Valley. Details of the peoples who occupied and cultivated the valley are few, but the fine architecture of the archaeological sites gives modern visitors a vivid

impression of the area's beauty and importance. Pisaq with its spacious terraces and spectacular views (fig. 147), the great megalithic wall and hillside storehouses of Ollantaytambo, the high terraces of the ruler's fields at Yucay—all illustrate the intricate planning and massive effort that went into this breadbasket of the capital.

The most famous site of the valley lies near its end. Beyond Machu Picchu the combination of rough terrain and thick vegetation makes the lower valley almost impenetrable. Machu Picchu remains almost as mysterious as it was when Hiram Bingham brought it to the world's attention in 1911. What is not in question is its spectacular beauty. Few towns in the world so successfully integrate architecture into the landscape. Its narrow terraces probably did not produce a surplus significant enough for shipping agricultural products to Cuzco. The clues to its meaning must lie in its location in the clouds at the edge of the empire and in the extraordinary care of its planning and construction. Temples perched on precipices (fig. 150), water flowed through stone channels and fine cisterns, sculpture was carved in living rock (fig. 149). All of this underscores the integration of land with people and culture. One

147 The terraces of Pisaq, northeast of Cuzco, form part of a dispersed set of fine buildings. Pisaq was constructed as an estate for Inka royalty.

148 The carved stone known as Intiwatana ("hitching post of the sun") at Machu Picchu. The name is probably modern. The stone's specific function is unknown, but it was probably the scene of offerings and ceremonies. Carved rocks and boulders were imbued with ritual significance in Inka religion.

149 At Machu Picchu, a "cave" beneath one of the principal structures, known as the Torreón, or tower, incorporates extraordinary carving in its stone. The cave also has several large trapezoidal niches where mummies may have been kept.

150 The wall of the Torreón encloses a sacred rock outcrop.

151 A sacred rock at Machu Picchu. The platform built around the rock emphasizes its special nature. This rock may have been modified to imitate the contours of the mountains beyond it.

carved stone even seems to echo the hills behind it (fig. 151). Whatever else Machu Picchu may have been, it was permeated with symbolism and not easily explainable in strictly utilitarian terms.

CHINCHA AND HUANUCO

Archaeological information from two regions much farther from Cuzco than the Urubamba Valley suggests additional ideas about the economic and political workings of Tawantinsuyu. Examining them allows us to address two questions related to the expansion and prosperity of the empire. What were the bases of the rulers' authority, and what were the sources of revenue that allowed growth of the governmental apparatus and support of the elite?

One part of Tawantinsuyu that has yielded substantial information, as a result of studies by the American Museum of Natural History, is the Chincha region on the south coast of Peru. Before its incorporation into the Inka Empire, Chincha was a rich desert kingdom (as discussed in chapter 8). Cuzco and Chincha evidently enjoyed close and friendly relations. Indeed, the lord of Chincha was traveling with the Inka Atawalpa at the time of the fateful encounter with Pizarro in Cajamarca. Two of the critical factors that determined relations between the Inka and the peoples they brought into Tawantinsuyu were the size of the conquered

group and the degree to which authority was centralized within it. The incorporation of Chincha into the empire seems to have been basically peaceful. The archaeological record also suggests a long tradition of sociopolitical complexity and centralized authority in the Chincha area, which the Inka were able to exploit. Establishing themselves at the top of the pyramid of power, they probably exerted some control over the process of selecting local people for positions of authority. But rule was essentially indirect, using an existing structure of power and administration.

152 The main Inka sector at La Centinela, in the Chincha Valley of Peru, was added to the massive complex built long before Inka domination of the valley. South coast, Peru.

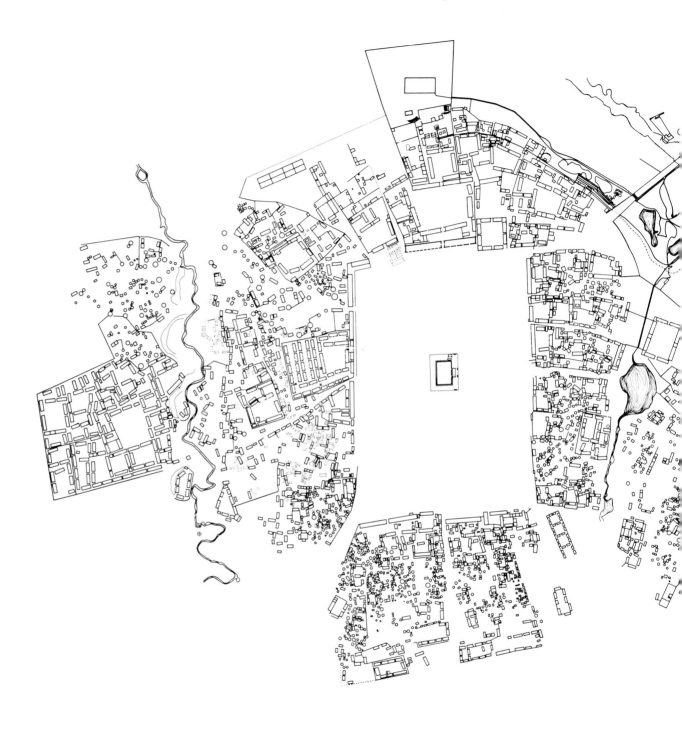

153 Plan of the Inka administrative center of Huánuco Pampa. The site lies at an altitude of more than 3,800 meters (12,470 feet) and has nearly four thousand buildings arranged around a large rectangular plaza. Built by the Inka using a preconceived plan, it is an excellent example of Inka planning. Central highlands, Peru.

N

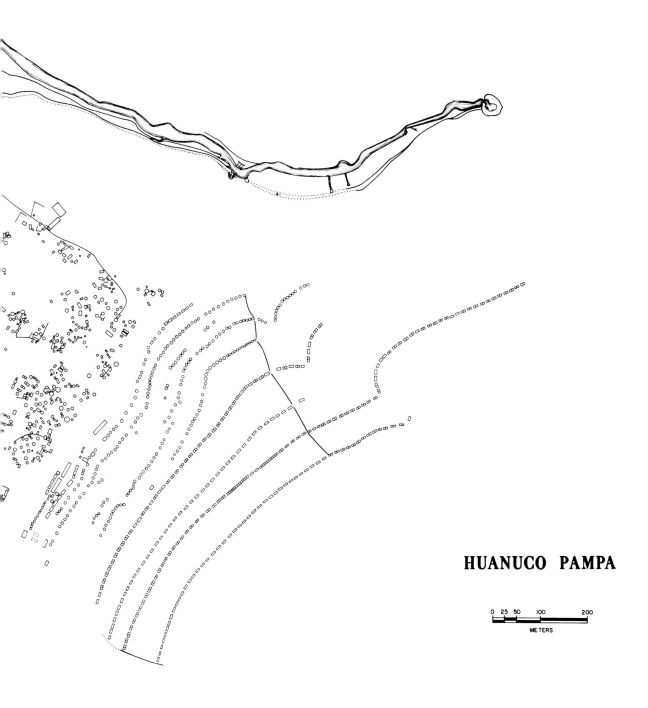

HUANUCO PAMPA

0 25 50 100 200
METERS

Chincha's capital, now the archaeological site of La Centinela, consists of a group of impressive locally built compounds, which continued to function during the period of Inka domination. In the midst of these the Inka built a compound of their own. While the earlier Chincha construction was of the coursed adobe known as tapia, the Inka compound was constructed of adobe bricks. It had a rectangular plaza, and trapezoidal niches and doorways typical of Inka architecture decorated its buildings. Alongside the structures that seemed to have served as an Inka palace stood a pyramidal platform more reminiscent of Chincha architecture, despite its construction of adobe bricks and its formal function within the compounds of the dominant Inka. Several of the compounds built of tapia had been modified with adobe bricks, in two cases extensively, indicating Inka alteration of existing structures. We suspect that these local compounds were related to Chincha social units and were the settings for important ceremonies and rituals, probably including initiation, marriage, and other rites of passage. Differences in Inka architectural modifications of the Chincha compounds may have been related to differences in the ways the Inka supported and controlled various groups. Though the Inka exerted control indirectly, they were obviously not content to leave its implementation entirely in local hands. Elements of Inka identity were made evident at many points in the social and political ceremonies that held together the upper levels of the local societies.

A second example of how distant provinces were ruled comes from the site of Huánuco Pampa in the Peruvian north-central highlands more than 600 kilometers (375 miles) north of Cuzco. Built by the Inka state on a high pampa, or plain, more than 3,800 meters (12,470 feet) above sea level, Huánuco Pampa served as a provincial capital, the city from which several small conquered groups were administered. Though it probably housed only a small permanent population, its nearly four thousand structures provided for the many thousands of people who came for the ceremonial festivities of state, filling the city at intervals with color and life.

More than ten years of research, also by the American Museum of Natural History, have shown that the great central plaza and the buildings around it served these public ceremonies, including the festivals of the elaborate ritual calendar and possibly also the ritual battles that helped define relations among groups in the region. Royal dwellings and temples formed a compound at the city's eastern edge. Thousands of jars for maize beer and nearly as many plates found in buildings around the smaller plazas, between the royal compound and the central plaza, suggest that public feasts were held in these areas. Nearly five hundred warehouses held food and other supplies to support the city's elaborate feasts. A compound of fifty houses provided work and living space to a group of women weavers and brewers, who produced the cloth and maize beer that conferred prestige on their recipients and gave respect and power to the Inka who provided them.

Archaeological sites of local, non-Inka peoples in the region near Huánuco Pampa contrast markedly with the center the Inka built. Most of these sites offer no evidence of the existence of Tawantinsuyu. Local towns continued to be inhab-

154 Beside or within the main
plazas of most Inka cities
there was a platform, or
ushnu. The ushnu were centers of ceremonial activities
and symbolized the Inka
state. The rectangular ushnu
at Huánuco Pampa is laid
out with great accuracy.

155 The shape of this ceramic jar and some elements of its painted design copy the ceramics of Cuzco. Other features reflect local influences. Inka period, Curua-cancha, Island of the Sun, Lake Titicaca, Bolivia.
H. 22 cm. (8.7 in.) D. 18 cm. (7.1 in.) 41.0/423

156 Modeled pumas form the handles of this pair of ceramic bowls with stylized maize or Spondylus shell molded on the interiors. Pumas, symbols of power and authority, were often associated with the ruling Inka. Lake Titicaca region, Bolivia.
D. (base) 15 cm. (5.9 in.) B/5700, 5701

ited by the same groups that had occupied them for centuries, and the ceramic vessels they used remained essentially unchanged. Early in the Colonial period the Spanish government ordered an inspection of part of the Huánuco region. That inspection, carried out by Iñigo Ortiz de Zúñiga in 1562, supplied important information on the organization of the local people. We can identify, for example, the towns where the local leaders lived. An archaeological survey based on the Ortiz inspection discovered quantities of pottery based on the designs of Cuzco ceramics in the ruins of the town of Ichu. At the time of the European invasion, Ichu had been home of the leader of the Chupaychu, one of the many small groups the Inka ruled through Huánuco Pampa. Ceramic vessels in this "state style" neatly followed the lines of power and authority—right into the household of the leader of a small polity. Apparently the brightly painted pots, plates, and jars allowed the local leader to symbolize the Inka's hospitality to his own followers.

The contrasts between the Huánuco and Chincha regions exemplify Inka flexibility in adapting policies and strategies of rule to the great variety of situations they encountered as the empire expanded. If a region was viewed as critical but its people recalcitrant, the Inka were capable of making bloody wars. This seems to have happened in the Cañete Valley, just north of Chincha, where a garrison town (now the archaeological site of Inkawasi) was built specifically to subjugate the area. If a region was wealthy and important, as well as amenable to collaboration, a course of closely integrated alliance might be pursued, as in Chincha itself. If a region was fragmented into

numerous small polities, the Inka could implement a strategy of sociopolitical combination. This strategy was aimed at bringing groups together and organizing them hierarchically into larger units, with their own internal administrative levels that were more easily governed by the Inka.

 ## THE ECONOMY OF THE EMPIRE

As in most premodern states, the Inka did not strive for an appearance of separation between the political and economic aspects of their relations with the people they ruled. On the contrary, gifts and state hospitality involving large quantities of goods were a basic element of Inka power. As we saw at Huánuco Pampa, the state distributed large quantities of food and maize beer to accompany activities in the impressive public section of the city. Written sources tell of massive issues and gifts of cloth to state officials, the army, and newly conquered or incorporated peoples.

The major problem facing the state economy was how to provide for these enormous outlays of hospitality and the living costs of increasingly large numbers of leaders, bureaucrats, and others who served the state. In theory the state functioned without tribute of goods. Its revenues were based on labor given by the subjects to till the state's fields, care for its herds, make its cloth, and build its roads, bridges, and cities. Lands

157 Silver kero, one of a pair, in the form of a human head. Keros were used for ceremonial drinking. Peru.
H. 23.7 cm. (9.3 in.) 41.2/7602

throughout the empire were divided into several classes. Lands of local communities provided subsistence for the great majority of the people; lands linked to religion provided goods related to various cults; state lands of various kinds supported the Inka rulers, their armies, and the massive labor forces who worked for the state. How much land belonged in each category is not known, nor do we have many details about the acquisition of state and religious lands. It seems clear that some of the land that passed into state use must have been used for local purposes before the Inka expansion. Additional land for farming was created or greatly improved by the Inka through terracing and irrigation projects as the state devoted some of its labor revenues to projects that increased production.

The labor tax was an outgrowth of Andean principles, probably centuries old, whereby leaders received labor from the people of their communities. In return, the leader was expected to support the people generously while they worked for him. Such support usually was not limited to mere subsistence rations. Instead, people did their work in a festival context with food, drink, and music. In this way, economics, politics, and religion were wrapped in an elaborate package of work, ritual, and festival. The evidence for feasting and drinking found at Huánuco Pampa exemplifies the state's enlarged version of these principles played out against the backdrop of an imperial city.

Most of the labor for the state came from able-bodied male heads of household, who served the state in turns. This rotating labor system, called *mit'a,* was used to cultivate the state's fields and to carry out its many construction projects.

159 Miniature tunics and bags of camelid fiber, made as garments and accessories for metal figurines used as offerings. They employ typical Inka designs: the checkerboard (left) and the Inka key (right). Provenience unknown.
7.8 x 7 cm. (3.1 x 2.8 in.) (tunic) 41.2/7037
2.5 x 2.7 cm. (.98 x 1.1 in.) (bag) 41.2/7038
6.6 x 5.7 cm. (2.6 x 2.2 in.) (tunic) 41.2/904
3.2 x 3.6 cm. (1.3 x 1.4 in.) (bag) 41.2/905

Similarly, the army was staffed by soldiers serving in rotation. Other workers devoted full time to Inka projects. The most famous group of these workers chosen for full-time state service were women known as *mamakuna* or *aqllakuna.* They are sometimes referred to in popular literature as "virgins of the sun." This term suggests dual requirements: they were unmarried women, and many of their duties related to religious functions that included worship of the sun. These requisites led the Spanish to draw a parallel between the mamakuna and nuns. Written sources note that these women were also spinners and weavers and brewers of maize beer. Excavation of a place where they lived and worked at Huánuco Pampa uncovered hundreds of spinning and weaving implements and large numbers of broken jars once used in brewing. Clearly, the women's economic importance at least equaled that of their religious duties. Frequent mention of the mamakuna in censuses, inspections (*visitas*), and other administrative documents makes clear their large numbers and pervasive role in the Inka state economy. They seem to have lived mainly in cities and towns along the Inka roads, where they could be carefully controlled by the state.

Members of certain classes of mamakuna may have had their celibate status abruptly ended. The Inka apparently gave mamakuna in marriage to local leaders as a means of forming or reinforcing alliances. Just how often this happened is difficult to gauge, but as both real and fictive kinship were important in Andean political relations, the Inka logically would have found a way to arrange kinship through such marriages. The large numbers of single women in service to the state not only would have provided the state with a substantial reserve of female workers and functionaries but also given the rulers the opportunity to adjust and create social relations for their own benefit. As with most other state workers, the Inka rulers maintained the mamakuna, providing them with food, clothing, and housing. While these women had little in the way of personal liberty, they apparently enjoyed a relatively lavish standard of living.

We have less evidence for a second category of people, the *yanakuna,* who worked full time for the state. One of their major services was caring for the royal herds. The yanakuna were men, and some accounts of the Inka have tended to equate them with slaves. Like the mamakuna, the yanakuna were dependent on the wishes of the state in a wide range of their activities. But the Inka had no concept of property as an asset to be bought and sold, much less of people as property. Interestingly, the right to service by yanakuna was not exclusive to the rulers of the Inka state. These men sometimes served local leaders as well. Their marital status seems to have been more flexible than that of the mamakuna; often they seem to have been married.

A final category of labor service is especially interesting because it involved entire communities rather than individuals or families. These groups were the *mitmakuna,* discussed above in relation to the resettling of the Urubamba Valley near Cuzco. On state orders the mitmakuna often were moved hundreds of kilometers, and they played major roles in the political and economic development of newly incorporated areas.

These categories of workers satisfied most of the state's needs for subsistence and crafts goods, with the state supplying land and raw materials. Some specialized artisans had their own titles, such as *kumpikamayoq,* the weavers of fine cloth. It is not always clear how these skilled people fit into, or cross-cut, the other categories through which human energy flowed to the state. The result, however, was very clear: The state commanded enormous wealth. Evidence of this is in the rich cities with their palaces, temples, and more gold than the Europeans had seen amassed under a single authority. Further evidence is in the feasts that the Inka provided and the system of warehouses that guaranteed the ability to do so. These storehouses were found throughout much of Tawantinsuyu, especially in areas where climatic or socioeconomic conditions made the reliability of supplies questionable.

Many storehouses can still be seen in orderly rows above the ruins of Inka provincial centers. Excavations of some of these storehouses have uncovered primarily maize and other foodstuffs. Huánuco Pampa has been estimated to have warehouses with a capacity of almost 40,000 cubic meters (52,320 cubic yards). The realm as a whole must have stored many tons of goods in its warehouses, assuring that the state would be able to supply its workers and armies and fulfill its feast obligations during times of the year when food was scarce. The role of state warehousing in preventing hunger during times of famine may have been exaggerated by writers who mistakenly believed that the Inka had a welfare state. The Inka actually

preferred to leave responsibility for local subsistence in local hands. But in times of crisis the state could still expand its role by increasing its hospitality and perhaps its use of labor as well.

One measure of the success of an economic system is the wealth it can produce and accumulate. By this measure the success of the Inka is clear. Another measure is distribution of sufficient wealth so that the people are well provided for and content. There is not enough information to suggest what the standard of living of the common people was during Inka times. But European inspectors and observers recorded enough complaints contrasting Inka and Colonial times to leave little doubt that for the great majority life had been better under the Inka. Yet another measure of economic success is how economic practices drew on available resources to maximize their use but not deplete them for future generations. The European invasion deprived us of the opportunity to analyze the long-term impact of Inka economic practice. The productivity of the Inka economy, however, depended on careful management of the great mosaic of Andean ecological zones and an almost equal diversity of human labor resources. Combining all these mosaic bits into a coherently assembled picture required sensitivity to individual local circumstances and careful monitoring of results. It was not something that could be achieved through simple adherence to a single set of principles. While there had been economic cycles, many of the same practices in the hands of previous Andean cultures had assured thousands of years of long-term growth in an environment Europeans found to be fragile. The European invaders brought many useful techniques, but their success in assuring the continuing well-being of the people and their environment has not so far matched that of the Inka and their Andean predecessors.

A society sustains its social and economic functioning through relationships based on communication among its members. Communication depends on a series of shared symbols, and language is the primary example of a symbolic system that allows a society to function. Complex societies like those of the Inka and their immediate predecessors not only had a large total population but also a great number of groups based on ethnicity, social class, and economic specialization. A means of communicating and mediating within and among all of these groups was neces-

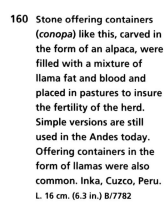

160 Stone offering containers (*conopa*) like this, carved in the form of an alpaca, were filled with a mixture of llama fat and blood and placed in pastures to insure the fertility of the herd. Simple versions are still used in the Andes today. Offering containers in the form of llamas were also common. Inka, Cuzco, Peru. L. 16 cm. (6.3 in.) B/7782

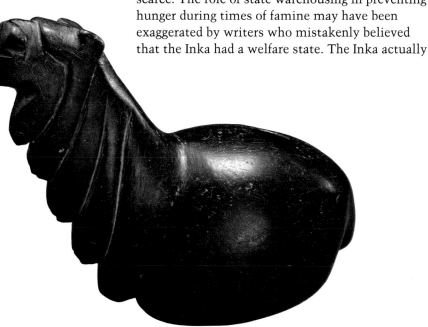

161 Jar painted in the style typical of the Lake Titicaca region. Such vessels were frequently quite large, holding seventy-five liters (twenty gallons) and more, and were used for storing grains and for liquids like chicha. The pointed base, which facilitates tilting the vessel for pouring, could be lodged in a separate cylindrical base of hard earth to keep the container upright. The constricted neck reduces evaporation and spillage. Inka period, Lake Titicaca region, Bolivia.
H. 40.6 cm. (16 in.) B/1890

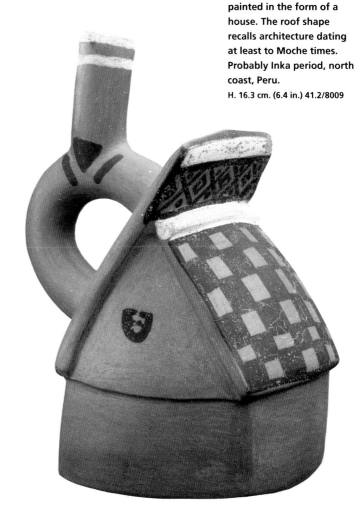

162 Ceramic bottle modeled and painted in the form of a house. The roof shape recalls architecture dating at least to Moche times. Probably Inka period, north coast, Peru.
H. 16.3 cm. (6.4 in.) 41.2/8009

sary to attain the society's ends: a government and an economy in which all groups participated and to a degree cooperated. There had to be a set of shared ideas about group identities and appropriate behavior within and among groups. In an expanding state that was continually incorporating new groups, the system of communication and the means of maintaining order had to be flexible and creative in order to realign positions and create new policies. These requirements called for an alignment between an efficient communication system and a system that enabled decisions to be reached at the places and times they were needed.

 ## ART AND COMMUNICATION

Most ancient complex societies developed writing systems. They were able to record laws and send written messages and orders from one area and one group to another. They kept records on tribute, population, and economic transactions. They recorded their calendar, the rites and activities it regulated, and they set down the events and transitions of their history—or at least the version of their history that they wanted to communicate to succeeding generations.

Given their management skills and their virtuosity in many areas, it is somewhat surprising that Andean peoples never developed writing, if it is defined as a set of codes that can record spoken language. Although the Inka had no writing, they did have elaborate symbolic systems that coded identities and relationships, and a system of knotted strings, or khipu (see chapter 7; figs. 163, 164), that recorded numbers and perhaps other kinds of information. Inka khipu used standardized types of knots and clusters of knots to indicate numbers; the position of the knot clusters signified the number's position in a decimal system of notation. Secondary cords and summary cords allowed the recording of complicated numerical information, and the order in which the cords were attached to the main cord probably referred to a tradition of categories of information and their relative importance. Khipu could be rolled up and stored and carried from one place to another; in many instances, they substituted for writing.

A vast system of roads was as important as the khipu. John Hyslop shows that the Inka road system consisted of more than 23,000 kilometers (14,260 miles) of roads and incorporated way stations and messengers to link one part of the realm with another. This infrastructure for transportation and communication was remarkable for its day. Built into this system were regional administrative centers like Huánuco Pampa that allowed many decisions to be made and carried out locally by various levels of provincial authorities. In terms of decision making and communication the Inka sought a balance between the efficiency of local control and the security of frequent checks by central authorities. They maintained the flexibility of adapting to local circumstances within a context of large-scale and long-term planning.

Symbols incorporated into clothing, ornaments, buildings, and items of daily use were one of the most important methods of establishing identities and relationships. At a glance they signaled the group of origin, or status, of Inka officials and the ruling elite. The function of clothing was not limited to warmth; that of buildings, to shelter; or that of ceramic and metal vessels, to containing food and drink. The designs we regard as decoration or art were filled with meaning. An abundance of crafted goods was richly imbedded with codes that allowed immediate identification of people and groups. With this information in hand they would know, or at least could learn, how to behave in various kinds of encounters with other peoples and groups.

Clothing and other items of dress were primary among objects that carried insignia of social identity. In Tawantinsuyu our own modern saying "you are what you wear" carried an almost literal validity: "The men and women of each nation and province had their insignias and emblems by which they could be identified, and they could not go around without this identification or exchange their insignias for those of another nation, or they would be severely punished. They had this insignia on their clothes with different stripes and colors, and the men wore their most distinguishing insignia on their heads." (Cobo, 1983 [1653]:196)

The *unqo*, or tunics (figs. 140, 173), encoded distinctions of status for their wearers. In the case of high officials some tunics may have been worn only on special occasions. As Cobo has stated, headdress was a primary indicator of membership in the many non-Inka groups. Belts, slings, and

163 Khipu of knotted cotton cords. Khipu were rolled for storage. Inka style, Media Luna, central coast, Peru.
L. 43 cm. (16.9 in.) B/8713

164 This khipu includes several colors of knotted cotton cords. Inka style, Peru.

L. (main cord) 63 cm. (24.8 in.)
41.2/6996

165 Headband of camelid fiber with cut pile. The royal headband, worn by the Inka ruler, supposedly had a red fringe that hung in front of the eyes and a golden plume mounted in the top center above the fringe. Inka style, Peru.

bags also were clues to group identities. Inka rulers often bestowed gifts of cloth and clothing on the non-Inka whom they incorporated into their empire. We have little specific information on the designs of these gifts, but it seems likely that they were of state production and state design. If so, their function may have been not just to honor the recipient but to furnish new insignia that would shift his or her sociopolitical identity.

We have already explored the custom in many Andean communities and states of building settlements within territories chiefly occupied by others, a practice that gave access to a wider range of environments and natural resources. Given the pattern of intermeshing, it was particularly important to identify settlements with the group that built and used them. Insignia on clothing could send the message when the towns were occupied, but since many towns were occupied only part of the time, the stamp of identity came through architecture and often through ceramic vessels and other objects as well. The architecture of imperial Inka settlements, with its simple but elegant rectangular buildings and its frequent use of fine dressed-stone masonry, is very well known. The use of trapezoidal windows, niches, and doorways is also a mark of Inka builders. Throughout Tawantinsuyu the centers built by the state are easy to distinguish from the towns of the local people who lived in the region during Inka domination. Even when Inka buildings were placed in an existing local settlement, as was the case in Chincha, the identity is evident. Architecture was a clear signal that the Inka

had arrived and established their presence. It was also probably an indication of the activities and relationships that were expected in those newly built centers.

The central part of Huánuco Pampa, for example, was planned around large open plazas, gateways, and spacious public structures. It was a public city designed for the gathering of large groups. In that sense it was reminiscent of architecture and planning at Tiwanaku. However, the plan also contained numerous courtyard groups, not so rigidly organized as those of Wari centers but nonetheless giving the impression of control, probably of groups of workers and participants in rituals.

The design of the ceramic vessels for state-sponsored feasts also often followed state-prescribed patterns of shape and painted decoration. It was important that the source of the hospitality be clearly recognized. The architecture of the setting and the tableware in which food and drink were provided constantly reminded the recipient of the provider's identity. Even the warehouses so prominently displayed on the hills above many Inka cities conspired to instill the image of the generous, wealthy providers. Moreover, the music and the ritual performances were probably tailored to reflect the state's image and aims. All were part of the state's propaganda and communication with its people, the means of conveying the obligation to reciprocate with work and loyalty.

167 Painted catfish and modeled snails decorate this ceramic plate. Inka period, south coast, Peru.

D. 15.2 cm. (6 in.) 41.0/1056

166 A *kallanka*, one of two large halls on the eastern side of the main plaza at Huánuco Pampa. It seems to have served as a temporary residence for large numbers of people.

168 Llama constructed of pieces of sheet silver joined by soldering. The cinnabar and gold inlay on its back probably represents the red blanket of the royal (*puka*) llama. Inka period, Lake Titicaca region, Bolivia.

IDEOLOGY OF THE EMPIRE

Every society has a set of overall principles that govern its functioning, even though most members of the society are not consciously aware of them. Young members of the society learn these principles as they grow up and play increasingly complex roles in social and economic life. When a state society is expanding, as was Tawantinsuyu, those rules must quickly be absorbed by a large group of new participants. More difficult still, the principles must be adjusted and expanded to match the new scale of the society. This change of scale is particularly important for smaller societies not accustomed to participation in a large, state-level polity.

The city plan of Huánuco Pampa may have reflected some of the basic Inka organizational principles. No written evidence exists to determine whether that was in fact the case, and archaeology alone cannot be conclusive in such matters. Certain aspects of the spatial organization of Huánuco Pampa's plan (fig. 153), however, follow the principles of arrangement of the shrines around Cuzco. These similarities are probably intentional. The main north-south Inka road clearly divides Huánuco Pampa into two parts. Each part is subdivided into halves, and the resulting quarters are again divided into three parts, for a total of twelve. These principles are best documented for the Cuzco shrines and the organization of their use for worship, but they also

pervade other aspects of Inka organization and ideology, such as the calendar.

More effective Inka rule in the provinces would have been achieved with a hierarchical order instituted among the small local groups, allowing the state to deal with fewer local leaders. It is intriguing to speculate that the city plan might have been used not just as an expression of important ideological principles but also to place groups of people in physical relationships that mirrored the social relationships the Inka state wanted them to assume. This placement could then have been reinforced through participation in the many ceremonies prescribed in the ritual calendar. Seen in this light the city plan becomes a diagram of sociopolitical ideology and a template for the creation of actual social, political, and economic organization.

Such features as site plans, the elaborate road system, and khipu give us clues to the ways the Inka controlled people, space, and goods. They also structured time to take advantage of the seasons, another important element of coordination. Details of the complex calendar they used for this purpose are still being deciphered by ethnohistorian Tom Zuidema and others. It seems that the Inka used two twelve-month calendars: a daytime calendar based on the yearly cycle of the sun and a nighttime calendar linked to cycles of the moon and certain stars. Through these two interlocked calendars people integrated their conception of society and nature and effectively managed their world.

The daytime calendar—marked by periodic sacrifices of llamas—scheduled a series of feasts, pilgrimages, and exchanges of goods related to

169 Crimped silver sheet metal suggests the long, hanging fleece of this long-haired llama. These special llamas were the source of unusually long, fine fibers. The state, individual families, and important local leaders all controlled large flocks of llama and alpaca for fiber, transportation, sacrifices, and food. Lifesize figures of llamas and alpacas in gold and silver are among the objects on lists of precious metals melted down by the Spaniards.
23.8 x 20.6 cm. (9.4 x 8.1 in.) B/1619

170 Ceramic bottle in the form of a feline head. Felines symbolize authority in the Andes. Culture uncertain, central coast, Peru.
H. 13 cm. (5.1 in.) B/9103

important economic activities. These events helped coordinate diverse kinds of work, such as agriculture, herding, travel and transportation, mining, construction, and warfare. The nighttime calendar concerned natural forces: wind, water, and sacred places. Ceremonies imploring help from these forces were enacted in an ordered sequence of various sacred sites, or *zeques*, thus creating a calendar of religious events. Because this calendar used twelve periods, based on observations of the moon and stars, it did not account for thirty-seven days in the solar year. This period is related to the disappearance of the Pleiades from the night sky. Details of how the Inka coordinated these two calendrical systems is not yet well understood.

The Inka combined diverse landscapes and peoples in intricate and ingenious ways to create a large and wealthy empire. Behind them lay at least two thousand years of experience by Andean peoples whose varied environments and incredibly rich history were both wrought through conflict and forged through cooperation. The roads, rituals, site planning, and calendars that helped the Inka achieve their empire were part of a long evolution, though the present archaeological record does not allow us to trace their development in detail. The objects that people made and used were imbued with symbols integral to the ways individuals and groups communicated with one another.

Every successful society has a set of beliefs and visions that help justify its structures of rule and guide its activities. For the Inka, these were embodied in religion and in the myths that validated the rulers' right to rule and to cast the political and social order of the empire as part of the natural order. Sociopolitical growth and agricultural growth were analogous processes. The sun, the moon, thunder, rain, earth, stone, and other elements of nature all became part of the system, and an attempt was made to rationalize human activities so that they fit harmoniously into nature's scheme.

The long route toward understanding how the Inka fell victim so quickly to the invading Europeans points to two fundamentally different kinds of societies. The Inka could no better understand the ends and means of the invaders than the invaders understood those of the Inka. A system that had grown up mainly by weaving a delicate, complex balance of opposing forces was helpless to compete in a confrontation with a society interested primarily in immediate gain through force. Much of the region's future prosperity was blindly sacrificed for present aggrandizement, with no concern for lessons from the past. One continent shamelessly stole the riches of another.

CLOTH OF MANY KINDS, CLOTH FOR MANY PURPOSES

THE SYMBOLISM AND TECHNOLOGY OF TEXTILES

The quality of the clothing has been seen in Spain from samples that were taken there after this kingdom was conquered. The clothing of these Incas was shirts of this wool [of the camelids], some of them adorned with gold embroidery, others with emeralds and precious stones, and others with feathers; some were plain. For these garments they had such perfect dyes—red, blue, yellow, black, and other colors—that they truly excel those of Spain (Cieza, 1959 [1553]:177).

The beauty and technical virtuosity of Andean textiles have attracted acclaim since Europeans first saw them in the sixteenth century. Brilliant colors and intricate designs emerged from threads spun so finely and woven so tightly that the thread count in some fabrics reached five hundred per inch. Many different textile structures were developed, some so complex as to be weavers' tours de force. Textiles rank first in the repertory of Andean arts and technologies in both quantity and quality. The Spaniards found enormous storehouses filled with cloth at the time of the invasion. Tombs have yielded many thousands of garments and wrappings from pre-Inka periods. For preindustrial times, the scale of textile production was enormous.

John V. Murra has pointed out that during the time of the Inka Empire textile manufacture was the second most important economic priority. Only agriculture consumed more time and energy than cloth production. Although weaving was sometimes done by men, it was the principal activity of women. Even today the image of Andean women with their spindles in never-idle hands, spinning as they walk or engage in other activities, is a symbol of the region's productivity.

Textiles have been of great importance to Andean cultures since the beginning of cloth making in the region more than four thousand years ago. As a medium of artistic expression cloth preceded ceramics by more than a thousand years. Images, such as condors and two-headed serpents, created in textiles in the Preceramic period, were the basis of four millennia of Andean art. One of the richest finds of these early textiles was made by Junius Bird of the American Museum of Natural History at the Huaca Prieta site on the Peruvian north coast. Of the more than four thousand fabric fragments excavated and studied, he found that more than 70 percent were made by twining. In twining, two wefts are twisted over each other between the warp yarns, enclosing the warp as one passes behind and the other in front of it (fig. 172). Excavators also found weaving, looping, and knotting techniques. Looms and heddles (the latter lift some of the warp threads so that the weft threads can be passed through the warp easily and quickly) were invented several centuries later. Textiles in the earliest periods were rather small, until the looms and improved techniques made possible the enormous mummy wrappings and other large fabrics of later times.

Several factors may help to explain the unusual predominance of textiles in the Andes. Before the earliest textile production, mats were made by twining techniques that perhaps formed the basis for twined textiles. Once textile technologies began to emerge, their further development interrelated with other cultural processes. Cotton is perhaps most important among the early domesticated plants on the coast of the Peruvian

171 Model of a weaving scene illustrates the typical backstrap loom used for most Andean textiles. The two yarn figures of camelid fiber with needlework-covered faces wear cotton and camelid-fiber clothing that could have been woven on such a loom. The backstrap, or belt, allows the weaver to control the tension of the warp threads running between upper and lower loom bars. Chancay style, central coast, Peru.
32 x 35.5 x 23 cm. (12.6 x 14 x 9 in.) 41.2/5630

172 Twining. In twining, two wefts are twisted over each other between the warp yarns, enclosing the warp as one weft passes behind and the other in front of it.

Andes. Similarly, the domestication of camelids may be related to the use of their hair as textile fibers. The familiar idea that agriculture and herding serve primarily to secure a plentiful and stable food source is an oversimplification for the Andes, where providing fiber sources for textiles was almost equally important.

Once established, textile technology carried over into many areas, such as transportation engineering, architecture, and communication. Thatched roofs were built of grass bound together with rope in complex ways. Rope also bound together timber framing members, and sometimes it was incorporated within masonry walls to stabilize them. Bridges of braided rope stretched across many Andean rivers. Reed boats tied together with cords sailed on Lake Titicaca and up and down the Pacific coast. Accounts, and perhaps other information, were recorded on knotted and/or wrapped string khipu, as we have seen (see figs. 163, 164).

The tradition of creating fine textiles has proven to be one of the most durable of Andean achievements. Andean people still weave and wear cloth made in styles and techniques derived from customs that are thousands of years old. Much of our ability to appreciate and understand the extraordinary accomplishments of Andean fabric makers has been learned from modern Andean weavers. And the climate of the coastal deserts of Peru and Chile has contributed to the excellent preservation of ancient textiles. Ancient tombs provided dark, dry resting places where cloth was preserved with little humidity or temperature fluctuation.

The great textile achievements cannot be understood simply by looking at the fabrics and garments, however. Clearly, the Andean people appreciated the beauty of their weavers' products, but the importance of textiles lay not simply in the creation or possession of extraordinary objects. Like so many other aspects of life that we customarily separate in modern society, art was probably not a separate activity in the Andes. Textiles and other arts and crafts must be understood in their contexts—how they were used and what they meant in the culture of the time.

CLOTHING AND THE SYMBOLS OF DRESS

Andean textiles were used principally for clothing. Costume varied from place to place and from one period to another. Men commonly wore tunics over a large loincloth wrapped about the waist and groin. Tunics, at least in Inka times, were made from a single piece of cloth, doubled over, and sewn up the sides, with openings left for the arms; a slit in the center provided an opening for the head. Tunics were akin to the ponchos still used in most of the Andes. The length and width of tunics varied considerably with time and place. Although they never had cut and tailored sleeves, the tunics of Wari, Chimú, and some other cultures had short extensions over the arms. A man often wore a large cloak over his tunic in Inka times, especially

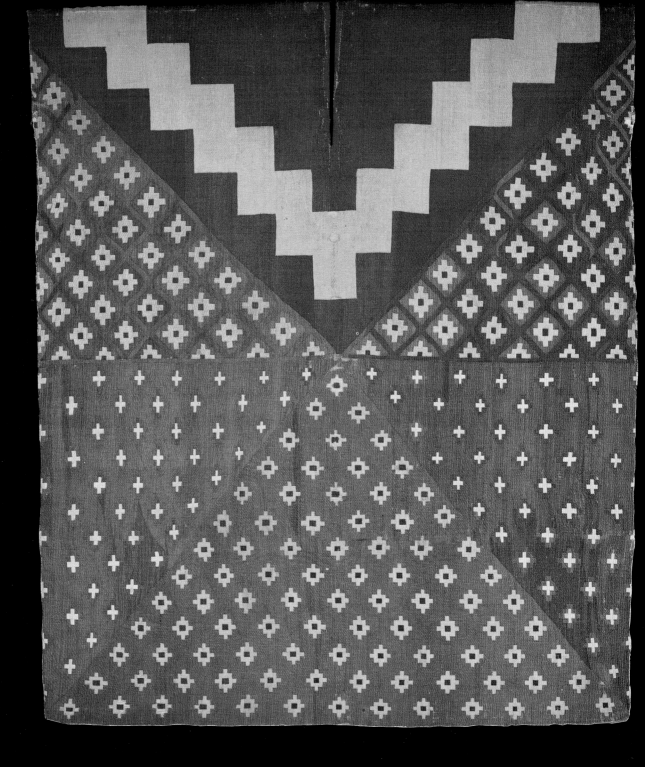

174 Shaped tapestry bag of camelid-fiber weft and cotton warp and tassels of twisted hide strips illustrates Andean excellence in tapestry weaving. Several techniques were sometimes combined to deal with the discontinuous wefts of the design. This bag, for example, has slits but also interlocking and dovetailing between the colors. Late Nazca style, south coast, Peru.

31 x 24 cm. (12.2 x 9.5 in.)

41.2/7682

in cold weather. In the Paracas period, men's garments included a wraparound kilt or skirt. Four-cornered caps made of knotted fabric, often covered with pile (see fig. 110), were characteristic of Tiwanaku and Wari cultures, but headdresses varied greatly. Sometimes they were simple cloth bands; but occasionally members of the nobility wore metal crowns decorated with cloth and feathers. Head adornment was the major index of ethnicity or class. In Inka times people were forbidden to wear the headdress of a group other than their own.

Women's garments tended to be larger and longer than men's. Inka women wrapped a large rectangle of cloth around their body, pinning it over the shoulders and tying it with a belt at the waist. This garment looked rather like a dress, though it was untailored. It was complemented by a mantle worn over the shoulders and fastened in front by a simple *tupu*, or pin, of copper, silver, or gold. Both sexes sometimes wore sandals with cord or leather soles and tied with cords; often elaborate, the cords were fashioned of camelid fiber, cotton, and other plant fibers.

Designs on clothing were richly symbolic in Inka times (see pages 174–177). Distinct patterns signaled differences in group membership. Some patterns symbolized the royal *panaqa*—the organizational divisions of the ruling elite. Certain garments were reserved for the ruler, and some of the royal vestments were used only once, for special rituals and calendar events. The description by Francisco de Jérez of the Inka ruler Atawalpa and his retinue entering the plaza of the city of Cajamarca, just before they were captured by Francisco Pizarro, not only gives an impression of the brilliance and color of the Inka court, but also implies that people dressed according to status and duties (see page 151).

The exact meanings of the designs on most Andean textiles will never be deciphered. Early Europeans were more concerned with subjugation and exploiting the great wealth of the New World than with understanding the details of the cultures that had accumulated such riches. Whatever their precise meanings, it seems that there was considerable standardization of the designs on tunics worn by Inka men. This practice assumed the use of visual insignia of group membership as a basic function of garments. Bright and highly visible designs told knowledgeable observers at a glance the ethnic identity and other key social and political characteristics of the people they encountered. Such designs also allowed them to perceive quickly the composition of a large group, such as the functionaries and officials Jérez saw accompanying Atawalpa. The capacity to communicate social identity quickly was essential, given the complex, patchwork quality of Tawantinsuyu and some of the earlier large states.

Symbols produced and reproduced in textiles were also important for communication between members of the groups who employed the weavers. We cannot yet trace the evolution of this use of symbols, but we know that their meanings depended on the social identities of the peoples producing them, and that both symbols and meanings changed over time. A few investigators have claimed that the meanings of some designs on Inka cloth were so standardized as to be a form of writing. Most, however, agree that the system of signs was not sufficiently complete, or flexible, to constitute writing in the sense of a system of codes for replicating spoken language.

While the bold, abstract symbols on Inka textiles seem to have had secular contexts, symbols and images on textiles from earlier Andean cultures appear to have had more religious content. Paracas textile designs incorporate rich imagery of plants, and especially animals, that populated the land, ocean, and sky and were part of the way of life of the people who buried their dead in the Paracas desert cemeteries. Anne Paul has suggested that many Paracas images portray humans, probably lords or rulers, dressed in the elaborate costumes of their ritual obligations of office. Some of these costumes enhanced their ability to impersonate the animals that probably played roles in their myths and related rituals. The symbolic images made the rituals clearer and easier to remember, and they probably also identified the roles of the various players.

Images on Paracas textiles seem rather directly representational. This tradition of animal imagery continued on the south coast into Nazca times (A.D. 100–700). Wari (A.D. 600–800) achieved what was perhaps the technological apex of Andean textiles. Wari weavers borrowed some of the imagery and brilliant coloring of the Nazca style along with imagery and ideas from other sources, particularly Tiwanaku. They created designs more complex and rigorously ordered than those from earlier periods. Rituals in which the textiles and their weavers played a part were apparently one aspect of a systematic religion. Religion and its accompanying ceremony (see chapter 7) was probably a central feature of Wari imperial expansion. The symbols associated with the state thus include images of gods and other representations related to religious ideas. By Inka times, textile designs became simplified and more abstract.

This simplicity allowed them to be interpreted more quickly by a larger number of people. The messages they bore were tied more to social, political, and ethnic concerns than to religion.

Textiles that look so bright, and often modern, in museum displays must be looked at in their Andean contexts. Their meanings changed substantially through the centuries, but their importance to communication and to Andean historical developments remained paramount. By helping define individuals and the groups they belonged to, textiles became vital to the way states and other political units functioned.

 ## BURIAL WEALTH

Most of the great wealth of Andean textiles now in museums was found in burials. Many are garments interred with the dead. Some are elaborate wrappings made for mummies. Peoples of the Paracas and Nazca cultures created spectacular mummy wrappings; many of them were made more than two thousand years ago. Mummies were tightly arranged into an almost fetal position and then wrapped with multiple layers of cloth and clothing, including large mantles or shrouds. Sometimes more than sixty layers of textiles covered a single mummy. Early burial mantles were often large (see fig. 42). Typically they measured about 2.3 to 2.8 meters (7.5 to 9 feet) by 1 to 1.4 meters (3.25 to 4.5 feet). The most spectacular examples were executed in polychrome embroidery on solid-color backgrounds. The images on these mantles are of fanciful animals and creatures that combine human and animal figures, probably representing people dressed in ritual attire. The animals include felines, two-headed snakes, birds, and foxes. Elements of conflict are noticeable and perhaps refer to ritual battle. Humans with spear-throwers are common, and they sometimes carry severed human heads.

 ## RITES OF PASSAGE: PERSONAL, POLITICAL, RELIGIOUS

Cloth as clothing and burial wrappings only begins to convey the multiple uses and meanings of textiles. Virtually all significant events in the life of an individual or a social group were marked by giving or exchanging textiles. The designs of the textiles that were exchanged as well as the occasions for passing them from one person to another were both special, and the textiles became enduring symbols of the event they marked. Ultimately, it was the pervasive social importance of cloth that led to both its quantitative importance in Andean economies and to the extraordinary flowering of textile technologies.

Victorious Inka rulers often gave rich gifts of cloth to their defeated foes as a way of initiating more peaceful relations. Such gifts were offered frequently, underscoring the mutual dependence of state and local officials at many levels of Inka society. What we might call diplomatic and administrative protocol depended greatly on textiles.

Cloth was as important to religion as it was to politics. Societies usually offer in sacrifice things that they consider especially valuable. In his 1653 account of Inka sacrifice, Father Bernabé Cobo tells of the importance of cloth:

[Offerings of] Fine clothing [were] just as common as that of the most frequent offerings. It was a part of nearly every sacrifice. Clothing was made for this purpose with certain ceremonies and in different ways. Part of it was men's garments and part of it women's; some of the garments were large and some small. They dressed the bodies of the idols and of the lords in this clothing, and put alongside them folded garments. Thus, not counting the garment that each idol already had, they put another garment next to it. However, the amount of clothing that was burned was so much greater that there was no comparison. In this there was also diversity. Sometimes they burned clothing alone, and other times they set fire to statues of men and women made of carved wood, dressed in this clothing, and in this way they burned them (Cobo, 1990 [1559]:117; see fig. 159).

Cloth and clothing also marked the great turning points of life, designating and confirming a new status: "The Inka and the people of Cuzco used to pierce the ears of their sons after they reached the age of fourteen, more or less, and give them silver and clothing. . . . Also it is common at the age of fourteen or fifteen to put the loincloth [*pañete*] on their sons with certain ceremonies which they call *warachikuy*" (Polo, 1916 [1567]:200).

As in most societies, Andean weddings required special textiles. Cloth used in weddings meant much more than rich and elaborate costume for the ceremonies. Social and economic relationships between the bride and groom and their relatives were underscored symbolically and economically with textiles. Of all the rites of passage, death was perhaps most elaborately marked by textiles. The extraordinary wealth of tombs at Paracas and elsewhere amply demonstrates this final tribute.

 ## CLOTH PRODUCTION

The Andean kingdoms invested enormous resources in producing cloth. Using textile techniques not very different from those of pre-Columbian times, Junius Bird calculated that more than five hundred hours of labor went into spinning and weaving a single poncho. We have only limited evidence on how the societies organized the massive labor effort needed for such an immense output. Spindles, spindle whorls, and weaver's tools are relatively common in the archaeological record, from all periods after the earliest textile production began. Centralized production of cloth in large quantities probably came only with large kingdoms, where it was important to make textiles with the imprint of the ruling elite. Evidence of what these textile workshops may have been like was found in excavations at the Inka city of Huánuco Pampa (see chapter 9). A walled textile workshop containing fifty structures served as the center's major production facility. A group of

women weavers, thought to be mamakuna, lived there on a full-time basis and seem to have formed one of the most important segments of the center's population. At the time, the Inka state was investing its enormous supply of labor to produce goods of special importance for economic and political growth. The rulers had to assure their supply of official garments and cloth gifts. Although as far as we know none of the cloth woven at Huánuco Pampa has been found, the circumstances of its production clearly testify to the state's strict control over the symbols used in textile designs.

Part of the Inka rulers' interest in state-centralized cloth production thus related to its economic and symbolic importance and to the advantage of stockpiling large quantities of textiles as gifts to their subjects. But a further interest was to create and control a series of essential signs and symbols important for defining and maintaining the ties between rulers and ruled. Future studies of earlier periods will perhaps explain the development of these symbolic and social aspects of cloth and clothing and the relationship of changes in the production system to such developments.

 ## THE TECHNOLOGY OF CLOTH PRODUCTION

The broad spectrum of uses and the great depth of meaning that textiles were given in Andean society translated into an extraordinary fiber technology. The Andean peoples used this technology to make many objects of daily use. Producing these objects required not only exceptional dexterity and artistic ability but also mathematical and engineering skills. As the importance and complexity of the Andean textile tradition has come to be appreciated, a number of specialists have conducted important research into its history and technology. It is impossible here to cover in depth the great diversity of techniques invented by Andean cloth makers. The following overview is drawn largely from texts and labels prepared by William Conklin, Consulting Curator for Textiles, and Vuka Roussakis, Textile Conservator, for the Hall of South American Peoples at the American Museum of Natural History. From it the reader can begin to understand the scale of Andean achievements in textiles.

 ## FIBERS FOR CLOTH

A wide choice of fibers was available in the Andes from both wild and domesticated plants and animals. Andean thread was among the finest in the world, and the great range of colors the Andean people achieved shows exceptional skill in dyeing. Ancient Andean cloth makers invented almost every known technique of weaving and textile structure. In the 1960s Junius Bird pointed out that the textile tradition "became almost a competition in ingenuity . . . an honored and remarkable combination of art and craftsmanship" (Bennett and Bird, 1964:193).

In the course of Andean textile history, every available plant and animal material with fibrous qualities was probably tested. Gradually, textile makers discovered the characteristics of each material and learned to make appropriate choices for constructing each textile. The earliest fiber used in the Andes was cotton. Probably domesticated there, *Gossypium barbadense,* or native Peruvian cotton, was cultivated in at least five natural shades ranging from white to dark brown. Soft, strong, flexible, absorbent, and easy to spin, it was used widely. The equivalent of wool in the Andes came from the hair of Andean camelids: the domesticated llama and alpaca and the wild vicuña. Camelid fiber is warm, resilient, and easy to dye. Adopted early in the highlands, it became the predominant textile material there, both because of its desirable qualities and because the camelids were best adapted to high altitudes, whereas growing cotton there was difficult or impossible.

Other fibers were sometimes used to make cloth and other textile products. In at least one instance, the fine hair of the viscacha, a burrowing rodent of the Chinchilla family, was combined with cotton and camelid wool to produce a bag. At times human hair was twisted and braided into cords; it was also used in wigs, headdresses, and other accessories. At other times it was woven into a loose-weave cloth. There is no evidence of this kind of cloth in some periods and areas, which suggests that some peoples may have had a taboo against using human hair.

Possibly the most exotic fiber used was bat hair. Bird, however, was convinced that it would be impossible to spin bat hair and that mention of

it in historical accounts probably referred to wrapping small pieces of bat hide around other fibers. The idea is nevertheless intriguing and suggests the extremes in unusual fibers that might be considered:

While Atahualpa was held prisoner by the Spaniards in Cajamarca, one day it happened that while he was eating in the presence of Spaniards who were guarding him, as he was taking a bite of food, a drop fell on the clothes that he was wearing, and, waving his hand to the maid who was holding his plate, he left the table and went to his chambers to change clothes, and he came out again wearing a dark gray shirt and cloak, and, noticing that it was softer than silk, [a Spaniard] asked him what his clothes were made of, the Inca responded that they were made from some birds that fly about at night in Puerto Viejo and Tumbez and bite people. In pursuing the matter, he said that it was from bat wool, and when the Spaniard asked him where so many bats could be gathered, he answered with these words: "What else would these dogs from Tumbez and Puerto Viejo have to do but catch these birds to make clothing for my father Guyna Capac?" (Cobo, 1983 [1653]:245)

Fibers from the thick, fleshy, often sword-like leaves of furcraea plants were often used in making items that required strength. The furcraeas are succulents closely related to the sisal-yielding agaves. Furcraea fibers commonly went into rope, slings, nets, sandals, mats, suspension bridges, and bags. Ritual artifacts, such as wigs on false mummy-bundle heads, sometimes also were made from furcraea fiber.

Stalks from a variety of sedges, another group of wild plants, were worked into basketry and used as a framework under woven cloth or wrapped yarn for objects, such as dolls, requiring support and shape but also pliability. In the textile fragments from Huaca Prieta, bast—fiber from the stem of certain plants—was sometimes combined with cotton to lend strength.

Textiles often incorporated feathers, some of them from birds of the Andean coast and highlands but most imported from tropical regions of the Amazon and the Ecuadorian coast. The bright feathers of macaws and parrots were assembled into accessories, such as plumes and fans, and used in ornamental apparel, such as earspools and headdresses. Often they entirely covered pieces of cloth and garments such as tunics and mantles (fig. 175). Accounts by the Spanish chroniclers indicate that people in Inka times especially prized feather textiles. Textiles were sometimes decorated with plaques of gold and other metals, bringing together the two realms in which Andean arts and technologies achieved particular distinction and illustrating their special genius in combining materials.

175 Amazonian parrot tail feathers attached to plain-weave cotton cloth with paired warps form this small, open-sided tunic. The feather quills are folded in rows over a thin cord, each knotted in place with another cord, and the row stitched to the cloth with a third cord. Amazonian parrot tail feathers are naturally green. The yellow color here was obtained by "tapirage": plucking the bird's feathers and rubbing the skin with toad skin secretion and a plant dye. The new feathers that grow back are yellow with a soft pink center. Chimú style, probably Chan Chan, north coast, Peru.
31 x 30 cm. (12.2 x 11.8 in.)
B/3165

177 Simple looping. Looped tunic of camelid fiber in geometric designs. Like twining, knotting, and wrapping, looping is not produced on a loom. In simple looping, the fabric is made with one continuous thread that forms rows of interconnected loops. Paracas style, Cerro Uhle, Ica Valley, south coast, Peru. 78 x 72 cm. (30.7 x 28.4 in.) 41.2/6083

176 Crossed looping. A human figure of camelid fiber with headdress, *tumi* knife, and staff, constructed by crossed looping. Such figurines were probably attached in a fringelike row to the edges of cloth. An amazing technical invention, this form of looping was done with a needle and thread, enabling textile artists in Paracas times and later to produce tiny but very detailed three-dimensional figures. These figures provide us with extensive information on costume and imagery. Nazca style, south coast, Peru.

5 x 4.5 cm. (2 x 1.8 in.) 41.2/6322

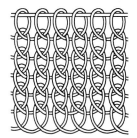

 # THE WEAVING PROCESS

Making cloth was one of the fundamental inventions of ancient peoples. It opened new horizons for producing useful goods and provided a major medium for aesthetic expression. Andean peoples devised an incredible variety of distinct ways of turning threads into fabrics. Each age and culture developed its characteristic techniques and designs.

Weaving, the most common process for making cloth, involves two sets of threads, the warp and the weft. Cloth making begins with the selection of the appropriate fibers for spinning thread. The fibers are then spun or twisted into threads of requisite strength, color, and flexibility. In Andean societies, women used a rotating stick, or spindle, to twist the fiber into a coherent yarn. The spindle whorl, a small flywheel that keeps the spindle rotating evenly, helped make the spinning consistent. Rotation could be clockwise or counterclockwise. Clockwise rotation forms what textile specialists call an S-trending spiral and counterclockwise rotation a Z-trending spiral. Both S and Z spinning relate to habit and tradition, not to the strength of the yarn. Usually, however, two yarns were twisted together, or plied, to form a stronger thread, which is especially important to the warp threads.

In the weaving process, the warp is a set of parallel threads held in place between the loom bars. The threads that cross over and under the warp at more or less right angles are called the weft. Except for the early periods of Andean weaving, yarn of dyed camelid fiber was often used for the weft to achieve brilliantly colored weft patterning. Little is known of dyeing procedures, but we know that dyers used mordants to fix the colors. Most of the dyes were derived from plants, but the cochineal insect was one source of red hues and a marine snail the source of purples in certain textiles. Blue was the only dye used for the Preceramic cotton textiles from Huaca Prieta. This blue dye has not been identified, but the indigo plant was the source of most blues in later Andean textiles.

 # TEXTILE STRUCTURE

Figures 172, 176, 177, 179, 180, 182, 183, 185, and 186 with their accompanying diagrams and descriptions illustrate the great range of textile structures used in the Andes and the magnitude of Andean achievements in both the art and technology of cloth making. In addition to twining, referred to early in this chapter, there were several other techniques for making textiles that did not involve using a loom. Two that were used often in Andean textiles are looping and crossed looping (figs. 176 and 177 and their diagrams). Wrapping, braiding, and knotting are other non-loom structures that were used throughout the history of Andean textiles. Loom techniques range from plain weaves of simple warp and weft structure through weaves of great complexity as the illustrations show.

178 Plain-weave triple-cloth band of camelid fiber features stylized sun faces. Three separate layers of gold, green, and brown, each with its own warp and weft, are woven together so that they go under and over each other to form the designs. Paracas style, probably Ica Valley, south coast, Peru.

89 x 7 cm. (35 x 2.8 in.)

41.2/5496

REGIONAL TEXTILE TECHNIQUES

Textile designs varied from one area of the ancient Andes to another. These regional variations often remained quite stable over time, although they slowly changed as new materials and techniques were discovered or introduced from other areas. Design variations reflected iconographies related to differences in religious images and in the symbols associated with group memberships. Specific textile structures also predominated in certain regions as did the direction of spinning thread.

The textiles of the south coast of Peru, which included the Paracas and Nazca cultures, showed the great inventiveness of these early peoples. Most of the techniques used in later textile production had already been invented. This advanced development began on the south coast during the Chavín period, when designs were made by wrapping colored camelid-fiber yarns around cotton warps, by slit tapestry, and by painting. The momentum of early textile development along the south coast continued through Wari times. Throughout this long complex history, individual threads were usually spun in a counterclockwise, or Z, direction.

Like the south coast, the central coast of Peru had a weaving history of at least 3,500 years before the Spanish arrived. Most early textiles were made of cotton, but camelid fiber was introduced from the highlands by about 300 B.C. and commonly used by A.D. 1000. Slit tapestry was a common technique (fig. 180). During the last three

179 Double cloth. Stylized birds
are among the figures in
this plain-weave double-
cloth pouch of cotton. In
double cloth, two separate
layers of weaving in con-
trasting colors, each with its
own warp and weft, are
woven together (under and
over each other) to form
the designs. The dark blue
and tan of this pouch
reverse on opposite sides.
Paracas style, Chongos,
Pisco Valley, south coast,
Peru.
41 x 41 cm. (16.1 x 16.1 in.)
41.2/7036

180 Slit tapestry. Half of a slit-tapestry tunic of cotton with camelid-fiber fringe features three standing figures wearing tunics and elaborate headdresses. In tapestry weave, the weft is compacted, or pushed tightly together, to cover the warp completely. The design is formed by discontinuous wefts of several colors. In slit-tapestry weaving, different colors of weft are separated between the warps. Central coast, Peru.
51.5 x 60 cm. (20.3 x 23.6 in.)
B/7781

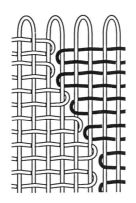

hundred years before the Spanish conquest, the central coast cultures, such as Chancay, were deeply influenced by the Chimú culture of the north coast. In early textiles from the region, both spinning directions occurred, but with Chimú influence **Z** spinning gradually decreased.

Some of the most interesting textiles on the central coast have been found in the graves of women. These cotton squares were woven as head-cloths in both plain weave and gauze. The almost transparent gauze fabrics (fig. 182), were sometimes tie-dyed—patterned by tying threads around selected portions of cloth to resist the dye.

The Moche and Chimú cultures of the north coast of Peru produced some of the most elaborate costumes of the ancient world. Most notable were the Chimú brocades and their use of supplemental materials and objects as attachments to basic textiles (fig. 183). Fringes of bells and tassels, surfaces of feathers, beads, and metal ornaments characterized many of their costumes, though Chimú weavers occasionally created austerely beautiful white costumes as well. Friezes on many of the adobe walls at Chan Chan, the Chimú capital, were probably patterned after textile designs. On the north coast, individual threads were normally spun in a clockwise, or **S**, direction, and their warps were often a pair of single threads rather than the plied threads common in other areas.

Textiles from the cultures of the highlands, such as Tiwanaku, Wari, and Inka, are rarely preserved because of the moist soils. However, garments suitable for their elite have been recovered from dry coastal tombs. Highland weavers made early and extensive use of warp patterning (figs. 184, 185), though tapestry with interlocked wefts was used for their highest-status textiles. Interlocked tapestries (fig. 186) distinguish highland weaving from coastal slit tapestries. Threads were normally **Z**-spun but then plied in pairs in the opposite direction, and most warps were of camelid fiber.

Weavers in the highlands of Bolivia and Peru today continue to make cloth in a style closely related to the pre-Hispanic tradition. The use and meaning of this weaving provide insights into the ancient significance of textiles. Evidence suggests, for example, that reversing the normal direction of spin in the creation of yarn makes it into a "magic" yarn, which can affect the spirits.

The incredible mastery of textile production achieved by ancient Andean women and men is one of the ancient world's greatest technological and artistic accomplishments. Textiles of cotton and camelid-fiber threads, bright colors, and frequent use of feathers and other decorative elements symbolize the ability of Andean peoples to combine materials from their varied lands. An occasional borrowing of techniques and styles from one area to another, while maintaining the integrity of local regional styles and techniques, is typical of the way the Andean world was organized. Local identities were retained while the advantages of interregional collaborations were kept open.

181 A flounderlike fish is painted on this plain-weave fragment of cotton. Chancay style, Surco, central coast, Peru.
55 x 35 cm. (21.7 x 13.8 in.)
B/4522

182 Gauze. Detail of a gauze headcloth of cotton. In gauze weave, the warps are not parallel but cross and recross each other and are held in place with interlaced wefts. Gauze weave lends itself to the creation of light, open fabrics that resemble lace. Designs in gauze can be geometric, like this one, or figurative, featuring humans and animals. Junius Bird noted that the eyes of figures on some gauzes had been created with added threads that had been spun in the opposite direction from the cloth itself. He suspected that this had been done for magical reasons. Chancay style, Chancay Valley, central coast, Peru.
62 x 56 cm. (24.4 x 22.1 in.)
41.2/6812

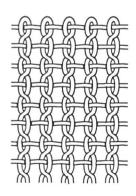

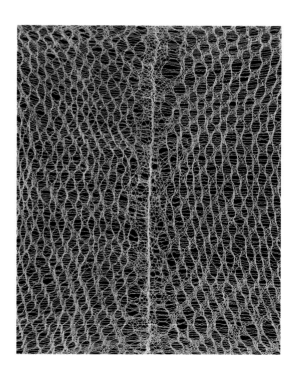

183 Brocade. Plain-weave cloth fragment of cotton with a camelid-fiber brocaded design of a standing male figure wearing a tunic, an elaborate headdress, and earspools. The plain weave was embellished by supplementary weft patterning, a technique in which the decorating weft is usually aligned with the weft threads and incorporated into the textile as weaving progresses. Introducing this weft only in certain areas to create individual designs, like the figure on the fragment, is a form of this technique called brocade. Chimú style, Paramonga, north-central coast, Peru.
43 x 22.5 cm. (16.9 x 8.9 in.)
41.1/223

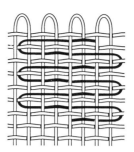

184 Warp-faced, plain-weave tunic of camelid fiber has discontinuous warps of different colors dovetailed around a common weft. The warps of warp-faced weaves entirely cover the wefts. When the warps of two adjacent colors alternately turn back around the weft separating the two color areas, they are dovetailed. Inka period, local highland style, Caudevilla, Peru.
35.5 x 77 cm. (14 x 30.3 in.)
41.2/7400

185 Warp patterning. Warp-faced plain-weave bag of camelid fiber with warp-patterned design bands, looped cotton fabric around the opening, and camelid-fiber braid on the edge. Inka bags are often warp-faced. To create the patterns, more than one set of warps can be used on the loom and interworked in various ways. In this example the S shapes and the eight-pointed stars are achieved by warp substitution: two sets of warps of contrasting color interlace with the weft one color at a time. Warp patterning, which grew in popularity during the Wari period, is the dominant textile structure used by highland weavers today. Inka style, Peru. 40 x 29 cm. (15.8 x 11.4 in.) 41.2/839

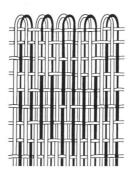

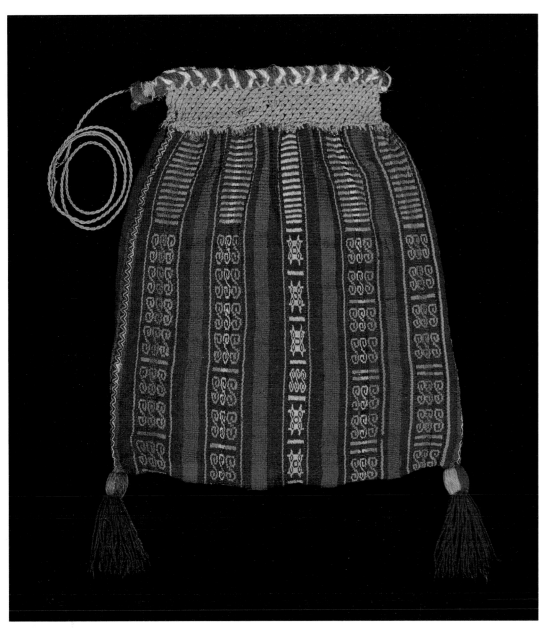

186 Interlocked tapestry. In many Andean textiles, the image reflects the textile structure. In this interlocked-tapestry tunic of camelid-fiber weft and cotton warp, for example, one of the repeated designs shows two double-headed, interlocked snakes. To make interlocked tapestry, the wefts are linked, or interlocked, at points of color change, creating a strong, clear color separation. Wari style, coast of Peru. 106 x 95 cm. (41.7 x 37.4 in.) 41.2/8604

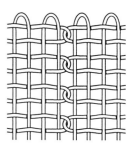

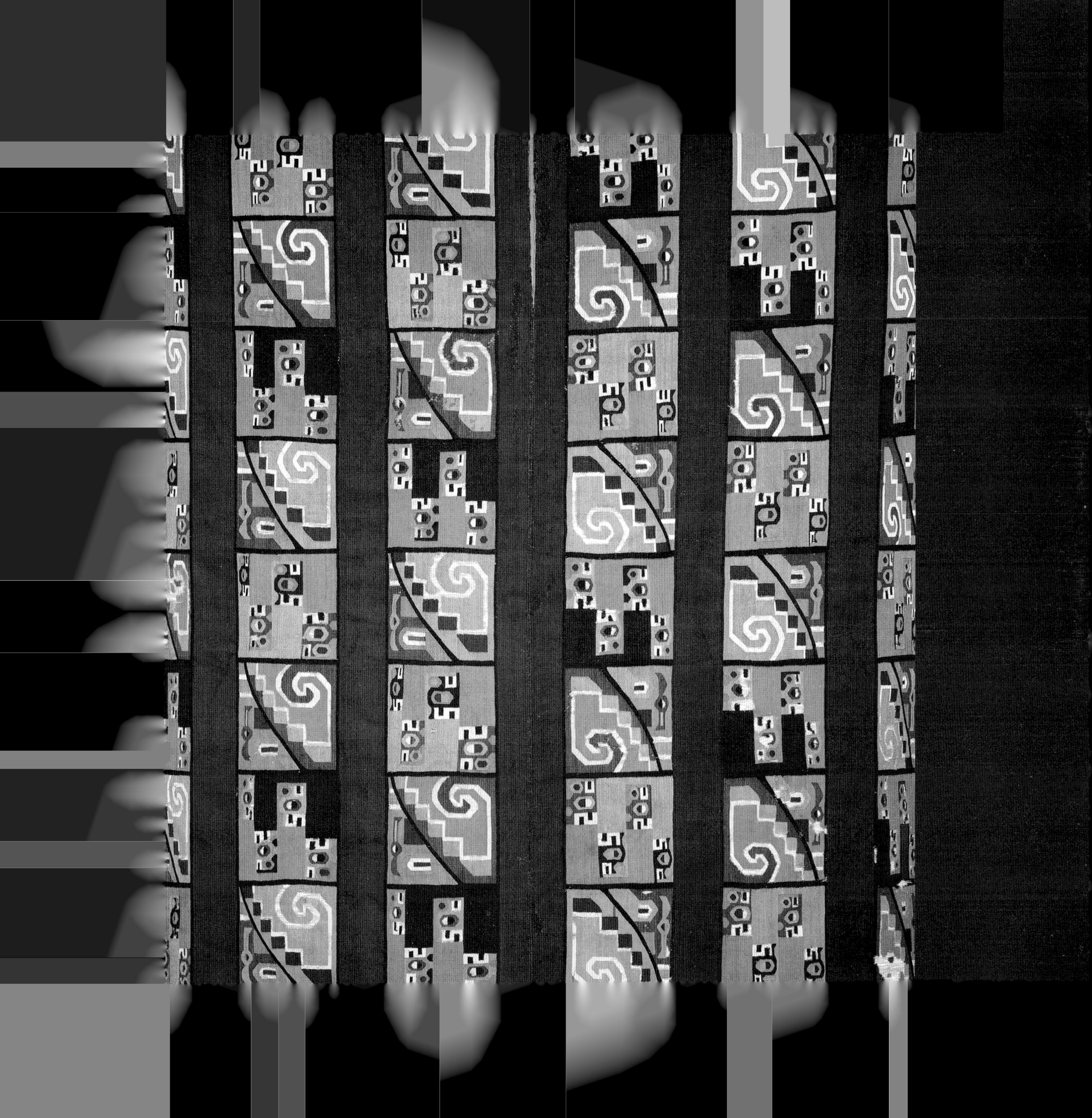

FLUTES, PANPIPES, AND DRUMS

THE INSTRUMENTS AND MUSIC OF CEREMONY

BY PETER KVIETOK

After having eaten and drunk repeatedly, and all being drunk, including the Inca and the high priest, joyful and warmed by the liquor, a little after midday the men assembled and began singing in a loud voice the songs and ballads which had been composed by their forebears, the burden of all being their gratitude to their gods and promises to return the benefits received. They also had many drums of gold, some of them set with precious stones, which were played by the women, who together with the sacred mamaconas took part in the singing. (Cieza, 1959 [1553]:182).

Accounts like this one by the sixteenth-century Spanish chronicler and soldier Pedro de Cieza de León are the richest indications we have for understanding the context of ancient Andean music. Many of the early Colonial documents describe the pageantry of state ceremonies in which music played the important role of transmitting a people's identity and pride. Others allude to different moods, such as the expression of sadness in funeral music. Written by Europeans and men of mixed European-Indian parentage, these early Colonial chronicles often are weighted by Western cultural bias. Certain largely descriptive passages, however, are models for reconstructing the use of musical instruments and song.

Ancient Andean musical traditions are preserved in part through the many musical instruments that still survive. They include ceramic and cane panpipes, conch-shell and ceramic trumpets, metal and bone flutes, and numerous other wind and percussion instruments. The variety of musical instruments used by the Inka show no great innovations or changes from those of their predecessors. Indeed, relatively few musical instruments from the Inka period have been found that match the technical levels and aesthetic qualities of earlier examples from the many coastal peoples. This lack of evidence may be explained in part by the Spaniards' intentional destruction of many musical instruments and by the natural deterioration of instruments made of perishable materials such as wood, gourd, cane, and hide. We have, however, vivid sixteenth-century descriptions of the components and construction of instruments and of their use and ceremonial maintenance.

They had drums made of the bodies of their principal rebels and traitors and they called these runatinya, they were intact as in life and with their own arms beat on their stomach, with skulls of other rebels they made vessels to drink corn beer and flutes from their bones. (Waman Puma de Ayala, 1980 [1615]: 164)

The earliest examples of musical instruments come from the south-central coast of Peru and consist of bone flutes found in a grave about 5,700 years old. The earliest musical instruments from the highlands are a bone whistle and an unfired clay whistle from the Temple of the Crossed Hands at Kotosh, dating to 2500 B.C. Evidence from early periods suggests that all Andean music was based on a combination of wind and percussion instruments. This combination was used throughout most of the Americas. The string instruments currently used in the Andes, one of which, the *charango*, is unique to the region, were introduced after the Spanish invasion.

187 Trumpet of *Strombus galeatus* shell with copper alloy mouthpiece has two human figures incised on the surface. Moche style, Peru.
L. 24 cm. (9.5 in.) B/9164

188 Incised and painted ceramic figure of a panpipe player. Paracas style, south coast, Peru.

H. 22.3 cm. (8.8 in.) 41.2/7944

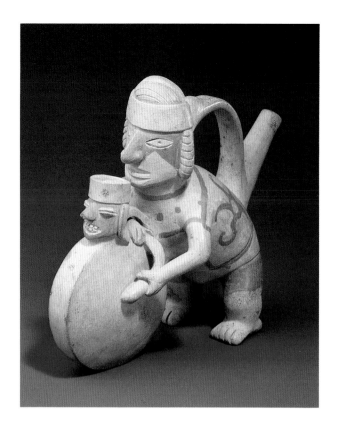

189 Stirrup-spout ceramic bottle modeled and painted in the form of a man playing a drum adorned with a human head. Salinar style, north coast, Peru.

H. 19.3 cm. (7.6 in.) 41.2/8673

The most common Andean wind instruments are *kenas*, notched and unnotched end flutes; *antaras* or *sikus*, panpipes; *guepas*, trumpets; and *ocarinas*, whistles that produce a variety of tones. These instruments are made of diverse materials including bone, cane, fired clay, gourd, hide, metal, wood, and even the quills of bird feathers. Percussion instruments include two basic categories: membranophones and idiophones. Membranophones produce sound through the vibration of a membrane with an attached resonance chamber, and idiophones, through the direct contact of two surfaces that can vary in elasticity.

Membranophones used in pre-Columbian times were various kinds of drums, with a membrane or skin head, made of animal or sometimes human skin, and a resonance chamber of reinforced hide, wood, ceramic, bone, or metal. Drums were especially important, as indicated by the vivid descriptions in the early Spanish documents and the elaborate archaeological examples that survive today.

Idiophones included a seemingly infinite variety of bells, clappers, dangles, rattles, and the like. These were used not only as separate instruments but also as parts of implements, dress, elements of architecture, and, in general, as attachments to almost any ritual object that was moved during its use or presentation. These nonmelodic, rhythm-producing instruments seem to have been especially favored by the northern peoples, such as the Moche, who used a rich array of idiophones during their many rituals and public ceremonies.

Andean instruments usually were played by groups of performers. The composition of these groups cannot be established with certainty, although it is clear that percussion and wind instrument pairing existed since the earliest evidence of musical performance in the Andean world. Images of large musical groups include varied combinations of wind and percussion instruments. Perhaps one of the more interesting details that we can reconstruct for such a group is the idea of paired, or dual, instruments that presumably were played in a way that allowed completion of a full scale. Evidence for this technique (also called musical dialogue, or playing in hocket) is most frequent in ancient representations of paired panpipe players, although matched pairs of ancient trumpets have also been found. This playing technique survives today in the Andean altiplano and in the Amazon basin. It allows each musician brief periods of rest that are extremely important in otherwise sustained playing with no substantial rest intervals. This dialogue in Andean music might also relate to the binary nature of Andean social and political organization.

Music provides a way to enhance the beliefs, values, and aspirations of a participant group. It is also unifying because its performance creates a ritual framework that encourages intergroup communication and thereby social cohesion. Musical instruments are often associated with concepts of power and authority as well as with the spiritual realm (the Andean *pututu*, or conch-shell trumpet; see fig. 187).

Instrumental music, song, and dance were woven into the fabric of Andean religious, social,

190 Blackware ceramic *kena*, a type of flute, with an incised design and a modeled animal figure near the mouthpiece. Probably Inka period, Ica Valley, south coast, Peru.
L. 22.2 cm. (8.7 in.) 41.0/1625

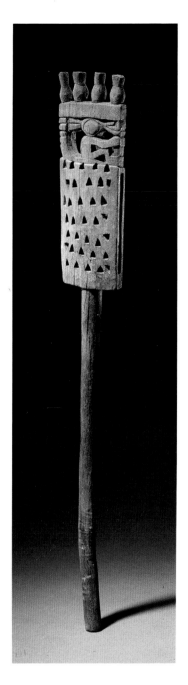

191 Carved wooden rattle
stick, decorated with a
seated human figure.
Seeds or pebbles
inside the rattle pro-
duce the sound. Cul-
ture uncertain, coastal
Peru.
L. 66.1 cm. (26 in.)
B/5600

and ceremonial life. It has been argued that musical traditions in the Andes manifest one of the more conservative aspects of culture, showing great continuity through the centuries. The decision by the Spaniards to ban musical performances in homage to ancestors and to burn instruments indicates the importance of music as a form of resistance to Western influence. In the second half of the sixteenth century a messianic movement called *Taki Onqoy,* or dance fever, achieved wide popularity in the Andes. Participants in this revitalization movement were known to enter into uncontrollable dance frenzies, after being possessed by the resident spirits of *wakas,* or ancient shrines. In the most extreme cases, possessed people hurled themselves from high peaks or into raging rivers with the conviction that the yoke of Spanish subjugation was soon to be overcome.

An analogous present-day example is the Dance of the Scissors, a highland dance thought to have pre-Hispanic roots. In this dance, participants wearing elaborate costumes engage in competitive paired movements while manipulating scissors that make sounds, as the dancers perform to the accompaniment of Andean harp and violin. Dancers often are said to enter into a pact with supernatural forces, such as the spirits of sacred mountains, to gain the strength and endurance to withstand and surpass their competitors' dance movements and self-inflicted, pain-invoking acts. The dance's symbolism reaffirms the power of the ancient earth spirits who can help conquer all enemies. These examples illustrate the role of musical performance in affirming identity, an important element of Andean music.

Written sources from the period immediately after the Spanish Conquest indicate that musical performance formed a part of nearly every Inka event or ceremony of public significance. Some of the ceremonies documented for the Inka period include funerals of important persons, ancestor worship, and musical performances related to ritual battles and military victories. Music also was a major feature of countless ritual events scheduled by the solar and lunar calendars. Such performances were enacted to communicate with the supernatural forces believed to control the life cycle. These rites pervaded every level of Andean society, and they were vital in preserving social groups, organizing labor, and marking political and religious change. Colonial documents indicate that dance was an integral part of these public ceremonies. The dancers' movements and elaborate costumes, in combination with instrument playing and singing, helped to transmit the ritual significance of an event. Although it is difficult to ascertain the relative importance of dance in these ancient rituals, the Quechua word *taki,* which means both "singing" and "dancing to the rhythm of song," implies that dancing was inseparable from singing.

The sung recital of historical events by poets was an especially important means of remembering and perpetuating Inka mythical history. These chants were performed for Inka nobility at state ceremonies, such as the Inti Raymi, or winter solstice festival; and they were part of the prolonged lamenting that occurred at the death of an Inka. The chants could be performed to include and encourage group response, and often they were accompanied by drum playing and dancing.

Musical performance was unquestionably a vital part of the diverse ceremonies that marked and—to a degree—structured life throughout the ancient Andes. In some images painted on pottery, musicians are depicted in scenes that seem to commemorate successful harvests and other events of the agricultural cycle. Unfortunately, we have only scattered fragments of such depictions and scant evidence from archaeological sites where the instruments that appear in such scenes were found.

Many of the images of the ceremonies in which music played an important role involve a supernatural element, either through figures with nonhuman attributes or the depiction of activities associated with, or directed toward, supernatural forces. Some of these images show that music was a powerful element in the human sacrifice rituals that led to the presentation of blood-filled goblets to priests or rulers as well as for the display of severed heads or human offerings atop high mountain peaks.

In the frequent depictions of funerary ceremonies in the Moche culture, and to a lesser degree in Nazca, performance on a wide variety of musical instruments accompanies the presentation of diverse offerings and other ritually prescribed behavior. These depictions also must be understood in the context of ancestor worship, an important aspect of Inka religion and cosmology, and presumably of many earlier Andean cultures. Music may have been the medium of communication with deceased ancestors, who were believed to

192 Single-piece ceramic drum, with deerskin drumhead. Paracas style, south coast, Peru.
L. 63 cm. (24.8 in.) 41.2/6220

remain active in ritual life. The significance of certain ceremonial songs today among the Amuesha, an Amazonian group, provides an analogy. The Amuesha believe that these songs are the language of sacred power and the only means by which the deities communicate with one another and with mortals. Contemporary Chipaya groups from the southern altiplano consider the haunting sounds produced on their cane panpipes to be the sounds of their ancestors, the *apus,* and the sounds that express their collective memory.

Scenes that show military confrontations or conflict rarely include musicians, but in those that depict the proud heralding of the victor over the vanquished, orchestral assemblages mark the presentation and display of arms and captives. The spoils of war were meant to appease and supplicate the supernatural forces.

Some evidence suggests that spirit healers used rattles in their repertoire of sacred objects to summon supernatural forces, to fend off harmful spirits, and to purify the curing ceremony. The unrelenting rhythm of the rattle also helped to induce a trancelike state in the healer, and to a certain degree in the others present.

Musical instruments discovered by archaeologists at various sites offer another view of musical context. Intact musical instruments are found most often in tombs, implying a strong magico-religious value. Recent excavations at Sipán in the Lambayeque Valley and Kuntur Wasi in the north highlands have unearthed spectacular examples of musical instruments. One of the Moche lords buried at Sipán was accompanied by a gold and silver rattle. This instrument is covered with images of a ritualized and bloody scene of war captives being presented to a Moche lord. At the site of Kuntur Wasi three Strombus trumpets covered with cinnabar were among the objects found in the tomb of an ancient local ruler.

Large and open elevated plazas or patios were used for ceremonies that almost certainly had a strong musical component. After these ceremonies the instruments were intentionally smashed. Evidence for this custom is abundant in the coastal regions at sites such as the Pyramid of the Sun, a Moche ceremonial center, and the Nazca ceremonial center of Cahuachi. Similar rituals were also enacted in small, narrow subterranean structures built by the Recuay people. Numerous ceramic trumpet fragments have been found in these structures. Further evidence from such sites suggests that ritual feasting and drug consumption were some of the activities that accompanied musical performances. Although the most important role of music was ceremonial, systematic surveys in the past two decades have begun to provide evidence that it was also played in nonceremonial settings, probably for recreation and entertainment. Musical instruments found at residential sites lack the fine level of workmanship and elaborate finish of their ceremonial counterparts, but their acoustical properties remain true.

A sixteenth-century description emphasizes the strong regionalism of performance style in the Andes:

Inca Pachacutec came out to receive his brother and the prince, his son, with a solemn triumph and great festivities which had been prepared. . . . All the tribes who

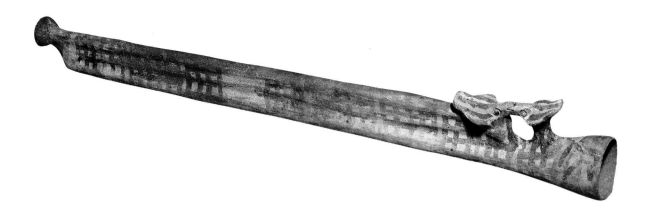

lived in the city and the curacas [local leaders] who came to take part in the celebrations marched in separate groups with their various instruments, drums, trumpets, horns and shells, according to local usage, with various new songs composed in their own language in praise of the deeds and excellencies of the captain general Cápac Yupanqui and his nephew, Prince Inca Yupanqui (Garcilaso de la Vega, 1966 [1609]:347).

Similarly, the illustrated manuscript of Felipe Waman Puma de Ayala provides vivid depictions of musical performances as regional identity markers. His drawings show musicians, singers, and dancers whose performances were characteristic of the four *suyus,* or quarters, of the Inka realm.

By consulting early documents it is possible to demonstrate certain correlations between pre-Hispanic musical preferences and language or ethnic groups. Among the best examples are the early Quechua and Aymara dictionaries, which show significant, distinct trends for these two groups. Among the Aymara, wind instruments, or different kinds of flutes, were known by a great variety of names, while the Quechua language is comparatively limited in assigning names to this instrument type. Furthermore, the generic term for "musician" in Aymara was *pincollori*—a player of the *pincollo,* or flute. In Quechua, by contrast, a musician was one who knew how to invent a song, or memorize great numbers of them. In further contrast, in Quechua the drum seems to have assumed primary importance, if we consider the varied compounds that were formed with the word *huancar,* or drum. Many compound word constructions incorporating terms for musical instruments entered Quechua and Aymara speech, attesting to their importance in daily life.

Recently discovered patterns of musical traditions from the earlier periods of Andean prehistory suggest similar regional distinctions. For instance, ceramic panpipes were common among nearly the entire central Andean coast, but it is in the Ica-Nazca region, from 300 B.C. to A.D. 500, that they were produced in great quantities and with exceptional technical and aesthetic sophistication. Wind instruments, in general, were common in the entire coastal region during this time span, but the preferred material for pipes in other areas was cane rather than clay. The northern cultures showed a preference for non-melodic, rhythmic sound in many ritual contexts, as seen in the large number of musical instruments and ornaments that produced rattling, clanging, and ringing sounds.

Variability is also evident throughout the last four thousand years of prehistory on the coast, where natural conditions have allowed the preservation of great quantities of ancient cultural materials. For instance, musicians in the pre-Chavín period seem to have developed and preferred a large variety of complex whistles, capable of producing a wide range of pitches. In later cultures these were replaced by flutes and panpipes.

Colonial documents provide extensive information about musical instruments, playing styles, and performance contexts, but there is virtually no evidence that offers even a tentative reconstruction of the sounds related to ancient musical

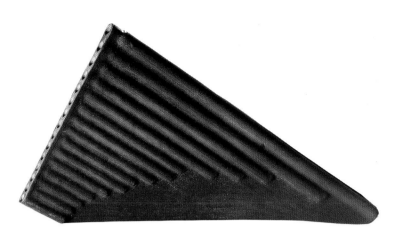

194 Each tube of this fifteen-tube ceramic panpipe with a slip-painted surface was individually formed and joined. Nazca style, south coast, Peru.

L. 49 cm. (19.3 in.) 41.2/7889

traditions. No notational system for music has been recovered from the pre-Hispanic period, and no melodies heard at the time of the Spanish Conquest were transcribed. During the centuries of contact with Western musical culture, under repressive Colonial rule, native musical expressions were profoundly altered.

There is therefore no possibility of listening to Inka music as an Inka audience would have heard it. Careful experimentation with ancient instruments, however, has led to some preliminary but important musicological conclusions. Among the results are the definition of the variety of sounds that any one instrument can produce (pitch registers); differences between the sounds (intervals) and the different ways of producing them; dimensional relationships between parts of an instrument and parts of a related instrument set; and possible acoustical relationships between similar instrument types. No doubt many of these technical qualities changed throughout prehistory as construction technology and acoustical sophistication evolved. Cultural preferences for different musical styles also influenced the complex process of change and permanence.

Experimental acoustical research has focused on the ancient panpipe, a wind instrument whose open-mouth and closed-end tubes can be grouped in diverse configurations and combinations. Attempts to fit specific musical elements, such as precise scales, to archaeological data are futile. Nevertheless, the work of many investigators supports the conclusion that the music cultures of Andean prehistory had multiple and different musical scales, and this can be observed today among many Andean musicians. Furthermore, defining a scale (a regular, fixed succession of intervals) is complicated by the fact that pitch varies considerably according to the construction details of the instrument, the positioning of its finger holes, and its intonation style. It is now clear that later and contemporary Andean musical scales produced by cane panpipes were and are simpler than the variety of scales developed by ancient musicians for their fired-clay panpipes.

Today, the rural immigrants who swarm into the coastal capital city of Lima arrive with much of their culture intact, and it is music that constitutes one of the most important symbols of their identity.

195 Matched rattles of copper
alloy with incised surface
designs. Moche style, north
coast, Peru.
L. 26.8; 27.8 cm. (10.6; 10.9 in.)
41.2/5430, 5431

ALL THAT GLITTERS

INVENTIONS AND USES OF METALLURGIES

The Inka treasure that so dazzled the gold-greedy Spanish invaders was created with techniques based on age-old Andean metalworking traditions. These traditions began some two millennia before Spanish ships began to prowl Peru's waters. Although metallurgies also existed in Colombia, Central America, and northwestern Argentina, the earliest metalworking technologies developed in the Central Andean region, including Peru and the southern altiplano area of Peru and Bolivia.

Both Peru and Bolivia abound in ores and native metals, and the earliest technologies arose in areas where these resources were readily available. By the fourth century A.D. north-coast metal smiths had developed a great many techniques to gild or silver copper. Toward the end of the first millennium technologies had emerged on the north coast to produce arsenic bronze, an alloy of copper and arsenic. At the same time, altiplano smiths had developed tin bronze, a metal that became one of the hallmarks of Inka expansion in the fifteenth century.

Metal in the Andes had a special status. It was a symbol of power and held religious significance among Andean peoples. Gold objects, such as headdresses, nose ornaments, or earspools were exclusively for the elite and conveyed social status. The Inka, for instance, reserved gold and silver earspools for their nobility. The Sicán people, who flourished on Peru's north coast four centuries before the Inka conquest of the region, buried their nobles with gold or gilded-copper funerary masks. Some Sicán tombs contained hundreds of metal offerings.

Gold was the earliest metal worked in the Andes, but copper provided the foundation for the emergence of one of the world's most sophisticated metallurgies. Copper served as the matrix metal for the important Andean alloys: copper-arsenic and copper-tin bronze, copper-silver, and copper-gold. The last two alloys figured prominently in Andean production of silver and gilt-metal objects. Those areas closest to specific raw materials developed independent traditions and innovations, based on readily available resources. Copper, for example, is abundant on Peru's north coast, both as carbonate and oxide ores, and it is found in veins of arsenic-rich sulfide ores in the highlands to the east. These sulfide ores were used to produce arsenic bronze. Cassiterite, the oxide of tin, is found in the altiplano, and the smiths there developed tin bronze. Gold was panned in rivers and extracted from mines, such as Pataz east of Trujillo, the Carabaya region east of the altiplano, and the area around La Paz, in what is now Bolivia. Innovations in metallurgy spread from the Central Andes north to Central America and south to northwestern Argentina and northern Chile. Imaginative Colombian smiths excelled at manufacturing gold objects using the lost-wax method, a technique that was known to Peruvian smiths but not as readily used.

Little is known of pre-Hispanic mining techniques, in part because many of the prehistoric mines were later exploited by the Spaniards, and most traces of pre-Hispanic mining have disappeared. Most often, miners followed the metallic-ore veins closely, excavating narrow tunnels to extract the richest mineral. An idea of the tools used by ancient miners can be surmised from the

196 This Vicús nose ornament representing a spread-winged owl is hammered from a single sheet of gold and decorated with dangles. The iconography recalls goldwork from the Lambayeque Valley site of Sipán. Northern Peru. H. 11.6 cm. (4.6 in.) 41.2/8692

215

197 Filigree decorates a Darien-
style gold pendant, made
by the lost-wax method.
The upper part may be a
headdress ornamented with
two large disks. Antioquia,
Colombia.
H. 13.5 cm. (5.3 in.) 41.0/1652

discovery in the last century of so-called Copper Man, a pre-Hispanic miner who died some fifteen hundred years ago as he was extracting atacamite, a copper ore. Copper Man was discovered near the mine of Chuquicamata, in the Atacama Desert, today Chile's largest copper mine. Arid conditions and alternating warm days and cold nights helped to preserve the body. Scattered about the miner were his tools: four hafted stone hammers, wooden scrapers and sticks, a hide bag, and four coiled baskets.

Documented discoveries of early metal finds in the Andes are widely scattered. Widespread looting since Colonial times, and especially in this century, has made it difficult to trace the provenience of the majority of Andean metal objects displayed in museums and private collections. But the recent scientific excavations of lavish, gold-filled tombs at Sipán, Kuntur Wasi, and Batán Grande will allow archaeologists, art historians, and other specialists to place such finds in context.

The earliest documented evidence for metalworking in the Andes comes from the site of Waywanka in Andahuaylas. There, archaeologist Joel Grossman uncovered pieces of hammered gold foil and gold-working tools made of stone. The finds have been dated to 1500 B.C. At Chavín de Huántar, Richard Burger found in an elite residence a sheet of hammered gold foil associated with Janabarriu phase ceramics (400–200 B.C.). This phase marks the beginning of the Chavín florescence and the next documented finds (see chapter 5) are all associated with the spread of the Chavín cult.

Chavín gold objects were made of hammered metal, indicating that this Andean tradition was already well established. Repoussé decoration was common and new techniques, such as soldering and welding, were commonly used. Earlier Chavín objects were made of native gold, while later pieces were crafted from gold-silver alloys. According to Heather Lechtman, the spread of the Chavín cult was tied to new techniques in metallurgy, and innovations in metalworking and weaving may be directly linked to the spread of portable Chavín-style objects crafted in metal and cloth. As discussed in chapter 5, the majority of objects from this period served either a ceremonial or an ornamental function.

At Kotosh, archaeologists found two sheets of gold and a gold ring dated to the Kotosh-Chavín phase. The most spectacular discoveries from this period, however, fall later in the Chavín sequence, sometime about 200 B.C. These discoveries are from a cache of gold objects said to come from a single grave at Chongoyape in the Lambayeque Valley. They include three crowns, a gold headband, gold tweezers, and four undecorated and seven decorated earspools. All were crafted from hammered sheet gold and decorated with repoussé images of jaguars in various guises.

Another group of objects, first described by S. K. Lothrop, is also said to be from Chongoyape. In this cache are pottery, a stone bowl, a spoon, a ring, an anthracite mirror, and various metal objects made of sheet gold. A third cache from the

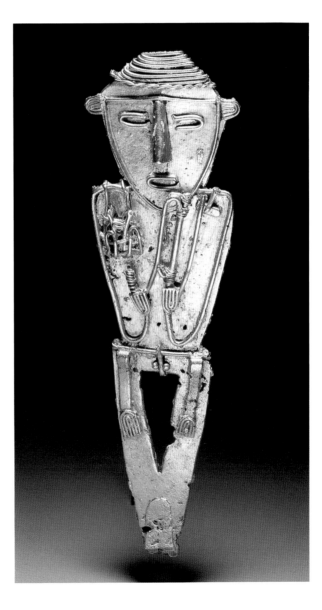

198 This gold *tunjo*, a type of figurine used as a religious offering, was cast from a wax model surrounded by a ceramic mold. When molten metal was poured into the ceramic mold, it melted the wax model inside. A few tunjos have been found on lake bottoms in highland Colombia. Provenience unknown.
L. 7 cm. (2.8 in.) 41.2/7713

same area includes gold nose ornaments, earspools, and spoons. Perched on one spoon, the hollow-gold figure of a man blows a silver Strombus trumpet. This spoon is now in the Robert Woods Bliss Collection of Pre-Columbian Art at Dumbarton Oaks. Most of the objects from this cache were made of gold with a high silver and low copper content and could be crafted either of a naturally occurring alloy or, in the case of one nose ornament, a deliberately produced alloy.

The Chongoyape area has produced other stunning gold objects. A set of seven hollow-gold jaguars was looted there in the late 1920s. Today these jaguars are scattered in museums and private collections around the world. Each jaguar is approximately 11 centimeters (4.4 inches) long and is made of twelve shaped pieces of hammered sheet gold. The two halves of the body are joined with pieces of copper-silver alloy solder while the legs, ears, and tail were assembled by the process known as sweat welding, in which edges are joined directly by melting their surfaces with high heat. Each jaguar has four pairs of suspension holes, two in the tail and two just above the foreleg, indicating that the jaguars formed part of a necklace. Inside the jaguars there are pebbles, and repoussé pelage marks delineate the irregular spots on their coats. Probably shaped over a carved wood or stone form, the jaguars are so similar that they seem to have been made in the same workshop. According to Lechtman, the closest stylistic and technical parallel is the gold spoon in the Bliss Collection, which also has suspension holes. There are stylistic and technical similarities, too, to the goldwork from the Lambayeque Valley site of Sipán (see chapter 6),

which included hollow-gold jaguar-head necklaces that rattle and are perforated with suspension holes.

In the southern highlands, smiths had already developed copper-working technology by 1000 B.C. Although there are no published analyses of the finds, Bolivian archaeologists report finding copper slag in the earliest levels at Wankarani and Pukará de Belén near Tiwanaku. Discoveries on Lake Titicaca's east shore record a similar date for copper ores found at Chiripa. In Cuzco, an area influenced by the Titicaca basin, advances in metallurgy are evidenced by the Echenique Plaque and the Oberti Disk looted in the last century. The Oberti Disk is crafted from a hammered copper alloy and decorated with an incised design. The Echenique Plaque is made of thin, hammered sheet gold and embossed with a repoussé decoration.

NORTHERN INNOVATIONS

From A.D. 1–600, particularly in the coastal valleys that once formed the heartland of the Moche realm, Andean metallurgy reached its pinnacle of creativity and technical mastery. Metalworking by the contemporary Nazca and earlier Paracas cultures of the south coast never reached the sophistication achieved by the northern smiths. The majority of metal finds from this area consist of hammered sheet-gold mouth masks and nose ornaments similar to those worn by deities portrayed on Nazca textiles and ceramics. At Paracas,

199 A shell container is decorated with gold sheet and shell inlays of different colors. Culture uncertain, northern Peru.

H. 7 cm. (2.8 in.) B/9318

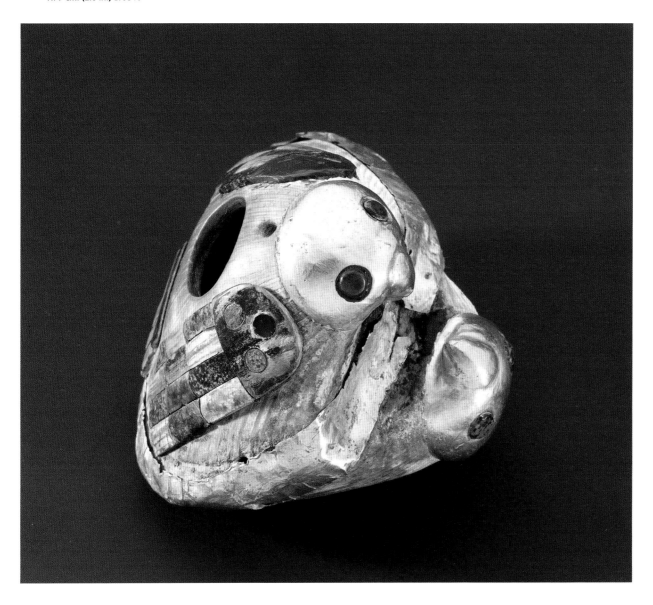

archaeologists found hammered-gold ornaments, including face and mouth masks, diadems, hair pendants, forehead ornaments, and miniature pieces of hammered gold wrapped among the layers of textile offerings in mummy bundles.

Until 1987, when archaeologists found the first tomb at Sipán, only a handful of Moche metal finds had come from controlled excavations. These include objects from Uhle's excavations at the pyramids at Moche; the tomb of the warrior priest in Virú; a burial excavated on the Huaca del Sol at Moche that contained a pair of gold earspools decorated with a mosaic inlay; and several Moche tombs excavated in the Santa Valley. Before Sipán, the largest group—more than five hundred objects—of Moche works of art in metal came from widespread looting in the 1960s of early Moche tombs in the Vicús area of northern Peru. The iconography and technology of the Vicús finds have been widely studied, but the context of these discoveries is still poorly understood. But, as discussed in chapter 6, the discoveries at Sipán and at the looted Jequetepeque Valley tomb site of La Mina are certain to shed new light on the Vicús enigma, since they show striking similarities to Moche metalwork and ceramics from Vicús.

Metallurgy in Ecuador and Colombia also influenced the smiths of northern Peru. Gold nose ornaments with filigree work from Vicús, for example, are similar to those found in Ecuador and Colombia (fig. 201), and a hollow-gold figurine, allegedly from Frias, near Piura, recalls ceramics and metalwork from Guangala in Ecuador.

Little is known of Moche metalworking sites, because no metalworking shops or smelters have been excavated. But one Moche ceramic vessel portrays four men manipulating metal objects that are lying over a domed structure.

With the exception of tin bronze, developed in the southern highlands, Moche smiths were familiar with almost every metalworking technology known to Andean metallurgists: the smelting of copper carbonates and oxides, the creation of copper-gold and copper-silver alloys, experimentation with copper-arsenic alloys, the casting of large objects, lost-wax casting, hammering, and annealing. Moche smiths also knew many techniques for assembling metal objects: soldering, welding, crimping, stapling, and the attachment of interlocking tabs. Although the Moche metalworking tradition, like those that preceded it, was based primarily on objects shaped from hammered sheet metal, Moche smiths also cast certain objects, such as agricultural tools and weapons, and used the lost-wax method to cast smaller and detailed decorative pieces.

Copper-gold alloys, also known as *tumbaga*, were produced by the Moche and later used extensively by Sicán and Chimú smiths. Tumbaga is well suited to the sheet-metal tradition, because it becomes hard when hammered but remains flexible when annealed. At the same time, these alloys allowed smiths to develop techniques for making the surfaces of objects that contained very little gold appear golden.

After ceramics, metal was the most common medium for Moche art. Moche smiths produced an array of objects from ceremonial and ornamental pieces to agricultural implements and weapons to utilitarian objects. Among the ceremonial and

200 This pair of copper owls with shell inlay probably formed part of a larger plaque. The hanging bangles may represent stylized feathers. Vicús style, northern Peru.
H. 8.4; 8.6 cm. (3.3; 3.4 in.)
41.2/8670, 8669

ornamental pieces are earspools, necklaces, rattles, plaques, masks, backflaps (apparently used by Moche warriors to cover their derrieres) nose ornaments, and headdresses. Agricultural tools and weapons include hoes, digging sticks, mace heads, spear-throwers, and spear points; domestic utilitarian objects include such items as tweezers.

Moche smiths developed several techniques to give a golden appearance to objects made from gold-silver-copper alloys or even pure copper. One of the most common techniques they used is depletion gilding, a method whereby an ingot of a gold-silver-copper alloy was repeatedly hammered and annealed into a thin sheet. Moche smiths removed the brown scale of oxidized copper formed on the surface of the sheet by pickling it in a weak corrosive solution, such as plant juice or stale urine, that dissolved the copper oxide. As the metal was reduced to the desired thickness by repeated hammering, annealing, and pickling, more and more surface copper was oxidized and removed, resulting in the formation of a thin layer of enriched gold and silver on the object's surface. To dissolve the silver remaining in this enriched surface layer, smiths applied corrosive mineral mixtures, such as ferric sulfate and salt to the surface. These techniques could produce a golden surface on an object made of a copper-silver-gold alloy with a gold content as low as about 15 percent of its weight.

Another, even more ingenious method used by Moche smiths to gild or silver objects made of copper sheet, is called electrochemical replacement plating. In this process, the gold or silver is dissolved in a highly acidic solution of water and corrosive minerals, such as salt, niter, and potash alum. A copper object dipped into this solution acts as a cathode. The gold and silver ions in solution, bearing a positive charge, are attracted to the negatively charged (cathode) surface of the object, and a metallic coating, or plate, results. Most Loma Negra objects were gilded or silvered by this method.

Surface fusion was still another technique used to coat copper objects with gold, which could be applied as foil or in a molten state. In this method, a thin gold foil was hammered onto the surface of the object, and then the object was heated, alloying the gold and copper by melting them together at the surface. Alternatively, molten gold was spread over the surface by dipping the object into the molten metal, or by flushing the gold onto its surfaces.

Few ancient peoples developed the imagination, artistry, and skill of the northern metal smiths. The Chongoyape jaguars, the lavish finds from Sipán, and the vast numbers of metal objects that accompanied the burials of important Sicán lords at Batán Grande indicate that the Lambayeque area had become a center of metalworking by late Chavín times. This age-old tradition was based on ready access to gold and copper sources, skilled craft specialists, abundant labor to work the mines, and trade links with highland communities.

Analyses by Lechtman of cast objects from the Moche site of Huaca de la Luna indicate that in late Moche times, smiths were beginning to experiment with arsenic bronze. It is uncertain, however, whether these bronzes were accidental or

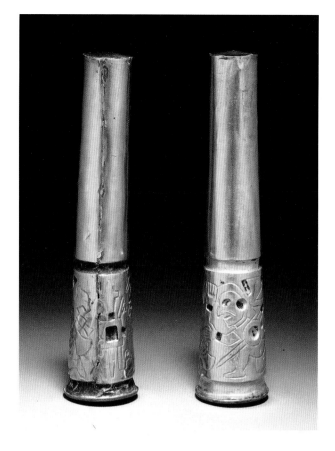

201 The tiny spheres of metal
on this hammered-gold
nose ornament were joined
by complex soldering or
sweat-welding techniques
to achieve a delicate filigree
effect. Vicús style, northern
Peru.
D. 2.5 cm. (1 in.) 41.2/6985

202 Earspools were worn as a
sign of status in ancient
Peru. This pair of ear ornaments was crafted of ham-
mered sheet gold and
adorned with an incised
design that includes a
human figure. Moche style,
northern Peru.
L. 13.3; 13.4 cm. (5.2; 5.3 in.)
41.2/8646 a, b

were produced intentionally. But by A.D. 900, some two hundred years after the fall of Moche, copper-arsenic bronze had largely replaced copper as the mainstay of north-coast metallurgy.

SICAN SMITHS

After Moche rule in the Lambayeque area languished, the Sicán culture established its center at the La Leche Valley site of Batán Grande, where it flourished from about A.D. 850 until the Chimú conquest of the region in approximately 1375. Batán Grande's excavator, Izumi Shimada, has described Batán Grande as the center of a culture that promoted stability in the area through religion, long-distance trade, and the mass production of crafts. Sicán traders may have even exchanged copper blanks, a form of primitive money known as *naipes*, for the much sought-after Spondylus, the coral-rimmed seashell found only in warm Ecuadorian waters, as well as for emeralds from Colombia (see chapter 8).

So famed is the Sicán culture for the sheer volume and wealth of metal goods it produced that its pyramids and cemeteries have been ransacked since Colonial times. Today, loot from Batán Grande fills the dazzling collections of Lima's Museo de Oro, where archaeologists estimate that over 90 percent of the museum's inventory is treasure plundered from Batán Grande. Batán Grande's very name reflects its metalworking tradition. *Batanes*, large flat-topped stones used by the ancient smiths to grind ores and slag, litter the

hills and metalworking shops to the east of the site.

Shimada has counted over a hundred thousand looters' pits at Batán Grande. In the folklore surrounding the major tombs plundered at the site, Shimada and his colleagues have been able to reconstruct three especially lavish burials. One, looted in late 1959, contained more than 150 gold and silver keros, or beakers, 1,000 gold beads, 20 necklaces, a *tumi*, or ceremonial knife, made mostly of gold and portraying a seated Sicán lord, as well as emeralds, pearls, and ceramics. Sicán funerary masks are elaborate objects made from sheet metal and encrusted with semiprecious stones and shells, metal spangles, and colorful feathers. The masks are often painted bright red with cinnabar, an ore that contains mercury. But the looting at Batán Grande has been so intense

203 Spider of hammered copper sheet with gold-plated surfaces. The surface is now covered by copper corrosion products. Moche style, north coast, Peru.
L. 5.5 cm. (2.2 in.) 41.2/8540

and systematic that archaeologists believed few royal tombs had survived the plunder. In 1991, however, Shimada discovered an intact elite Sicán burial, the first of its kind excavated there by archaeologists.

The tomb dates to the Middle Sicán period (A.D. 900–1100). The Sicán lord who lies at the center of the 12-meter-deep (40-foot-deep) tomb was a man forty to fifty years old who was accompanied by several other burials. Bright red cinnabar covered the lord's body, and remains of necklaces crafted from amethyst, sodalite, and Spondylus beads adorned his chest. His head was hidden by a gold funerary mask, and in his left hand he held a

silver tumi. A cloth covered with gold, silver, and bronze spangles once cloaked the body. Other offerings in the burial chamber included a cache of six golden crowns, gold earspools, an undecorated solid silver tumi, gold shin guards, and a pair of ceremonial gloves made of tumbaga.

But the opulent ornaments from this tomb are only part of the wide-ranging repertory of metal objects produced by Sicán smiths. Silver, gold, and tumbaga were reserved to manufacture objects for the tombs of the elite, but arsenic bronze, mass-produced at Sicán, was the primary metal used for an array of objects ranging from implements of everyday use like cups and bowls to tools like chisels, digging sticks, hoes, and lance points.

By excavating workshops used for metal smithing and smelting, Shimada and his team have been able to trace the evolution of metalworking at Batán Grande from A.D. 900 to 1500. At the Huaca del Pueblo de Batán Grande, Shimada found four smelting furnaces. Known as bowl furnaces, they were used to smelt copper ore. Smiths heated the furnaces with charcoal made from the wood of the algarrobo tree, which abounds in the area, and then added a smelting charge composed of crushed ores of copper, arsenic, and iron. The iron served as the flux, fusing with nonmetallic substances in the smelting charge to separate them from the resultant copper-arsenic alloy. The smiths then increased the heat of the furnace by blowing through blow tubes that end in ceramic tips, commonly referred to as *tuyères*. The smelting charge became a thick slag that contained prills, or droplets of nearly pure arsenical copper. When the slag cooled, the smiths crushed it on batanes and

204 The Middle Sicán culture (A.D. 900–1100) flourished in Lambayeque, on Peru's northern coast, where metal smiths produced vast quantities of elaborate funerary offerings, such as this pair of gold keros.
H. 14; 14.8 cm. (5.5; 5.8 in.)
41.2/7588, 7589

removed the prills. The prills were then melted to form ingots, which, in turn, were cast or hammered in the manufacture of metal objects. Experiments by Shimada and his colleagues indicate that each smelting session would have required four to five people working three to four hours to produce 300 to 500 grams, or less than a pound, of arsenical copper.

At the nearby site of Cerro de los Cementerios, Shimada and his team found ancient roads leading to pre-Hispanic and Colonial mines as well as hammerstones similar to those found with Copper Man in northern Chile. Llamas carried the ores to the smelting sites.

As discussed in chapter 8, about A.D. 1375, when the Chimú conquered the Sicán heartland, the center of north-coast metal production shifted south to the Chimú capital at Chan Chan in the Moche Valley. Although the Chimú occupied Batán Grande and even continued to produce metal objects, Batán Grande's most skilled smiths were taken to Chan Chan. There they produced grave goods for their Chimú masters and passed on their metalworking skills. When the Inka conquered the Chimú in the mid-1460s, they in turn took Chimú smiths to the Inka capital at Cuzco. According to some accounts, the Inka plundered the royal Chimú tombs at Chan Chan and took the booty to Cuzco.

INKA METALWORKING

The sixteenth-century Spanish chronicler Pedro de Cieza de León relates that the Inka emperor Pachakuti brought architects from the Titicaca basin to rebuild Cuzco. Pachakuti's building plans for Cuzco were intended to reflect Cuzco's new-found status as the center and architectural showcase of an ever-expanding Inka realm. The architects, heirs of Tiwanaku's builders, introduced the use of copper clamps to join stone blocks. The T-shaped perforations, so common at Tiwanaku, can still be seen in some stones at Cuzco's Korikancha, or Temple of the Sun, and at Ollantaytambo, the Inka fortress and ceremonial center in the Urubamba Valley. The Inka also borrowed tin-bronze technology from Titicaca smiths, a technology that soon replaced arsenic bronze in the former Chimú heartland as well as

in other areas of the Inka realm. Lechtman calls tin bronze the "stainless steel" of the Inka Empire. It was used for ornaments and for cast and hammered implements, such as axes, chisels, tweezers, tumis, and *tupus* (pins used to fasten women's cloaks). Bronzes with a high tin content are strong but brittle, and they develop a golden color; bronzes with a low tin content are more suited to cold working, because they are malleable when hammered. Indeed, cold-hammered tin bronze can be as hard, or harder, than iron and may have been used by Inka builders to dress stone.

The few Inka metal objects excavated by archaeologists include gold and silver offerings buried at the Island of the Sun on Lake Titicaca, the legendary birthplace of the founders of the Inka Empire (fig. 207). The Inka also buried gold and silver figurines in mountaintop sanctuaries. These sanctuaries were built to honor mountain gods, believed by the Inka and other Andean peoples to control fertility and rainfall. On the summit of Copiapo, high in the Chilean Andes, archaeologists uncovered a silver figurine of a woman wrapped in miniature woven garments fastened with silver tupus and topped by a feather headdress.

Precious metals and luxury goods were restricted by Inka sumptuary laws to the emperor

205 Smiths formed the thirteen hollow gold beads of this necklace by hammering thin sheets of metal over a wooden or stone mold and joining the two halves with a solder. Culture uncertain, northern Peru.
D. (single bead) 2.7 cm. (1.1 in.)
B/9449

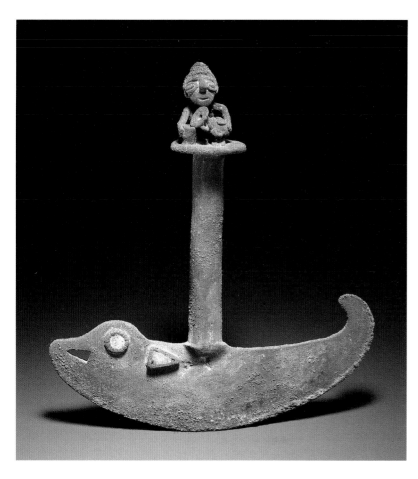

206 The blade of this copper-tin tumi, or ceremonial knife, has the form of a fish, and a human figure perches on the handle. Copper-tin, the hardest metal of the Andes, was a hallmark of fifteenth-century Inka expansion. Chimú-Inka style, north coast, Peru.
H. 16.2 cm. (6.4 in.) 41.2/6733

207 Miniature objects, like this silver llama, were deposited as ritual offerings at ceremonial sites throughout the Inka Empire. X-radiography studies show that the llama's head, ears, neck, body, legs, feet, and tail are separate pieces of silver sheet metal connected by soldered joints. Inka style, Island of the Sun, Lake Titicaca, Bolivia.
H. 5 cm. (2 in.) B/1621

and nobility. Gold and silver were reserved for the nobility because of their links to the legendary ancestors of the realm. The Inka controlled the mining of ores as well as the production of metal objects. Cieza, who traveled throughout the ravaged remains of the Inka Empire only ten years after the invasion, wrote: "So well had the Incas organized this that the amount of gold and silver mined throughout the kingdom was so great that there must have been years when they took out over fifty thousand arrobas of silver, and over fifteen thousand of gold, and all this metal was for their use" (Cieza, 1959 [1553]:163).

The opulence of Inka Cuzco, especially that of Cuzco's most sacred building, the Korikancha, or Temple of the Sun, amazed the Spaniards:

In one of these houses, which was the richest, there was an image of the sun, of great size, made of gold, beautifully wrought and set with many precious stones. . . .

There was a garden in which the earth was lumps of fine gold, and it was cunningly planted with stalks of corn that were of gold—stalk, leaves, and ears. . . . Aside from this, there were more than twenty sheep [llamas] of gold with their lambs, and the shepherds who guarded them, with their slings and staffs, all of this metal. There were many tubs of gold and silver and emeralds, and goblets, pots, and every kind of vessel all of fine gold. . . . In a word, it was one of the richest temples in the whole world (Cieza, 1959 [1553]:146–47).

The Korikancha and other temples provided some of the booty amassed by the captive Inka emperor Atawalpa at Cajamarca, in a futile attempt to secure his freedom from the Spanish invaders. Noting the Spaniards' lust for precious metals, Atawalpa ordered gold and silver to be brought to Cajamarca, a ransom settlement at today's values of 30 to 50 million dollars in gold and 1.5 to 2 million dollars in silver. Historian S. K. Lothrop estimated that there was more gold en route to Cajamarca than finally arrived at its destination, and to this day folk legends and tales of buried treasure abound in the Andes.

The raison d'être of the Spanish conquest was to find new sources of precious metals to fill the coffers of the Spanish Crown, first with the lavish treasure looted from temples and tombs and later with the riches from the gold and silver mines. Cieza wrote: "There is no kingdom in the world so rich in precious ores, for every day great lodes are discovered, both of gold and of silver. . . . I do not know how many ships would have been needed to carry to Spain the vast treasures lost in the bowels of the earth, where they will remain, for those who buried them are now dead" (Cieza, 1959 [1553]:156–57).

Perhaps enterprising Spaniards took Cieza's words as a challenge, for, soon after the conquest, the Crown began to grant licenses to "mine" the treasures of the ancient huacas. A Colonial official oversaw the melting of the metal, and, as mandated by Colonial law, he reserved one-fifth for the Spanish Crown. In 1602 one group of entrepreneurs diverted the waters of Trujillo's Moche River, washing away roughly two-thirds of the imposing Huaca del Sol and recovering "800,000 ducats" (about 1,200 pounds) of plunder, including, according to one contemporary account, a large golden statue.

208 Copper-silver alloy funerary mask, originally attached to a mummy head. Eyebrows are of human hair; textile impressions on the metal suggest that it was originally covered with cloth. Culture uncertain. Ica Valley, southern Peru.
L. 21 cm. (8.3 in.) B/5837

The Spaniards, however, did not immediately melt down all the gold and silver they plundered from Inka Cuzco. Documents found at the Archive of the Indies in Seville account for the Crown's share of gold and silver sent in 1534 to Charles V by Francisco Pizarro. The share includes "an idol in the shape of a man, weighing eleven pounds . . . a gold maize stalk of 14cts. with three leaves and two ears, weighing ten marks . . . three sheep and a lamb, made of silver and weighing three hundred . . . marks . . . twelve female figures in silver, large and small, weighing nine hundred . . . marks." The corn stalks and the "three sheep" (early Spanish chroniclers referred to Andean camelids as "sheep of the land") recall Cieza's description of the Korikancha.

Once the Spaniards had exhausted treasure stolen from temples and tombs as easy plunder, they began to look for mines. In 1545 silver was discovered at Potosí, today in Bolivia. Silver and gold production flourished after 1564, when the Spaniards found mercury at Huancavelica, in what is now Peru. (Mercury is useful for winning silver and gold from their ores.) The arrival in 1570 of the Viceroy Toledo brought renewed hardship for an already beleaguered Andean people. In 1574, Toledo legalized the mine *mit'a*, the Inka institution of rotational labor twisted to suit Spanish needs. Many died on the long, forced march to Potosí, and two of every three Indians sent to Potosí died as a result of appalling working conditions in the mines. Huancavelica's Santa Barbara mercury mine soon became known as the "mine of death." Thousands of Indians died in the Huancavelica mines, asphyxiated by lethal fumes of cinnabar, arsenic, and mercury.

The gold and silver looted and mined by the Spaniards from the former Inka realm transformed Peru into Spain's most-treasured American possession. Indeed, the mineral wealth of the Andes financed Europe's largest empire for over two centuries. Most of Spain's newfound wealth, however, was lavished on wars with France, Italy, and the Netherlands, eventually forcing Spain to borrow money from Europe's newly established bankers. Cieza observed that "for what impoverishes princes and keeps them stripped of money is war. . . . Possessing more silver and gold than any king of Spain . . . none of them was as hard up as His Majesty [Charles V], and if he had no wars and remained in Spain, with the nation's revenues and what has come from the Indies, all Spain could be as full of treasure as was Peru in the days of its Incas" (Cieza, 1959 [1553]:156)."

EPILOGUE

When the Indians saw their lord [the Inka king] lying on the ground a prisoner and themselves attacked from so many sides and so furiously by the horses they so feared, they turned round and began to flee in panic (Zárate, 1968:104–5).

The events that followed the moments in Cajamarca recounted by Zárate were unlike any that had occurred in the thousands of years of Andean civilization. In the past there were times when a conquering people had encroached on the lands of others, drafting the labor of the conquered for their own purposes. But these new conquerors of the Andes came from an entirely different culture, from another continent and another world. The traditions of conquest, incorporation, and exploitation differed completely from those of Wari, Chimor, and Tawantinsuyu. Ideas of control and empire in sixteenth-century Europe were distinct from and, in the native Andean view, much more brutal than those described in the chapters on the Wari, the Chimú, and the Inka.

Two aspects of the European invasion were particularly devastating and foreign to the Andes. One was the nature of warfare itself. The technological and tactical superiority of soldiers carrying firearms and mounted on horses over foot soldiers armed with maces and slings is obvious. Added to this were the psychological effects of these new and frightening arms and tactics. The Europeans, strange foreign beings astride weird beasts, discharging noisy and deadly weapons, threw the Inka ruler and his orderly entourage into hopeless confusion.

The second aspect of this latest conquest that was new to the Andes was its economic outlook. The new conquerors, like earlier Andean conquerors, would eventually be interested in exploiting the labor of the natives. But the new conquerors assumed this labor to be a more abstract right, without the obligation to reciprocate in the way of earlier Andean conquerors. The conquered people were expected to deliver tributes of goods to the conquistadors from their own communities, but without receiving in return the gifts and hospitality that Andean tradition had usually bestowed. The Europeans did not understand, or did not recognize, their own obligations: peace and prosperity in Andean society required a generous ruler. Rulers had duties as well as rights. If a kingdom did not prosper, its rulers could not reign long. Andean kingdoms were at times authoritarian and brutal, but eventually reciprocal obligations had to be met. Just over the horizon were other rulers, potentially more generous and powerful. Therein lay both the success and the fragility of any Andean kingdom. The Spaniard who recorded the Naymlap myth (see page 129) noted that the people of Lambayeque had been "forgetful of the fidelity that is owed by vassals." The native Andean idea of services owed by the vanquished and what could be demanded of them because of difference in status or position, was on a different plane from that of the Europeans.

Differences in the values placed on goods were as critical as differences in military practices and traditional expectations regarding rights and responsibilities of rulers. The Spanish were accustomed to an economy with gold as the medium of exchange—the standard of value for everything. Sensing the opportunity to acquire untold quanti-

209 Painted wooden kero carved in the form of a feline head. Early Colonial period, Peru. H. 22 cm. (8.7 in.) B/9163

231

210 Seventeenth-century drawing by Waman Puma of the arrival of the Europeans in the Americas. Pizarro and Almagro, leaders of the invasion of the Andes, are shown with Columbus and other European explorers and conquistadors.

ties of this economic essence inspired the invaders to acts of unbridled greed. While many Spaniards in the clergy and elsewhere recognized the moral implications of the Europeans' treatment of the natives, for the most part religion became a pretext for the virtual enslavement of the indigenous population. The Andes was primarily a source of gold and silver to enrich the Crown and only secondarily a source of new souls for the Christian fold.

In Andean life, gold and other objects beautifully fashioned from scarce materials were valuable mainly because of their symbolic meanings. As we have seen, they mediated not just exchanges of goods but also those of human relations. To strip these treasures of their rich human, religious, and social context—gold was actually melted back into raw material—must have seemed to Andeans both immoral and insane.

As the years passed the Andean peoples began to understand the nature of their adversaries. Some rebelled, and their rebellions were more effective than the minimal resistance to the initial invasion. Such leaders as Tupac Amaru I are remembered as heroes who attempted to restore native rights and native rule. But the moment had been lost for sheer numerical superiority to turn the tide; the foreign rulers of the Andes were now entrenched. Other natives learned the ways of the Europeans and managed to acquire land and other commodities, particularly in the early years when their skills and collaboration were most needed. They used their positions in both the native and European worlds to collaborate with the conquerors for personal enrichment.

The human condition of the Andean peoples during the first centuries of Colonial rule was almost unremittingly bleak, as epidemics of new European diseases blighted the entire New World and added to the pain of subjugation. But even under these conditions there were brilliant moments of achievement as some native traditions continued to flourish. Indeed, in remote areas of the Andes the earliest Andean art form, the creation of textiles, is still practiced today with much of its vitality and virtuosity intact. Even when European and Andean traditions have blended, as they necessarily did in most areas of art and life, Andean ideas and values can be easily detected behind a veil of European canons and techniques. Often Andean colors and forms are only half-hidden within the apparently pure European and Christian subjects of the famous Cuzco school of Colonial painters. The new rulers also directed Andean techniques, labor, and wealth into monumental architecture, the magnificent churches of the Colonial period.

What was destroyed in the sixteenth century, perhaps irretrievably, was the way in which people and resources had been managed on a large scale. Native management of a complex set of diverse landscapes, with their natural and human resources, had produced thousands of years of growth in economy, government, and technology.

By the time of the last Inka rulers, there were attempts to coordinate peoples and resources over a vast area from within a single governing order. A complicated and beautiful system of symbols communicated the ideology of the rulers and structured human relations. And a huge storage system of food and other supplies was constructed to secure the generosity of Inka rulers even in times of environmental or political stress. The management system was beginning to take into account not only the enormous geographic diversity but also some of the variation over time that had made earlier Andean states unstable. For almost the last five hundred years the management of these resources, so rich but so variable over space and time, has been primarily in the hands of rulers who have yet to learn how to manage them effectively.

211 Painted wooden kero carved as a human head, possibly of a jungle warrior. Its form may relate to an Inka tradition of using a defeated enemy's skull as a drinking vessel. Colonial or early Republican period, Peru.

H. 14.8 cm. (5.8 in.) 41.2/7847

212 The curving stone walls of the Korikancha, or Temple of the Sun, in Cuzco were used by the Spanish for the Colonial church of Santo Domingo. When an earthquake toppled the church in the mid-twentieth century, the solid Inka masonry was only slightly damaged.

COLOMBIA

GUACA

QUITO

ECUADOR

Hatun Cañar (Ingapirca)

TOMEBAMBA (CUENCA)

TUMBES

PERU

BRAZIL

CAJAMARCA

Chiquitoy Viejo

Huánuco Pampa

PACIFIC OCEAN

LIMA

JAUJA

Pachacamac

Inkawasi

Tambo Colorado

CUZCO

BOLIVIA

VILCAS WAMAN

La Centinela

Hatun-Colla

Lake Titicaca

ATICO

CHUCUITO

CHUQUIABO (LA PAZ)

AREQUIPA

Paria

CHILE

AREA OF DETAIL

INKA EMPIRE

THE INKA ROAD SYSTEM

	Inka Road
Paria	Inka Site
LIMA	Modern City or Town
CUZCO	City or Town over Inka Site

0   400 MILES

0   600 KILOMETERS

SELECT BIBLIOGRAPHY

CHAPTER 2

Flannery, Kent V., Joyce Marcus, and R. G. Reynolds

1989　*The Flocks of the Wamani: A Study of Llama Herders on the Punas of Ayacucho, Peru.* New York: Academic Press.

Mannheim, Bruce

1991　*The Language of the Inka since the European Invasion.* Austin: University of Texas Press.

Murra, John V.

1972　"El control vertical de un máximo de pisos ecológicos en la economía de las sociedades andinas." In *Visita de la provincia de León de Huánuco,* vol. 2, pp. 429–76. Huánuco, Peru: Universidad Nacional Hermilio Valdizán.

Pulgar Vidal, Javier

1987　*Geografía del Perú: Las ocho regiones naturales.* Lima: Promoción Editorial Inca.

Thompson, L., L. Hastenrath, and B. Arno

1979　"Climate Ice Core Records from the Tropical Quelccaya Ice Cap." *Science* 203: 1240–43.

Thompson, L., E. Moseley-Thompson, and B. Koci

1985　"A 1,500 Year Record of Tropical Precipitation in Ice Cores from the Quelccaya Ice Cap, Peru." *Science* 229: 971–73.

CHAPTER 3

Allison, Marvin J.

1985　"Chile's Ancient Mummies." *Natural History* 94/10: 75–81.

Bird, Junius B.

1988　*Travels and Archaeology in South Chile,* edited by John Hyslop. Iowa City: University of Iowa Press.

Bonavia, Duccio

1991　*Peru: Hombre e historia. De los orígenes al siglo XV.* Lima: Fundación del Banco Continental para el Fomento de la Educación y la Cultura.

Chauchat, Claude

1988　"Early Hunter-Gatherers on the Peruvian Coast." In *Peruvian Prehistory,* edited by Richard W. Keatinge, pp. 41–66. Cambridge: Cambridge University Press.

Dillehay, Tom D.

1987　"By the Banks of the Chinchihuapi." *Natural History* 96/4: 8–12.

1989　*Monte Verde: A Late Pleistocene Settlement in Chile.* Washington, D.C.: Smithsonian Institution Press.

Lynch, Thomas F.

1980　*Guitarrero Cave: Early Man in the Andes.* New York and London: Academic Press.

1990　"Glacial Age Man in South America? A Critical Review." *American Antiquity* 55/1: 12–36.

Quilter, Jeffrey

1991　*Life and Death at Paloma: Society and Mortuary Practices in a Preceramic Peruvian Village.* Iowa City: University of Iowa Press.

Rick, John W.

1980　*Prehistoric Hunters of the High Andes.* New York and London: Academic Press.

1988　"The Character and Context of Highland Preceramic Society." In *Peruvian Prehistory,* edited by Richard W. Keatinge, pp. 3–40. Cambridge: Cambridge University Press.

CHAPTER 4

Bird, Junius B., John Hyslop, and Milica Dimitrijevic Skinner

1985　*The Preceramic Excavations at the Huaca Prieta, Chicama Valley, Peru.* Anthropological Papers of the American Museum of Natural History, vol. 62, pt. 1.

Burger, Richard L.

1985　"Prehistoric Stylistic Change and Cultural Development at Huaricoto, Peru." *National Geographic Research* 1/4: 505–34.

Burger, Richard L., and Lucy Salazar-Burger

1980　"Ritual and Religion at Huaricoto." *Archaeology* 33/6: 26–32.

1982　"The Early Ceremonial Center of Huaricoto." In *Early Ceremonial Architecture of the Andes,* edited by Christopher B. Donnan, pp. 111–38. Washington, D.C.: Dumbarton Oaks Research Library and Collection.

Feldman, Robert A.

1985　"Preceramic Corporate Architecture: Evidence for the Development of Non-Egalitarian Social Systems in Peru." In *Early Ceremonial Architecture of the Andes,* edited by Christopher B. Donnan, pp. 71–92. Washington, D.C.: Dumbarton Oaks Research Library and Collection.

Grieder, Terence, and Alberto Bueno

1981　"La Galgada: Peru before Pottery." *Archaeology* 34/2: 44–51.

1985　"Ceremonial Architecture at La Galgada." In *Early Ceremonial Architecture of the Andes,* edited by Christopher B. Donnan, pp. 93–110. Washington, D.C.: Dumbarton Oaks Research Library and Collection.

Izumi, Seiichi

1971　"Development of the Formative Culture in the Ceja de Montaña of the Central Andes." In *Dumbarton Oaks Conference on Chavin,* edited by Elizabeth P. Benson, pp. 49–72. Washington, D.C.: Dumbarton Oaks Research Library and Collection.

Matsuzawa, Tsugio

1978   "The Formative Site of Las Haldas, Peru: Architecture, Chronology, and Economy." *American Antiquity* 43/4: 652–73.

Moseley, Michael E.

1975   *The Maritime Foundations of Andean Civilization.* Menlo Park, Calif.: Cummings.

1985   "The Exploration and Explanation of Early Monumental Architecture in the Andes." In *Early Ceremonial Architecture of the Andes*, edited by Christopher B. Donnan, pp. 29–58. Washington, D.C.: Dumbarton Oaks Research Library and Collection.

1992   *The Incas and Their Ancestors: The Archaeology of Peru.* London: Thames and Hudson.

Pozorski, Shelia, and Thomas Pozorski

1987   *Early Settlement and Subsistence in the Casma Valley, Peru.* Iowa City: University of Iowa Press.

1990   "Reexamining the Critical Preceramic/Ceramic Period Transition: The Data from Coastal Peru." *American Anthropologist* 92: 481–91.

Quilter, Jeffrey

1985   "Architecture and Chronology at El Paraíso, Peru." *Journal of Field Archaeology* 12: 279–97.

Quilter, Jeffrey, Bernardino Ojeda E., Deborah M. Pearsall, Daniel H. Sandweiss, John G. Jones, and Elizabeth S. Wing

1991   "Subsistence Economy of El Paraíso, an Early Peruvian Site." *Science* 251: 277–83.

Williams, Carlos

1985   "A Scheme for the Early Monumental Architecture of the Central Coast of Peru." In *Early Monumental Architecture of the Andes*, edited by Christopher B. Donnan, pp. 227–40. Washington, D.C.: Dumbarton Oaks Research Library and Collection.

CHAPTER 5

Burger, Richard L.

1982   "Concluding Remarks: Early Peruvian Civilization and Its Relationship to the Chavin Horizon." In *Early Ceremonial Architecture of the Andes*, edited by Christopher B. Donnan, pp. 269–83. Washington, D.C.: Dumbarton Oaks Research Library and Collection.

1984   *The Prehistoric Occupation of Chavin de Huantar, Peru.* University of California Publications in Anthropology, vol. 14. Berkeley and Los Angeles: University of California Press.

1987   "The U-Shaped Pyramid Complex, Cardal, Peru." *National Geographic Research* 3/3: 363–75.

1988   "Unity and Heterogeneity within the Chavin Horizon." In *Peruvian Prehistory*, edited by Richard W. Keatinge, pp. 99–144. Cambridge: Cambridge University Press.

1989   "Long Before the Inca." *Natural History* 98/2: 66–72.

Conklin, William J.

1971   "Chavin Textiles and the Origin of Peruvian Weaving." *Textile Museum Journal* 3/2: 13–19.

Mohr Chavez, Karen

1988   "The Significance of Chiripa in Lake Titicaca Basin Developments." *Expedition* 30/3: 17–26.

Moseley, Edward M., and Luis Watanabe

1974   "The Adobe Sculptures of Huaca de los Reyes." *Archaeology* 27/3: 154–161.

Patterson, Thomas C.

1985   "The Huaca La Florida, Rimac Valley, Peru." In *Early Ceremonial Architecture of the Andes*, edited by Christopher B. Donnan, pp. 59–70. Washington, D.C.: Dumbarton Oaks Research Library and Collection.

Pozorski, Shelia G.

1979   "Prehistoric Diet and Subsistence of the Moche Valley, Peru." *World Archaeology* 2/2: 163–84.

Pozorski, Shelia, and Thomas Pozorski

1986   "Recent Excavations at Pampa de las Llamas-Moxeke, a Complex Initial Period Site in Peru." *Journal of Field Archaeology* 13/4: 381–401.

Pozorski, Thomas

1980   "The Early Horizon Site of Huaca de los Reyes: Societal Implications." *American Antiquity* 45/1: 100–161.

Pozorski, Thomas, and Shelia Pozorski

1988   "An Early Stone Carving from Pampa de las Llamas-Moxeke, Casma Valley, Peru." *Journal of Field Archaeology* 15: 114–19.

Reinhard, Johan

1985   "Chavin and Tiahuanaco: A New Look at Two Andean Ceremonial Centers." *National Geographic Research* 1/3: 395–422.

Rowe, John H.

1967   "Form and Meaning in Chavin Art." In *Peruvian Archaeology: Selected Readings*, edited by John H. Rowe and Dorothy Menzel, pp. 72–103. Palo Alto, Calif.: Peek Publications.

Samaniego, Lorenzo, Enrique Vergara, and Henning Bischof

1985   "New Evidence on Cerro Sechin, Casma Valley, Peru." In *Early Ceremonial Architecture of the Andes*, edited by Christopher B. Donnan, pp. 165–90. Washington, D.C.: Dumbarton Oaks Research Library and Collection.

Shimada, Izumi

1980   "Temples of Time: The Ancient Burial and Religious Center of Batan Grande, Peru." *Archaeology* 34/5: 37–45.

Terada, Kazuo

1985   "Early Ceremonial Architecture in the Cajamarca Valley." In *Early Ceremonial Architecture of the Andes*, edited by Christopher B. Donnan, pp. 191–208. Washington, D.C.: Dumbarton Oaks Research Library and Collection.

CHAPTER 6

Alva, Walter

1988   "Discovering the New World's Richest Unlooted Tomb." *National Geographic* 174/4: 510–48.

1989   "New Tomb of Royal Splendor." *National Geographic* 177/6: 2–15.

Aveni, Anthony

1990a   "An Assessment of Previous Studies of the Nazca Geoglyphs." In *The Lines of Nazca*, edited by Anthony Aveni, pp. 1–40. Memoirs of the American Philosophical Society, vol. 185. Philadelphia.

1990b   "Order in the Nazca Lines." In *The Lines of Nazca*, edited by Anthony Aveni, pp. 41–113. Memoirs of the American Philosophical Society, vol. 185. Philadelphia.

Brennan, Curtis T.

1980   "Cerro Arena: Rise of the Andean Elite." *Archaeology* 33/3: 6–13.

Clarkson, Persis

1990   "The Archaeology of the Nazca Pampa: Environmental and Cultural Parameters." In *The Lines of Nazca*, edited by Anthony Aveni, pp. 117–72. Memoirs of the American Philosophical Society, vol. 185. Philadelphia.

1991   "Nuevos datos relativos a la antigüedad de los geoglifos y pukios de Nazca, Peru." *Boletín de Lima* 78: 33–74.

Conklin, William J., and Michael Moseley

1988   "The Pattern of Art and Power in the Early Intermediate Period." In *Peruvian Prehistory*, edited by Richard W. Keatinge, pp. 145–63. Cambridge: Cambridge University Press.

Donnan, Christopher B.

1976   *Moche Art and Iconography.* Los Angeles: UCLA Latin American Center, University of California.

1988   "Unraveling the Mystery of the Warrior-Priest." *National Geographic* 147/4: 551–55.

1989   "Masterworks of Art Reveal a Remarkable Pre-Inca World."
       National Geographic 147/6: 16–33.

Franquemont, Edward M.

1986   "The Ancient Pottery from Pucara, Peru." *Nawpa Pacha* 24:
       1–30.

Grieder, Terence

1978   *The Art and Archaeology of Pashash.* Austin and London:
       University of Texas Press.

Hastings, Mansfield C., and Edward M. Moseley

1975   "The Adobes of Huaca del Sol and Huaca de la Luna." *Amer-
       ican Antiquity* 40/2: 196–203.

Lumbreras, Luis G.

1974   *The Peoples and Cultures of Ancient Peru,* translated by
       Betty J. Meggers. Washington, D.C.: Smithsonian Institution
       Press.

Mohr Chavez, Karen

1988   "The Significance of Chiripa in Lake Titicaca Basin Develop-
       ments." *Expedition* 30/3: 17–26.

Paul, Anne

1991   "Paracas: An Ancient Cultural Tradition on the South Coast
       of Peru." In *Paracas: Art and Architecture,* edited by Anne
       Paul, pp. 1–31. Iowa City: University of Iowa Press.

Reinhard, Johan

1988   *The Nazca Lines: A New Perspective on Their Origin and
       Meaning.* Lima: Editorial Los Pinos E.I.R.L.

Schreiber, Katharina J., and Josue Lancho Rojas

1988   "Los puquios de Nazca: Un sistema de galerias filtrantes."
       Boletín de Lima 59: 51–62.

Shimada, Izumi, Crystal Barker Schaaf, Lonnie G. Thompson, and
Ellen Mosley-Thompson

1991   "Cultural Impacts of Severe Drought in the Prehistoric
       Andes: Application of a 1,500-Year Ice Core Precipitation
       Record." *World Archaeology* 22/3: 247–70.

Silverman, Helaine

1988   "Cahuachi: Non-Urban Cultural Complexity on the South
       Coast of Peru." *Journal of Field Archaeology* 15/4: 403–30.

1990   "Beyond the Pampa: The Geoglyphs in the Valleys of Nazca."
       National Geographic Research 6/4: 435–56.

1991   "The Paracas Problem: Archaeological Perspectives." In
       Paracas: Art and Architecture, edited by Anne Paul, pp.
       349–415. Iowa City: University of Iowa Press.

CHAPTER 7

Anders, Martha B.

1990   "Maymi: Un sitio del Horizonte Medio en el valle de Pisco."
       Gaceta arqueológica andina 17: 27–39.

1991   "Structure and Function at the Planned Site of Azangaro:
       Cautionary Notes for the Model of Huari as a Centralized
       Secular State." In *Huari Administrative Structure: Prehis-
       toric Monumental Architecture and State Government,*
       edited by William H. Isbell and Gordon F. McEwan, pp.
       165–97. Washington, D.C.: Dumbarton Oaks Research
       Library and Collection.

Arellano, Jorge L.

1991   "The New Cultural Contexts of Tiahuanaco." In *Huari
       Administrative Structure: Prehistoric Monumental Architec-
       ture and State Government,* edited by William H. Isbell and
       Gordon F. McEwan, pp. 259–80. Washington, D.C.: Dumb-
       arton Oaks Research Library and Collection.

Benavides, Mario

1991   "Cheqo Wasi, Huari." In *Huari Administrative Structure:
       Prehistoric Monumental Architecture and State Govern-
       ment,* edited by William H. Isbell and Gordon F. McEwan, pp.
       55–69. Washington, D.C.: Dumbarton Oaks Research Library
       and Collection.

Bennett, Wendell C.

1936   *Excavations in Bolivia.* Anthropological Papers of the Amer-
       ican Museum of Natural History, vol. 35, pt. 4. New York.

Browman, David

1980   "New Light on Andean Tiwanaku." *American Scientist* 69:
       408–19.

Conklin, William J.

1991   "Tiahuanaco and Huari: Architectural Comparisons and
       Interpretations." In *Huari Administrative Structure: Prehis-
       toric Monumental Architecture and State Government,*
       edited by William H. Isbell and Gordon F. McEwan, pp.
       281–91. Washington, D.C.: Dumbarton Oaks Research
       Library and Collection.

Cook, Anita G.

1983   "Aspects of State Ideology in Huari and Tiwanaku Iconography:
       The Central Deity and Sacrificer." In *Investigations of the
       Andean Past,* edited by Daniel Sandwiess, pp. 161–85. Ithaca,
       N.Y.: Latin American Studies Program, Cornell University.

1992   "The Stone Ancestors: Idioms of Imperial Attire and Rank
       Among Huari Figurines." *Latin American Antiquity* 3/4:
       341–64.

Denevan, William, K. Mathewson, and G. Knapp, eds.

1987   *Prehistoric Agricultural Fields in the Andes.* Oxford: British
       Archaeological Reports.

Diez de San Miguel, Garci

1964   [1567] *Visita hecha a la provincia de Chucuito. . . .* Docu-
       mentos Regionales para la Etnología y Etnohistoria Andina,
       vol. 1, pp. 1–299. Lima: Casa de la Cultura.

Erickson, Clark L.

1985   "Applications of Prehistoric Andean Technology: Experi-
       ments in Raised Field Agriculture, Huatta, Lake Titicaca:
       1981–2." In *Prehistoric Intensive Agriculture in the Tropics,*
       edited by Ian Farrington, pp. 209–32. British Archaeological
       Reports, International Series, no. 232. Oxford.

Goldstein, Paul

1993a "Tiwanaku Temples and State Expansion: A Tiwanaku
       Sunken-Court Temple in Moquegua, Peru." *Latin American
       Antiquity* 4/1: 22–47.

1993b "House, Community, and State in the Earliest Tiwanaku
       Colony: Domestic Patterns and State Integration at Omo
       M12, Moquegua, Peru." In *Domestic Architecture, Ethnicity
       and Complementarity in the South-Central Andes,* edited by
       Mark S. Aldenderfer, pp. 25–41. Iowa City: University of Iowa
       Press.

Isbell, William H.

1988   "City and State in Middle Horizon Huari." In *Peruvian Pre-
       history,* edited by Richard W. Keatinge, pp. 164–89. Cam-
       bridge: Cambridge University Press.

1991   "Huari Administration and the Orthogonal Cellular Architec-
       ture Horizon." In *Huari Administrative Structure: Prehistoric
       Monumental Architecture and State Government,* edited by
       William H. Isbell and Gordon F. McEwan, pp. 293–315. Wash-
       ington, D.C.: Dumbarton Oaks Research Library and Collec-
       tion.

Isbell, William H., Christine Brewster-Wray, and Lynda E. Spickard

1991   "Architecture and Spatial Organization at Huari." In *Huari
       Administrative Structure: Prehistoric Monumental Architec-
       ture and State Government,* edited by William H. Isbell and
       Gordon F. McEwan, pp. 19–53. Washington, D.C.: Dumbarton
       Oaks Research Library and Collection.

Kolata, Alan

1986   "The Agricultural Foundations of the Tiwanaku State: A
       View from the Heartland." *American Antiquity* 51: 748–62.

1991   "The Technology and Organization of Agricultural Produc-
       tion in the Tiwanaku State." *Latin American Antiquity* 2:
       99–125.

1993   "Understanding Tiwanaku: Conquest, Colonization, and Clientage in the South-Central Andes." In *Latin American Horizons*, edited by Don S. Rice, pp. 193–224. Washington, D.C.: Dumbarton Oaks Research Library and Collection.

Lumbreras, Luis G.

1974   *The Peoples and Cultures of Ancient Peru*, translated by Betty J. Meggers. Washington, D.C.: Smithsonian Institution Press.

McEwan, Gordon F.

1991   "Investigations at the Pikillacta Site: A Provincial Huari Center in the Valley of Cuzco." In *Huari Administrative Structure: Prehistoric Monumental Architecture and State Government*, edited by William H. Isbell and Gordon F. McEwan, pp. 93–119. Washington, D.C.: Dumbarton Oaks Research Library and Collection.

Menzel, Dorothy

1964   "Style and Time in the Middle Horizon." *Nawpa Pacha* 2: 1–105.

1968   "New Data on the Huari Empire in Middle Horizon Epoch 2A." *Nawpa Pacha* 6: 47–114.

Moseley, Michael E., Robert A. Feldman, Paul S. Goldstein, and Luis Watanabe

1991   "Colonies and Conquest: Tiahuanaco and Huari in Moquegua." In *Huari Administrative Structure: Prehistoric Monumental Architecture and State Government*, edited by William H. Isbell and Gordon F. McEwan, pp. 121–40. Washington, D.C.: Dumbarton Oaks Research Library and Collection.

Mujica, Elías

1985   "Altiplano-Coast Relationships in the South-Central Andes: From Indirect to Direct Complementarity." In *Andean Ecology and Civilization*, edited by Shozo Masuda, Izumi Shimada, and Craig Morris, pp. 103–40. Tokyo: University of Tokyo Press.

Ponce Sanginés, Carlos

1970   *Acerca de la procedencia del material lítico de los monumentos de Tiwanaku*. La Paz: Academia Nacional de Ciencias de Bolivia.

1972   *Tiwanaku: Espacio, tiempo y cultura*. Publicación no. 30. La Paz: Academia Nacional de Ciencias de Bolivia.

Pozzi-Escot, Denise

1991   "Conchopata: A Community of Potters." In *Huari Administrative Structure: Prehistoric Monumental Architecture and State Government*, edited by William H. Isbell and Gordon F. McEwan, pp. 81–92. Washington, D.C.: Dumbarton Oaks Research Library and Collection.

Schreiber, Katharina J.

1991   "Jincamocco: A Huari Administrative Center in the South-Central Highlands of Peru." In *Huari Administrative Structure: Prehistoric Monumental Architecture and State Government*, edited by William H. Isbell and Gordon F. McEwan, pp. 199–213. Washington, D.C.: Dumbarton Oaks Research Library and Collection.

Shimada, Izumi

1990   "Cultural Continuities and Discontinuities on the Northern North Coast of Peru, Middle-Late Horizons." In *The Northern Dynasties: Kingship and Statecraft in Chimor*, edited by Michael E. Moseley and Alana Cordy-Collins, pp. 297–392. Washington, D.C.: Dumbarton Oaks Research Library and Collection.

Topic, John R.

1991   "Huari and Huamachuco." In *Huari Administrative Structure: Prehistoric Monumental Architecture and State Government*, edited by William H. Isbell and Gordon F. McEwan, pp. 141–64. Washington, D.C.: Dumbarton Oaks Research Library and Collection.

CHAPTER 8

Bueno, Alberto

1982   *El antiguo valle de Pachacamac: Espacio, tiempo y cultura*. Lima: Editorial Los Pinos.

Conrad, Geoffrey W.

1982   "The Burial Platforms of Chan Chan: Some Social and Political Implications." In *Chan Chan: Andean Desert City*, edited by Michael E. Moseley and Kent C. Day, pp. 87–117. Albuquerque: University of New Mexico Press.

Day, Kent C.

1982   "Ciudadelas: Their Form and Function." In *Chan Chan: Andean Desert City*, edited by Michael E. Moseley and Kent C. Day, pp. 55–66. Albuquerque: University of New Mexico Press.

Donnan, Christopher B.

1990   "An Assessment of the Validity of the Naymlap Dynasty." In *The Northern Dynasties: Kingship and Statecraft in Chimor*, edited by Michael E. Moseley and Alana Cordy-Collins, pp. 243–74. Washington, D.C.: Dumbarton Oaks Research Library and Collection.

Earle, Timothy K., Terence N. D'Altroy, Catherine J. LeBlanc, Catherine J. Scott, Cathy L. Costin, Glenn S. Russell, and Elsie Sandefur

1987   *Archaeological Field Research in the Upper Mantaro, Peru, 1982–1983: Investigations of Inka Expansion and Exchange*. Monograph 28. Los Angeles: Institute of Archaeology, University of California, Los Angeles.

Hyslop, John

1977a   "Chulpas of the Lupaca Zone of the Peruvian High Plateau." *Journal of Field Archaeology* 4: 149–70.

1977b   "Hilltop Cities in Peru." *Archaeology* 30/4: 218–26.

Jiménez Borja, Arturo

1985   "Pachacamac." *Boletín de Lima* 7/38: 40–54.

Kolata, Alan L.

1990   "The Urban Concept of Chan Chan." In *The Northern Dynasties: Kingship and Statecraft in Chimor*, edited by Michael E. Moseley and Alana Cordy-Collins, pp. 107–44. Washington, D.C.: Dumbarton Oaks Research Library and Collection.

McEwan, Gordon F.

1990   "Some Formal Correspondences Between the Imperial Architecture of the Wari and Chimu Cultures of Ancient Peru." *Latin American Antiquity* 1/2: 97–116.

Mackey, Carol J.

1982   "The Middle Horizon as Viewed from the Moche Valley." In *Chan Chan: Andean Desert City*, edited by Michael E. Moseley and Kent C. Day, pp. 321–31. Albuquerque: University of New Mexico Press.

1987   "Chimu Administration in the Provinces." In *The Origins and Development of the Andean State*, edited by Jonathan Haas, Shelia Pozorski, and Thomas Pozorski, pp. 121–29. Cambridge: Cambridge University Press.

Mackey, Carol J., and A. M. Ulana Klymyshyn

1990   "The Southern Frontiers of the Chimu Empire." In *The Northern Dynasties: Kingship and Statecraft in Chimor*, edited by Michael E. Moseley and Alana Cordy-Collins, pp. 195–226. Washington, D.C.: Dumbarton Oaks Research Library and Collection.

Morris, Craig

1985   "From Principles of Ecological Complementarity to the Organization and Administration of Tawantinsuyu." In *Andean Ecology and Civilization*, edited by Shozo Masuda, Izumi Shimada, and Craig Morris, pp. 477–90. Tokyo: University of Tokyo Press.

1988   "Más allá de las fronteras de Chincha." In *La frontera del estado Inca*, edited by Tom D. Dillehay and Patricia

Netherly, pp. 131–40. British Archaeological Reports, International Series, no. 442. Oxford.

Netherly, Patricia J.

1990 "Out of Many, One: The Organization of Rule in the North Coast Polities." In *The Northern Dynasties: Kingship and Statecraft in Chimor*, edited by Michael E. Moseley and Alana Cordy-Collins, pp. 461–87. Washington, D.C.: Dumbarton Oaks Research Library and Collection.

Paredes B., Ponciano, and Régulo Franco

1987 "Pachacamac: Las pirámides con rampa, cronología y función." *Gaceta arqueológica andina* 4/13: 5–7.

Parsons, Jeffrey R., and Charles M. Hastings

1988 "The Late Intermediate Period." In *Peruvian Prehistory*, edited by Richard W. Keatinge, pp. 190–229. Cambridge: Cambridge University Press.

Richardson, James B., III, Mark A. McConaughy, Allison Heaps de Peña, and Elena B. Décima Zamecnik

1990 "The Northern Frontier of the Kingdom of Chimor: The Piura, Chira, and Tumbez Valleys." In *The Northern Dynasties: Kingship and Statecraft in Chimor*, edited by Michael E. Moseley and Alana Cordy-Collins, pp. 419–45. Washington, D.C.: Dumbarton Oaks Research Library and Collection.

Rostworowski de Diez Canseco, María

1970 "Mercaderes del valle de Chincha en la época prehispánica: Un documento y unos comentarios." *Revista española de antropología americana* 5: 135–78.

Shimada, Izumi

1991 "Pachacamac Archaeology: Retrospect and Prospect." In Max Uhle, *Pachacamac: A Reprint of the 1903 Edition*, pp. xv–lxvi. Philadelphia: University Museum of Archaeology and Anthropology.

Stanish, Charles, Edmundo de la Vega, and Kirk Lawrence Frye

1993 "Domestic Architecture on Lupaqa Area Sites in the Department of Puno." In *Domestic Architecture, Ethnicity, and Complementarity in the South-Central Andes*, edited by Mark S. Aldenderfer, pp. 83–93. Iowa City: University of Iowa Press.

Topic, John R.

1990 "Craft Production in the Kingdom of Chimor." In *The Northern Dynasties: Kingship and Statecraft in Chimor*, edited by Michael E. Moseley and Alana Cordy-Collins, pp. 145–76. Washington, D.C.: Dumbarton Oaks Research Library and Collection.

Topic, Theresa Lange

1990 "Territorial Expansion and the Kingdom of Chimor." In *The Northern Dynasties: Kingship and Statecraft in Chimor*, edited by Michael E. Moseley and Alana Cordy-Collins, pp. 177–94. Washington, D.C.: Dumbarton Oaks Research Library and Collection.

CHAPTER 9

Acosta, José de

1954 [1590] *Historia natural y moral de las Indias*. Biblioteca de Autores Españoles, vol. 73. Madrid: Atlas.

Agurto Calvo, Santiago

1987 *Estudios acerca de la construcción, arquitectura y planeamiento incas*. Lima: Cámara Peruana de la Construcción.

Cieza de León, Pedro de

1959 [1553] *The Incas*, translated by Harriet de Onis, edited by Victor W. von Hagen. Norman: University of Oklahoma Press.

Cobo, Bernabé

1983 [1653] *History of the Inca Empire*, translated by Roland Hamilton. Austin and London: University of Texas Press.

D'Altroy, Terence N.

1992 *Provincial Power in the Inka Empire*. Washington, D.C.: Smithsonian Institution Press.

Dillehay, Tom D.

1977 "Tawantinsuyu Integration of the Chillon Valley, Peru: A Case of Inca Geo-Political Mastery." *Journal of Field Archaeology* 4: 397–405.

Gasparini, Graziano, and Luise Margolies

1977 *Arquitectura inka*. Caracas: Centro de Investigaciones Históricas y Estéticas, Facultad de Arquitectura y Urbanismo, Universidad Central de Venezuela. (Reprinted as *Inca Architecture*, translated by Patricia J. Lyon. Bloomington: Indiana University Press, 1980.)

González, Alberto Rex, and Antonio Cravotto

1977 *Estudio arqueológico e inventario de las ruinas de Inkallajta*. UNESCO Informe Técnico PP/1975–76/3.411.6. Paris.

Hyslop, John

1985 *The Inka Road System*. New York: Academic Press.

1990 *Inka Settlement Planning*. Austin: University of Texas Press.

Jerez, Francisco de

1917 [1534] *Verdadera relación de la conquista del Perú*. Lima: Imprenta y Librería Sanmarti.

Julien, Catherine J.

1983 *Hatunqolla: A View of Inka Rule from the Lake Titicaca Region*. Berkeley: University of California Publications in Anthropology.

Menzel, Dorothy

1959 "The Inca Occupation of the South Coast of Peru." *Southwestern Journal of Anthropology* 15/2: 125–42.

1966 "The Role of Chincha in Late Pre-Spanish Peru." *Nawpa Pacha* 4: 63–76.

Morris, Craig

1974 "Reconstructing Patterns of Non-Agricultural Production in the Inca Economy: Archaeology and Documents in Institutional Analysis." In *The Reconstruction of Complex Societies. An Archaeological Symposium*, edited by Charlotte Moore, pp. 49–60. Chicago: The American Schools of Oriental Research.

1982 "The Infrastructure of Inka Control in the Peruvian Central Highlands." In *The Inca and Aztec States, 1400–1800*, edited by George A. Collier, Renato I. Rosaldo, and John D. Wirth, pp. 153–71. New York and London: Academic Press.

1992 "The Technology of Highland Inka Food Storage." In *Inka Storage Systems*, edited by Terry Y. LeVine, pp. 237–58. Norman: University of Oklahoma Press.

Morris, Craig, and Donald E. Thompson

1985 *Huánuco Pampa: An Inca City and Its Hinterland*. London: Thames and Hudson.

Murra, John V.

1965 "Herds and Herders in the Inca State." In *Man, Culture, and Animals*, edited by Anthony Leeds and Andrew P. Vayda, pp. 185–216. Washington, D.C.: American Association for the Advancement of Science.

1975 *Formaciones económicas y políticas del mundo andino*. Lima: Instituto de Estudios Peruanos.

1980 *The Economic Organization of the Inca State*. Greenwich, Conn.: JAI Press.

Niles, Susan A.

1987 *Callachaca: Style and Status in an Inca Community*. Iowa City: University of Iowa Press.

Pease G. Y., Franklin

1992 *Curacas, reciprocidad y riqueza*. Lima: Pontificia Universidad Católica del Perú.

Rostworowski de Diez Canseco, María

1988 *Historia del Tahuantinsuyu*. Lima: Instituto de Estudios Peruanos.

Rowe, John H.

1946 "Inca Culture at the Time of the Spanish Conquest." In *The Andean Civilizations*, vol. 2 of *Handbook of South American Indians*, gen. ed. Julian H. Steward, pp. 183–330. Bureau of American Ethnology, Bulletin 143. Washington, D.C.: Smithsonian Institution.

1979 "An Account of the Shrines of Ancient Cuzco." *Nawpa Pacha* 17: 2–80.

Sandweiss, Daniel H.

1992 *The Archaeology of Chincha Fishermen: Specialization and Status in Inka Peru.* Bulletin of the Carnegie Museum of Natural History, no. 29. Pittsburgh.

Salomon, Frank L.

1980 *Los señores étnicos de Quito en la época de los Incas.* Otavalo, Ecuador: Instituto Otavaleño de Antropología.

Silverblatt, Irene

1987 *Moon, Sun and Witches: Gender Ideologies and Class in Inca and Colonial Peru.* Princeton: Princeton University Press.

Zárate, Augustin de

1968 [1555] *The Discovery and Conquest of Peru*, translated by J. H. Cohen. Harmondsworth, Middlesex: Penguin Books.

Zuidema, R. Tom

1990 *Inca Civilization in Cuzco*, translated by Jean-Jacques Decoster. Austin: University of Texas Press.

CHAPTER 10

Bennett, Wendell C., and Junius B. Bird

1964 *Andean Culture History.* New York: Natural History Press.

Bird, Junius B.

1973 "Fibers and Spinning Procedures in the Andean Area." In *The Junius B. Bird Pre-Columbian Textile Conference*, edited by Ann Pollard Rowe, Elizabeth P. Benson, and Anne-Louise Schaffer, pp. 13–17. Washington, D.C.: The Textile Museum and Dumbarton Oaks, Trustees for Harvard University.

Bird, Junius B., and Louisa Bellinger

1954 *Paracas Fabrics and Nazca Needlework, 3rd Century B.C.– 3rd Century A.D.* Washington, D.C.: National Publishing Co.

Conklin, William J.

1971 "Chavin Textiles and the Origins of Peruvian Weaving." *Textile Museum Journal* 3/2: 13–19.

1975 "An Introduction to South American Archaeological Textiles with Emphasis on Materials and Techniques of Peruvian Tapestry." In *Irene Emery Roundtable on Museum Textiles, 1974 Proceedings, Archaeological Textiles*, edited by Patricia L. Fiske, pp. 17–30. Washington, D.C.: The Textile Museum.

1984 "The Mythic Geometry of the Ancient Southern Sierra." In *The Junius B. Bird Conference on Andean Textiles*, edited by Ann Pollard Rowe, pp. 123–36. Washington, D.C.: The Textile Museum.

d'Harcourt, Raoul

1962 *Textiles of Ancient Peru and Their Techniques*, edited by Grace G. Denny and Carolyn M. Osborne, translated by Sadie Brown. Seattle: University of Washington Press.

Emery, Irene

1966 *The Primary Structures of Fabrics: An Illustrated Classification.* Washington, D.C.: The Textile Museum.

Frame, Mary

1990 *Andean Four-Cornered Hats: Ancient Volumes.* New York: Metropolitan Museum of Art.

King, Mary Elizabeth

1965 "Textiles and Basketry of the Paracas Period Ica Valley, Peru." Ph.D. diss., University of Arizona.

Murra, John V.

1962 "Cloth and Its Functions in the Inca State." *American Anthropologist* 64/4: 710–28.

Paul, Anne

1990 *Paracas Ritual Attire: Symbols of Authority in Ancient Peru.* Norman: University of Oklahoma Press.

Rowe, Ann Pollard

1977 *Warp-Patterned Weaves of the Andes.* Washington, D.C.: The Textile Museum.

1978 "Technical Features of Inca Tapestry Tunics." *Textile Museum Journal* 17: 5–28.

1984 *Costumes and Featherwork of the Lords of Chimor: Textiles from Peru's North Coast.* Washington, D.C.: The Textile Museum.

Rowe, John Howland

1973 "Standardization in Inca Tapestry Tunics." In *The Junius B. Bird Pre-Columbian Textile Conference*, edited by Ann Pollard Rowe, Elizabeth P. Benson, and Anne-Louise Schaffer, pp. 239–64. Washington, D.C.: The Textile Museum and Dumbarton Oaks, Trustees for Harvard University.

Stone-Miller, Rebecca

1992 *To Weave for the Sun: Andean Textiles in the Museum of Fine Arts, Boston.* Boston: Museum of Fine Arts.

CHAPTER 11

Bohague, Gerard

1982 "Folk and Traditional Music of Latin America: General Prospect and Research Problems." *The World of Music* 25/2.

Bolaños, Cesar

1988a *Las antaras nasca: Historia y análisis.* Lima: Instituto de Estudios Peruanos.

1988b "La música en el antiguo Perú." In *La música en el Perú*, pp. 1–64. Lima: Patronato Popular y Porvenir Pro Musica Clásica.

Garcilaso de la Vega, Inca

1966 [1609] *Royal Commentaries of the Inca and General History of Peru*, translated by Harold V. Livermore. Austin: University of Texas Press.

Guaman Poma de Ayala, Felipe [Waman Puma]

1980 [1615] *El primer nueva Coronica y buen gobierno*, edited by John V. Murra and Rolena Adorno. Mexico City: Siglo Veintiuno.

Haeberli, Joerg

1979 "Twelve Nasca Panpipes: A Study." *Ethnomusicology* 23/1: 37–74.

Jiménez Borja, Arturo

1950–1951 "Instrumentos musicales Peruanos." *Revista del Museo Nacional* 19–20: 37–190.

Mead, Charles W.

1924 *The Musical Instruments of the Inca.* Anthropological Papers of the American Museum of Natural History, vol. 15, no. 3. New York.

Silva Sifuentes, Jorge

1978 *Instrumentos musicales pre-colombinos.* Lima: Universidad Nacional Mayor de San Marcos, Gabinete de Arqueología.

Smith, Richard Chase

1981 "The Language of Power: Music, Order and Redemption." *Latin American Musical Review* 2.

Valencia Chacón, Américo

1989 *El siku o zampona. The Altiplano Bipolar Siku: Study and Projection of Peruvian Panpipe Orchestras.* Lima: Centro de Investigación y Desarrollo de la Música Peruana.

CHAPTER 12

Carcedo Muro, Paloma, and Izumi Shimada

1985 "Behind the Golden Mask: The Sican Gold Artifacts from Batan Grande, Peru." In *Art of Precolumbian Gold: The Jan Mitchell Collection*, pp. 60–75. London: Weidenfeld and Nicolson.

Donnan, Christopher B.

1973   "A Precolumbian Smelter from Northern Peru." *Archaeology* 26/4: 289–97.

Grossman, Joel W.

1972   "An Ancient Gold Worker's Tool Kit: The Earliest Metal Technology in Peru." *Archaeology* 25/4: 270–75.

Jones, Julie

1975   "Mochica Works of Art in Metal: A Review." In *Pre-Columbian Metallurgy of South America*, edited by Elizabeth P. Benson, pp. 53–104. Washington, D.C.: Dumbarton Oaks Research Library and Collection.

Lechtman, Heather

1976   "A Metallurgical Site Survey in the Peruvian Andes." *Journal of Field Archaeology* 3: 1–42.

1979   "Issues in Andean Metallurgy." In *Pre-Columbian Metallurgy of South America*, edited by Elizabeth P. Benson, pp. 1–40. Washington, D.C.: Dumbarton Oaks Research Library and Collection.

1980   "The Central Andes: Metallurgy without Iron." In *The Coming of the Age of Iron*, edited by Theodore A. Wertime and James D. Muhly, pp. 267–334. New Haven and London: Yale University Press.

Lechtman, Heather, Antonieta Erlij, and Edward J. Barry

1982   "New Perspectives on Moche Metallurgy: Techniques of Gilding Copper at Loma Negra, Northern Peru." *American Antiquity* 47/1: 3–30.

Lechtman, Heather, Lee A. Parsons, and William J. Young

1975   *Seven Matched Hollow Gold Jaguars from Peru's Early Horizon.* Studies in Pre-Columbian Art and Archaeology, no. 16. Washington, D.C.: Dumbarton Oaks, Trustees for Harvard University.

Lothrop, S. K.

1938   *Inca Treasure as Depicted by Spanish Historians.* Los Angeles: Southwest Museum.

1941   "Gold Ornaments of Chavin Style from Chongoyape, Peru." *American Antiquity* 6/3: 250–62.

1951   "Gold Artifacts of Chavin Style." *American Antiquity* 16/3: 226–40.

Porras Barrenechea, Raúl

1959   "Legend and Gold of Peru." Introduction to *The Gold of Peru*, by Miguel Mujica Gallo, pp. 12–32. Recklinghausen, Germany: Aurel Bongers.

Shimada, Izumi

1990   "Cultural Continuities and Discontinuities on the Northern North Coast of Peru, Middle-Late Horizon." In *The Northern Dynasties: Kingship and Statecraft in Chimor*, edited by Michael E. Moseley and Alana Cordy-Collins, pp. 297–392. Washington, D.C.: Dumbarton Oaks Research Library and Collections.

Shimada, Izumi, Stephen Epstein, and Alan K. Craig

1983   "The Metallurgical Process in Ancient North Peru." *Archaeology* 35/5: 38–45.

Shimada, Izumi, and John F. Merkel

1991   "Copper Alloy Metallurgy in Ancient Peru." *Scientific American* 265/1: 80–86.

EPILOGUE

Cook, Noble David

1981   *Demographic Collapse, Indian Peru 1520–1620.* Cambridge: Cambridge University Press.

Cummins, Thomas

1988   "Abstraction to Narration: Kero Imagery of Peru and the Colonial Alteration of Native Identity." Ph.D. diss., University of California, Los Angeles.

Hemming, John

1970   *The Conquest of the Incas.* New York: Harcourt Brace Jovanovich.

Spalding, Karen

1974   *De indio a campesino.* Lima: Instituto de Estudios Peruanos.

Stern, Steve J.

1982   *Peru's Indian Peoples and the Challenge of the Spanish Conquest: Huamanga to 1640.* Madison: University of Wisconsin Press.

INDEX

PHOTOGRAPHY CREDITS

All photographs courtesy of John Bigelow Taylor, with the exception of the following:

Bill Ballenberg, © 1988 National Geographic Society: fig. 72
Nathan Benn, © 1990 National Geographic Society: fig. 71
Junius B. Bird: figs. 11, 19 (drawing by Miguel Covarrubias)
© Marilyn Bridges: figs. 83, 84, 86
Martin Chambi: figs. 150, 212
William J. Conklin: fig. 89
Terence D'Altroy: fig. 138
Christopher B. Donnan: figs. 73, 74 (drawing by Donna McClelland)
Robert A. Feldman: fig. 21
Paul Goldstein: fig. 98
John Hyslop: figs. 4, 5, 8, 13, 18, 28, 87, 88, 139
Martin Lowenfish, American Museum of Natural History: fig. 146
© Loren McIntyre: fig. 1
Craig Morris: figs. 6, 152, 153 (drawing by Delfín Zúñiga), 154, 166
© Edward Ranney: figs. 22, 75, 115, 118, 127, 132, 136, 142, 143, 148, 149, 151
Johan Reinhard: fig. 24
John W. Rick: fig. 10
Shippee/Johnson, American Museum of Natural History: figs. 61, 107, 120, 121, 141, 145, 147
Adriana von Hagen: figs. 3, 7, 9, 16, 70 (drawing by Luis Caballero for the Proyecto Arqueológico El Brujo, Fundación Augusto N. Wiese; Instituto Regional de Cultura, La Libertad; and Universidad Nacional de Trujillo), 109

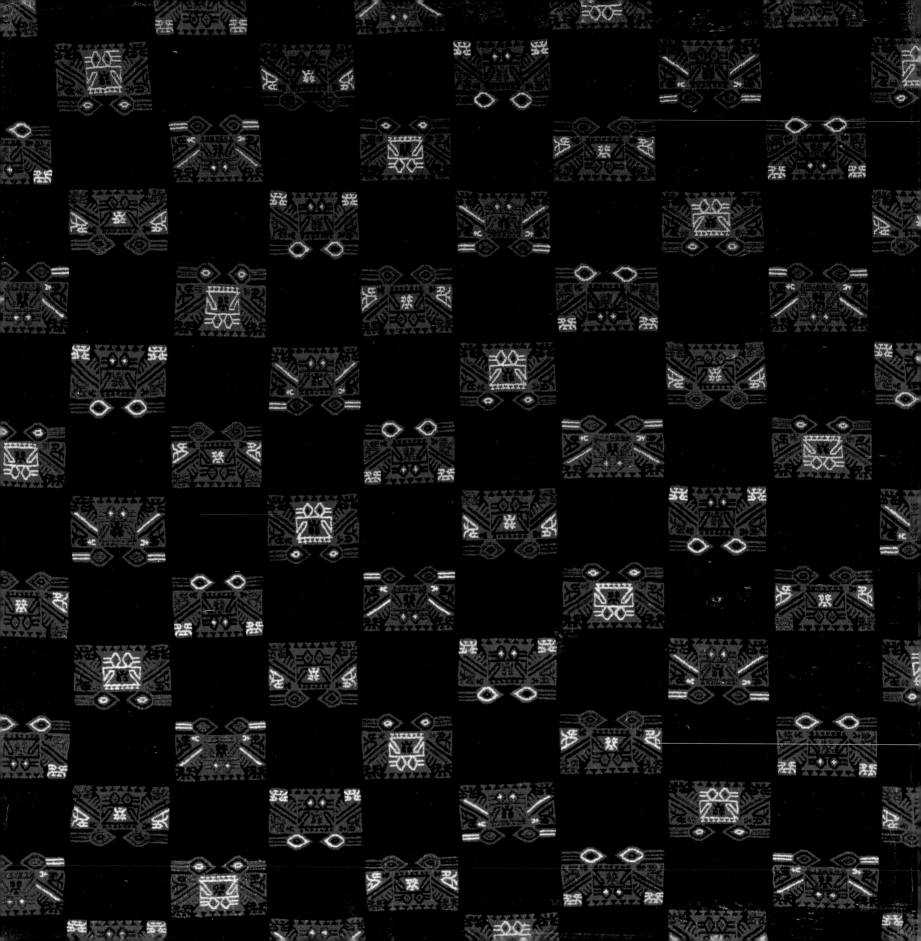